A NEW ACCOUNT OF THE EAST-INDIES

1688-1873

A NEW ACCOUNT OF THE EAST-INDIES

BEING THE

OBSERVATIONS AND REMARKS

OF

CAPT. ALEXANDER HAMILTON

FROM THE YEAR 1688-1723

TRADING AND TRAVELLING, BY SEA AND LAND, TO MOST OF THE COUNTRIES AND ISLANDS OF COMMERCE AND NAVIGATION, BETWEEN THE CAPE OF GOOD-HOPE AND THE ISLAND OF JAPAN

THE SECOND EDITION
IN TWO VOLUMES

VOLUME-II

GYAN

Published by

Gyan Publishing House
5, Ansari Road
Daryaganj, New Delhi-110002
Phone: 011-47034999, 9811692060
E-mail: books@gyanbooks.com

Distribution Network
gyanbooks.com
India, USA, Canada, UK, Australia, France

ISBN : 978-81-212-3817-5 (Set)
ISBN : 978-81-212-4741-2 (PB)
First Published, London, 1739

2nd Impression 2020

Printed at: Gyan Press, Delhi.

A New Account of the East-Indies Vol. II
Author: Capt. Alexander Hamilton

A NEW ACCOUNT OF THE EAST-INDIES:

BEING THE

OBSERVATIONS and REMARKS

OF

Capt. *ALEXANDER HAMILTON*,

Who resided in those Parts

From the Year 1688. to 1723.

Trading and Travelling by Sea and Land, to most of the Countries and Islands of COMMERCE and NAVIGATION, between the Cape of *Good-Hope*, and the Island of *Japan*.

The SECOND EDITION.

VOLUME II.

LONDON:

Printed for A. BETTESWORTH and C. HITCH, at the *Red-Lion* in *Pater-noster-row*. 1739.

THE CONTENTS OF THE Chapters of the Second VOLUME.

CHAP. XL.

CHAP. XLI.

CHAP. XLII.

CHAP. XLIII.

CHAP. XLIV.

CHAP.

CHAP. LI.

CHAP. LII.

CHAP. LIII.

CHAP. LIV.

A NEW ACCOUNT OF THE *Eaſt Indies*

CHAP. XXXIII.

Treats of the Towns, Cities, Country and Cuſtoms of Bengal, *particularly on thoſe near the famous* Ganges, *with ſome hiſtorical Accounts ancient and modern of Fort* William.

PIPLY lies on the Banks of a River ſuppoſed to be a Branch of the *Ganges*, about 5 Leagues from that of *Ballaſore*, formerly it was a Place of Trade, and was honoured with *Engliſh* and *Dutch* Factories. The Country produces the ſame Commodities that *Ballaſore* does, at present it is reduced to Beggary by the Factory's Removal to *Hughly* and *Calcutta*, the Merchants being all gone. It is now inhabited by Fishers, as are also *Ingellie*, and *Kidgerie*, two neighbouring Islands on the West Side of the Mouth of *Ganges*. These Islands abound also in tame Swine, where they are sold very cheap, for I have bought One and twenty good Hogs, between 50 and 80 Pound Weight each, for 17 Rupees, or 45 Shillings *Sterling*. Those Islands send forth dangerous Sand Banks, that are both numerous and large, and make the Navigation out and in to *Hughly* River, both troublesom and dangerous, and after we pass those Islands, in going up the River, the Chanel for Shipping is on the East-side, and several Creeks run from the Chanel among a great Number of Islands, formed by different Chanels of *Ganges*, two of which are more remarkable than the rest, *viz.* *Coxes* and *Sagor* Islands, where great Ships were obliged to anchor to take in Part of their Cargoes, because several Places in the River are too shallow for great Ships to pass over, when their whole Cargoes are aboard.

THERE are no Inhabitants on those Islands, for they are so pestered with Tigers, that there could be no Security for human Creatures to dwell on them; nay, it is even dangerous to land on them, or for Boats to anchor near them, for in the Night they have swimmed to Boats at Anchor, and carried Men out of them, yet among the *Pagans*, the

the Island *Sagor* is accounted holy, and great Numbers of *Jougies* go yearly thither in the Months of *November* and *December*, to worship and wash in Salt-water, tho' many of them fall Sacrifices to the hungry Tigers.

The first safe anchoring Place in the River, is off the Mouth of a River about twelve Leagues above *Sagor*, commonly known by the Name of *Rogues* River, which had that Appellation from some *Banditti Portugueze*, who were Followers of *Sultan Sujah*, when *Emirjemal*, *Aurengzeb*'s General, drove that unfortunate Prince out of his Province of *Bengal*, for those *Portugueze* having no Way to subsist, after their Master's Flight to the Kingdom of *Arackan*, betook themselves to Piracy among the Islands, at the Mouth of *Ganges*, and that River having Communication with all the Chanels from *Xatigam* to the westward, from this River they used to sally out, and commit Depredations on those that traded in the River of *Hughly*.

About 5 Leagues farther up, on the West Side of the River of *Hughly*, is another Branch of the *Ganges*, called *Gauga*, it is broader than that of *Hughly*, but much shallower, and more incumbred with Sand Banks; a little below the Mouth of it the *Danes* have a thatcht House, but for what Reasons they kept an House there, I never could learn.

Along the River of *Hughly* there are many small Villages and Farms, intersperst in those large Plains, but the first of any

Note on the River's Side, is *Culculla*, a Market Town for Corn, coarſe Cloth, Butter, and Oyl, with other Productions of the Country; above it is the *Dutch Bankſhall*, a Place where their Ships ride when they cannot get farther up for the too ſwift Currents of the River. *Culculla* has a large deep River that runs to the eaſtward, and ſo has *Juanpardoa*, and on the Weſt Side there is a River that runs by the Back of *Hughly* Iſland, which leads up to *Radnagur*, famous for manufacturing Cotton Cloth, and Silk *Romaals*, or Handkerchiefs. *Buſſundri* and *Treſindi*, or *Gorgat* and *Cottrong*, are on that River, which produce the greateſt Quantities of the beſt Sugars in *Bengal*.

A little higher up on the Eaſt Side of *Hughly* River, is *Ponjelly*, a Village where a Corn Mart is kept once or twice in a Week, it exports more Rice than any Place on this River; and five Leagues farther up on the other Side, is *Tanna* Fort, built to protect the Trade of the River, at a Place convenient enough, where it is not above Half a Mile from Shore to Shore, but it never was of much Uſe; for *in Anno* 1686. when the *Engliſh* Company quarrelled with the *Mogul*, the Company had ſeveral great Ships at *Hughly*, and this Fort was manned in order to hinder their Paſſage down the River. One 60 Gun Ship approaching pretty near the Fort, ſaluted it with a Broad-ſide, which ſo frightned the Governor and his Myrmidons, that they all deſerted their Poſt, and

and left their Caſtle to be plundred by the *Engliſh* Seamen. About a League farther up on the other Side of the River, is *Governapore*, where there is a little Pyramid built for a Land-mark, to confine the Company's Colony of *Calcutta*, or Fort *William*. On that Side, and about a League farther up, ſtands Fort *William*.

THE *Engliſh* ſettled there about the Year 1690. after the *Mogul* had pardoned all the Robberies and Murders committed on his Subjects. Mr. *Job Channock* being then the Company's Agent in *Bengal*, he had Liberty to ſettle an *Emporium* in any Part on the River's Side below *Hughly*, and for the ſake of a large ſhaddy Tree choſe that Place, tho' he could not have choſen a more unhealthful Place on all the River; for three Miles to the North-eaſtward, is a Salt-water Lake that overflows in *September* and *October*, and then prodigious Numbers of Fiſh reſort thither, but in *November* and *December* when the Floods are diſſipated, thoſe Fiſhes are left dry, and with their Putrefaction affect the Air with thick ſtinking Vapours, which the North-eaſt Winds bring with them to Fort *William*, that they cauſe a yearly Mortality One Year I was there, and there were reckoned in *Auguſt* about 1200 *Engliſh*, ſome Military, ſome Servants to the Company, ſome private Merchants reſiding in the Town, and ſome Seamen belonging to Shipping lying at the Town, and before the Beginning of *January* there were four hundred

dred and ſixty Burials regiſtred in the Clerk's Book of Mortality.

Mr. *Channock* chooſing the Ground of the Colony, where it now is, reigned more abſolute than a *Rajah*, only he wanted much of their Humanity, for when any poor ignorant Native tranſgreſſed his Laws, they were ſure to undergo a ſevere Whipping for a Penalty, and the Execution was generally done when he was at Dinner, ſo near his Dining-room that the Grones and Cries of the poor Delinquent ſerved him for Muſick.

The Country about being overſpread with *Paganiſm*, the Cuſtom of Wives burning with their deceaſed Husbands, is alſo practiſed here. Before the *Mogul's* War, Mr. *Channoch* went one Time with his ordinary Guard of Soldiers, to ſee a young Widow act that tragical Cataſtrophe, but he was ſo ſmitten with the Widow's Beauty, that he ſent his Guards to take her by Force from her Executioners, and conducted her to his own Lodgings. They lived lovingly many Years, and had ſeveral Children, at length ſhe died, after he had ſettled in *Calcutta*, but inſtead of converting her to *Chriſtianity*, ſhe made him a Proſelyte to *Paganiſm*, and the only Part of *Chriſtianity* that was remarkable in him, was burying her decently, and he built a Tomb over her, where all his Life after her Death, he kept the anniverſary Day of her Death by ſacrificing a Cock on her Tomb, after the *Pagan* Manner; this was and is the common Re-

Report, and I have been credibly informed, both by *Christians* and *Pagans*, who lived at *Calcutta* under his Agency, that the Story was really true Matter of Fact.

Fort *William* was built an irregular Tetragon, of Brick and Morter, called *Puckah*, which is a Composition of Brick-dust, Lime, Malasses, and cut Hemp, and when it comes to be dry, is as hard and tougher than firm Stone or Brick, and the Town was built without Order, as the Builders thought most convenient for their own Affairs, every one taking in what Ground best pleased them for Gardening, so that in most Houses you must pass through a Garden into the House, the *English* building near the River's Side, and the Natives within Land.

The Agency continued till the Year 1705. that the old and new Companies united, and then it became a split Government, the old and new Companies Servants governing Week about, which made it more anarchical than regular. Sir *Edward Littleton* was Agent and Consul for the new Company at *Hughly*, when this Union of the Companies was made, and then he was ordered to remove his Factory to *Calcutta*, and being of an indolent Disposition, had let his Accounts with the Company run behind. He was suspended, but lived at *Calcutta* till 1707. that he died there ; he was the only President or Precedent in the Company's Service, that lost an Estate of 700 Pounds *per Annum* in so profitable a Post in their Service.

This

THIS double-headed Government continued in *Calcutta*, till *January* 1709. that Mr. *Weldon* arrived with the Company's Commiſſion to ſettle it at *Bombay* and Fort St. *George*, which were under the Management of a Governor and Council, which thoſe of the Direction in *England* took to be a better Way to promote their own Creatures, as well as their own Intereſt. His Term of governing was very ſhort, and he took as ſhort a Way to be enriched by it, by haraſſing the People to fill his Coffers. There was one ſingular Inſtance of it. A poor Seaman had got a pretty *Muſtice* Wife, a little inclined to Lewdneſs in her Husband's Abſence. She entertained two *Armenians*, who were like to quarrel about ſharing her Favours, which coming to the Governor's Ears, he reprimanded them: However, by the ſtrong Perſwaſion of 500 Rupees paid in hand by one of them, he awarded him to have the ſole Right to her, and he carried her to *Hughly*, and bragg'd openly what his Purchaſe had coſt him, to the great Credit and Praiſe of the Governor; and when the poor Husband returned, he was forced to ſubmit to loſe his Mare, under the Pain of Flagellation: Yet he was very ſhy in taking Bribes, referring thoſe honeſt Folks, who traffick'd that Way, to the Diſcretion of his Wife and Daughter, to make the beſt Bargain they could about the Sum to be paid, and to pay the Money into their Hands. I could give many Inſtances of the Force of Bribery, both here and elſe-

elſewhere in *India*, but am loth to ruffle the Skin of old Sores.

ABOUT fifty Yards from Fort *William*, ſtands the Church built by the pious Charity of Merchants reſiding there, and the *Chriſtian* Benevolence of Sea-faring Men, whoſe Affairs call them to trade there; but Miniſters of the Goſpel being ſubject to Mortality, very often young Merchants are obliged to officiate, and have a Salary of 50 *L. per Annum* added to what the Company allows them, for their Pains in reading Prayers and Sermons on *Sundays*.

THE Governor's Houſe, in the Fort, is the beſt and moſt regular Piece of Architecture that I ever ſaw in *India*. And there are many convenient Lodgings for Factors and Writers, within the Fort, and ſome Store-houſes for the Company's Goods, and the Magazines for their Ammunition.

THE Company has a pretty good Hoſpital at *Calcutta*, where many go in to undergo the Penance of Phyſick, but few come out to give Account of its Operation. The Company has alſo a pretty good Garden, that furniſhes the Governor's Table with Herbage and Fruits; and ſome Fiſh-ponds to ſerve his Kitchin with good Carp, Calkops and Mullet.

MOST of the Inhabitants of *Calcutta* that make any tolerable Figure, have the ſame Advantages; and all Sorts of Proviſions, both wild and tame, being plentiful, good and cheap, as well as Clothing, make the Coun-

Country very agreeable, notwithſtanding the above mentioned Inconveniencies that attend it.

On the other Side of the River are Docks made for repairing and fitting their Ships Bottoms, and a pretty good Garden belonging to the *Armenians*, that had been a better Place to have built their Fort and Town in, for many Reaſons. One is, that, where it now ſtands, the After-noon's Sun is full in the Fronts of the Houſes, and ſhines hot on the Streets, that are both above and below the Fort, the Sun would have ſent its hot Rays on the Back of the Houſes, and the Fronts had been a good Shade for the Streets.

Most Gentlemen and Ladies in *Bengal* live both ſplendidly and pleaſantly, the Forenoons being dedicated to Buſineſs, and after Dinner to Reſt, and in the Evening to recreate themſelves in Chaiſes or *Palankins* in the Fields, or to Gardens, or by Water in their *Budgeroes*, which is a convenient Boat, that goes ſwiftly with the Force of Oars; and, on the River, ſometimes there is the Diverſion of Fiſhing or Fowling, or both; and, before Night, they make friendly Viſits to one another, when Pride or Contention do not ſpoil Society, which too often they do among the Ladies, as Diſcord and Faction do among the Men. And altho' the conſcript Fathers of the Colony diſagree in many Points among themſelves, yet they all agree in oppreſſing Strangers, who are conſigned to them, not ſuffering them to buy

or

or ſell their Goods at the moſt advantageous Markets, but of the Governor and his Council, who fix their own Prices, high or low, as ſeemeth beſt to their Wiſdom and Diſcretion: And it is a Crime hardly pardonable for a private Merchant to go to *Hughly*, to inform himſelf of the current Prices of Goods, altho' the Liberty of buying and ſelling is intirely taken from him before.

THE Gariſon of Fort *William* generally conſiſts of 2 or 300 Soldiers, more for to convey their Fleet from *Patana*, with the Company's Saltpetre, and Piece Goods, raw Silk and ſome Ophium belonging to other Merchants, than for the Defence of the Fort, for, as the Company holds their Colony in fie Tail of the *Mogul*, they need not be afraid of any Enemies coming to diſpoſſeſs them. And if they ſhould, at any Time, quarrel again with the *Mogul*, his prohibiting his Subjects to trade with the Company, would ſoon end the Quarrel.

THERE are ſome impertinent troubleſom *Rajahs*, whoſe Territories ly on the Banks of the *Ganges*, betwen *Patana* and *Caſſembuzaar*, who pretend a Tax on all Goods and Merchandize, that paſs by, or through their Dominions on the River, and often raiſe Forces to compel Payment; but ſome Forces from Fort *William* in Boats, generally clear the Paſſage, tho' I have known ſome of our Men killed in the Skirmiſhes.

IN *Calcutta* all Religions are freely tolerated, but the *Presbyterian*, and that they brow-

brow-beat. The *Pagans* carry their Idols in Proceſſion thro' the Town. The *Roman Catholicks* have their Church to lodge their Idols in, and the *Mahometan* is not diſcountenanced; but there are no Polemicks, except what are between our High-church Men and our low, or between the Governor's Party and other private Merchants on Points of Trade.

THE Colony has very little Manufactory of its own, for the Government being pretty arbitrary, diſcourages Ingenuity and Induſtry in the Populace; for, by the Weight of the Company's Authority, if a Native chances to diſoblige one of the Upper-houſe, he is liable to arbitrary Puniſhment, either by Fine, Impriſonment or corporal Sufferings. I will give one Inſtance, out of many, that I knew of the Injuſtice of a Governor of the double-headed Government *in Anno* 1706.

THERE was one Captain *Perrin* Maſter of a Ship, who took up about 500 *L.* on *reſpondentia* from Mr. *Ralph Sheldon* one of the Governors, on a Voyage to *Perſia*, payable at his Return to *Bengal*. *Perrin* having diſpatched his Affairs in *Perſia* ſooner than he expected, called at *Goa* in his Way Home, and bought a *Surat*-built Ship very cheap, and carried her to *Calecut*, and took in a Quantity of Pepper for the *Bengal* Market; and having brought in his other Ship, good Store of *Perſia* Wines, called at Fort St. *George* to diſpoſe of what he could there, but finding no Encouragement from that Market, carried it to *Bengal*. On his Arrival

val he complimented Mr. *Sheldon* with the Offer of his Pepper and Wine, but he declined meddling with that Bargain, farther than with as much of the Pepper, at the current Price, as would balance his Account of Principal and *respondentia*. Accordingly *Perrin* delivered so much Pepper, and, on the Delivery, required his Bond up, but the Governor told him, that he being a Fellow troubled with the Spirit of interlopping in buying Goods, and taking Freights where he could best get them, he would keep that Bond as a Curb on him, that he should not spoil his Markets for the future. Poor *Perrin* used all his Rhetorick to get his Bond up, but to no Purpose; and the Governor moreover gave his Wine a bad Name, so that he could not dispose of that either, and all this Oppression was in order to straiten him, that he might be obliged to sell his new purchased Ship, at a low Price, to him and his Associates, which, at last, he was obliged to do, holding a Quarter Part in his own Hands, to secure the Command of her to himself, which, after all, he could hardly do. *Perrin* made his Complaint to me, but I was in no Condition to assist him, because I, having three or four large Ships at *Bengal*, was reckoned a Criminal guilty of that unpardonable Sin of Interlopping; however, I advised *Perrin* to comply with his inexorable Master, on any Terms of Agreement whatsoever, which he endeavoured to do, that he might, at least, keep the Command of of his Ship, where he was ſo much concerned, and had hardly done it, but by Accident. One Day meeting me on the Green near the Fort, he ſtopt me to relate his Grievances, and begged, that, if he was turned out of his own Ship, he might have an Employ in one of mine, which I promiſed he ſhould.

Sheldon eſpied us, out of a Window, holding a long Confabulation, and being impatient to know about what, ſent a Servant to call *Perrin*, and he, obeying the Summons, was interrogated about what our Diſcourſe was; and he told the Promiſe I had made him. *Sheldon* told him, that he was as capable to employ him, as I could be. *Perrin* anſwered, that he knew that, but wiſhed that he would be as willing too; ſo *Sheldon* promiſed that he ſhould command his own Ship to *Perſia*.

But the Wine ſtill lay unſold, tho' it was ſcarce then in *Bengal*; but the Name that it got, firſt at Fort St. *George*, and afterward in Fort *William*, ſtuck ſo faſt to it, that none of it would go off at any Price, ſo I adviſed him to carry it off in the Night, in my Boats, on board of one of my Ships, and I would try if I could ſerve him in ſelling it, which accordingly he did, and two Gentlemen of the Council, being that Seaſon bound for *England*, coming one Day to dine with me, I treated them, and the reſt of my Company, with that *Perſia* Wine, which they all praiſed, and askt me where I got it. I told them, that,

that, knowing that good Wines would be scarce at *Bengal* that Year, I had provided a good Quantity at *Surat*, from whence I had come that Seaſon. Every one begged that I would ſpare them ſome Cheſts, which I condeſcended to do as a Favour, and next Day ſent them what they wanted, at double the Price the Owner demanded for it, while he had it, and ſo got off above 120 Cheſts, which enabled Mr. *Perrin* to ſatisfy moſt of his Creditors.

Sheldon provided a Stock and Freight for *Perrin* to *Perſia*, and put on board ſome rotten long Pepper, that he could diſpoſe of no other Way, and ſome damaged *Gunnies*, which are much in Uſe in *Perſia* for embaling Goods, when they are good in their Kind; but, *nolens volens*, *Perrin* muſt take them, and ſign Bills of Loading for good well conditioned Goods; and yet, after he was ready to ſail, he had been ſtopt, if he could not raiſe the Sum of 2500 Rupees, to diſcharge a Bill, that, at that Time, became due, and was indorſed to *Sheldon*. I alſo helped him out of that Difficulty, and took his Bond for the Sum, bearing Intereſt from the Date, at the current Intereſt of 1 *per Cent. per Menſem*, ſo *Perrin* proceeded on his Voyage to *Perſia*, but called at *Calecut* in his Way Home again, and laid up his Ship there, and took Protection of a *Nayer*, with the full Hand of 11000 *L. Sterl.* of *Bengal* Money, and wrote to Mr. *Sheldon*, that he might keep his former Bond, and he would take Care of his Part of the Stock in his Hands. He alſo wrote to me, that he would take particular Care to reimburſe me, but, in a ſhort Time after, he died, and his Effects came into the *Engliſh* Chief's Hands, who detained them ſeveral Years, denying that ever he had any, till Governor *Boone* came to the Government of *Bombay* in 1715. and then he made a lame Account. I have been ſo prolix and particular in this Story, that it may form an Idea of the Deformity and diſmal Image of Tyranny and Villany ſupported by a Power, that neither divine nor human Laws have Force enough to bridle or reſtrain.

The Company's Colony is limited by a Land-mark at *Governapore*, and another near *Barnagul*, about ſix Miles diſtant; and the Salt-water Lake bounds it on the Land Side. It may contain, in all, about 10 or 12000 Souls; and the Company's Revenues are pretty good, and well paid. They riſe from Ground-rents and Conſulage on all Goods imported and exported by *Britiſh* Subjects; but all Nations beſides are free from Taxes.

CHAP. XXXIV

Is a Continuation of the Deſcription of Bengal.

BARNAGUL is the next Village on the River's Side, above *Calcutta*, where the *Dutch* have an Houſe and Garden; and the

the Town is famously infamous for a Seminary of female Lewdness, where Numbers of Girls are trained up for the Destruction of unwary Youths, who study more how to gratify their brutal Passions, than how to shun the evil Consequences that attend their Folly, notwithstanding the daily Instances of Rottenness and Mortality that happen to those who most frequent those Schools of Debauchery. The *Dutch* Shipping anchors there sometimes, to take in their Cargoes for *Batavia*. And those are all that are remarkable at *Barnagul* or *Barnagur*.

THERE are several other Villages on the River's Sides, in the Way to *Hughly*, which lies 20 Miles above *Barnagul*, but none remarkable, till we come to the *Danes* Factory, which stands about four Miles below *Hughly*, but the Poverty of the *Danes* has made them desert it, after having robbed the *Mogul*'s Subjects of some of their Shipping, to keep themselves from starving.

ALMOST opposite to the *Danes* Factory is *Bankebanksal*, a Place where the *Ostend* Company settled a Factory, but, *in Anno* 1723. they quarrelled with the *Fouzdaar* or Governor of *Hughly*, and he forced the *Ostenders* to quit their Factory, and seek Protection from the *French* at *Charnagur*, where their Factory is, but, for Want of Money, are not in a Capacity to trade. They have a few private Families dwelling near the Factory, and a pretty little Church to hear

hear *Maſs* in, which is the chief Buſineſs of the *French* in *Bengal*.

ABOUT half a League farther up is the *Chinchura*, where the *Dutch Emporium* ſtands. It is a large Factory, walled high with Brick. And the Factors have a great many good Houſes ſtanding pleaſantly on the River's Side; and all of them have pretty Gardens to their Houſes. The *Chinchura* is wholly under the *Dutch* Company's Government. It is about a Mile long, and about the ſame Breadth, well inhabited by *Armenians* and the Natives. It is contiguous to *Hughly*, and affords Sanctuary for many poor Natives, when they are in Danger of being oppreſt by the *Mogul's* Governor, or his *Harpies*.

Hughly is a Town of a large Extent, but ill built. It reaches about 2 Miles along the River's Side, from the *Chinchura* before mentioned to the *Bandel*, a Colony formerly ſettled by the *Portugueze*, but the *Mogul's Fouzdaar* governs both at preſent. This Town of *Hughly* drives a great Trade, becauſe all foreign Goods are brought thither for Import, and all Goods of the Product of *Bengal* are brought hither for Exportation. And the *Mogul's Furza* or Cuſtom-houſe is at this Place. It affords rich Cargoes for fifty or ſixty Ships yearly, beſides what is carried to neighbouring Countries in ſmall Veſſels; and there are Veſſels that bring Salt-petre from *Patana*, above 50 Yards long, and 5 broad, and two and an half deep, and can carry above 200 Tuns. They come down in the

Month

Month of *October*, before the Stream of the River, but are obliged to track them up again, with Strength of Hand, about 1000 Miles. To mention all the particular Species of Goods that this rich Country produces, is far beyond my Skill; but, in our *East-india* Company's Sales, all the Sorts, that are sent hence to *Europe*, may be found; but Ophium, long Pepper and Ginger are Commodities that the trading Shipping in *India* deals in, besides Tobacco, and many Sorts of Piece Goods, that are not merchantable in *Europe*.

THE *Bandel*, at present, deals in no Sort of Commodities, but what are in Request at the Court of *Venus*, and they have a Church, where the Owners of such Goods and Merchandize are to be met with, and the Buyer may be conducted to proper Shops, where the Commodities may be seen and felt, and a Priest to be Security for the Soundness of the Goods.

NOW this being my farthest Travels up the famous *Ganges*, I must advance farther on the Report of others, and so I begin with *Cassembazaar*, about 100 Miles above *Hughly*, where the *English* and *Dutch* have their respective Factories; and, by their Companies Orders, the Seconds of Council ought to be Chiefs of those Factories. The Town is large, and much frequented by Merchants, which never fails of making a Place rich. The Country about it is very healthful and fruitful, and produces industrious People, who cultivate many valuable Manufactories.

Muxadabaud is but 12 Miles from it, a Place of much greater Antiquity, and the *Mogul* has a Mint there; but the ancient Name of *Muxadabaud* is changed for *Rajahmal*, for above a Century. It was, in former Times, the greateſt Place of Trade and Commerce on the *Ganges*, but now its Trade and Grandeur adorns *Caſſembazaar*.

About forty or fifty Miles to the Eaſtward of *Rajahmal*, on another Chanel of the *Ganges*, is *Maldo*, a large Town, well inhabited and frequented by Merchants, and the *Engliſh* and *Dutch* had Factories there, but whether they are continued ſtill, I know not.

Patana is the next Town frequented by *Europeans*, where the *Engliſh* and *Dutch* have Factories for Salt-petre and raw Silk. It produces alſo ſo much Opium, that it ſerves all the Countries in *India* with that Commodity. It is the Place of Reſidence of the Prince of *Bengal*, who is always of the Blood Royal. The Town is large, but the Houſes built at ſome Diſtance from one another. The Country is pleaſant and fruitful; and the Town lies in 26 Degrees of Latitude to the Northward of the Æquator.

Bannaras lies about 100 Miles farther up the River, celebrated for its Sanctity by all Perſons over *India*, where *Paganiſm* prevails. Here are Seminaries and Univerſities for the Education of Youth, and to initiate them into the Myſteries of their Religion. *Aurengzeb* reſtrained the Prieſts from ſhewing the Madneſs of their Zeal, for they found

out

out ſome weak Dotards, who, for Oſtentation, would go to the Top of an high Tower, and leap down where divers pointed Weapons were placed in the Spot they were to fall on, and among them they ended their ſilly Lives. It is ſtill in ſo much Veneration, that I have known young and old *Banyans* go from *Surat* thither over Land, out of Devotion, which is computed to be 400 Miles. The Prieſts fill Braſs and Copper Pots, made in the Shape of ſhort-necked Bottles, with *Ganges*'s Water, which they conſecrate and ſeal up, and ſend thoſe Bottles, which contain about 4 *Engliſh* Gallons, all over *India*, to their Benefactors, who make them good Returns, for whoever is waſht with that Water juſt before they expire, are waſht as clean from their Sins as a new-born Babe.

I have ventured ſo far into this *Terra incognita* on the *Ganges*, that I dare venture no farther, but muſt viſit *Dacca*, which lies under the Tropick of *Cancer*, on the broadeſt and eaſtermoſt Branch of *Ganges*. The City is the largeſt in *Bengal*, and it manufactures Cotton and Silk the beſt and cheapeſt. The Plenty and Cheapneſs of Proviſions are incredible, and the Country is full of Inhabitants, but it breeds none of tolerable Courage, for five or ſix armed Men will chaſe a Thouſand: Yet, about two Centuries ago, *Dacca* had its own Kings, but when *Jehan Guire*, the King of *Mogul*, over-ran *Bengal* with a victorious Army, a Detatchment of 20000 Men was ſent down to *Dacca*, on whose Approach the poor King surrendred his Kingdom, without once drawing his Sword in its Defence, and so it easily became annext to the *Mogul*'s Dominions.

THAT Branch of the *Ganges* disembogues into the Sea at *Chittagoung*, or, as the *Portugueze* call it, *Xatigam*, about 50 Leagues below *Dacca*; and this Place confines the *Mogul*'s Dominions to the Eastward. The Distance between *Sagor* the westermost Chanel of the *Ganges*, and *Xatigam* the eastermost, is about 100 Leagues, the maritim Coast being divided into many small Islands made by the Currents of the *Ganges*, but very few are inhabited, because they are so pestred with Tigers, that there is little Safety for other Inhabitants; and there are also many Rhinoceroses on those Islands, but they are not so dangerous Neighbours as the Tigers, yet, when provoked, they will assault any living Thing. Nature has endued him with two particular Rarities out of her Stores. One is a large Horn placed on his Nose. The second is a Coat of Mail to defend him from the Teeth or Claws of other fierce Animals. His Tongue is also somewhat of a Rarity, for, if he can but get any of his Antagonists down, he will lick them so clean, that he leaves neither Skin nor Flesh to cover their Bones; but he is seldom known to be an Aggressor, except when he meets with an Elephant, then he sharpens his Horn and assaults, tho' he is much inferior to the Elephant in Bulk and Strength, being no bigger than a

very

very large Ox, yet he often overcomes in ſpite of the Elephant's Teeth.

Sundiva is an Iſland four Leagues diſtant from the reſt, and ſo far it lies in the Sea, it is about 20 Leagues in Circumference, and has three Fathoms Water within a Mile of the Shore, and it may ſerve to ſhelter ſmall Ships from the raging Seas, and Winds of the South-weſt Monſoons. I was credibly informed by one that wintred there, that he bought 580 Pound Weight of Rice for a Rupee, or Half a Crown, eight Geeſe for the ſame Money, and ſixty good tame Poultry for the ſame, and Cloth is alſo incredibly cheap, it is but thinly inhabited, but the People ſimple and honeſt.

THE Religion of *Bengal* by Law eſtabliſhed, is *Mahometan*, yet for one *Mahometan* there are above an Hundred *Pagans*, and the publick Offices and Poſts of Truſt are filled promiſcuouſly with Men of both Perſwaſions.

THE *Gentiles* are better contented to live under the *Mogul*'s Laws than under *Pagan* Princes, for the *Mogul* taxes them gently, and every one knows what he muſt pay, but the *Pagan* Kings or Princes tax at Diſcretion, making their own Avarice the Standard of Equity; beſides there were formerly many ſmall *Rajahs*, that uſed, upon frivolous Occaſions, to pick Quarrels with one another, and before they could be made Friends again, their Subjects were forced to

open

open both their Veins and Purſes to gratifie Ambition or Folly.

And now having curſorily travelled over the moſt noted Countries and Towns in *Bengal*, with the beſt Remarks I could of their Government, only making a voluntary Omiſſion of many Oppreſſions and other Injuſtices that came within the Reach of my own Knowledge and Experiments, I take Leave of that earthly Paradiſe, and proceed.

CHAP. XXXV.

Gives an Account of Xatigam, *and the Kingdom of* Arackan, *ſome hiſtorical Obſervations on* Sultan Sujah's *Misfortunes there, and the Miſeries that Country fell under by Civil Wars.*

XATIGAM is a Town that borders on *Bengal* and *Arackan*, and its Poverty makes it a Matter of Indifference whom it belongs to. It was here that the *Portugueze* firſt ſettled in *Bengal*, but the Dangers their Ships run in coming thither in the South-weſt Monſoons, made them remove to the *Bandel* at *Hughly*. The *Mogul* keeps a *Cadjee* or Judge in it, to adminiſter Juſtice among the *Pagan* and *Mahometan* Inhabitants, but the Offspring of thoſe *Portugueze* that followed the Fortune of *Sultan Sujah*, when he was forced to quit *Bengal*, are the domineering Lords of it.

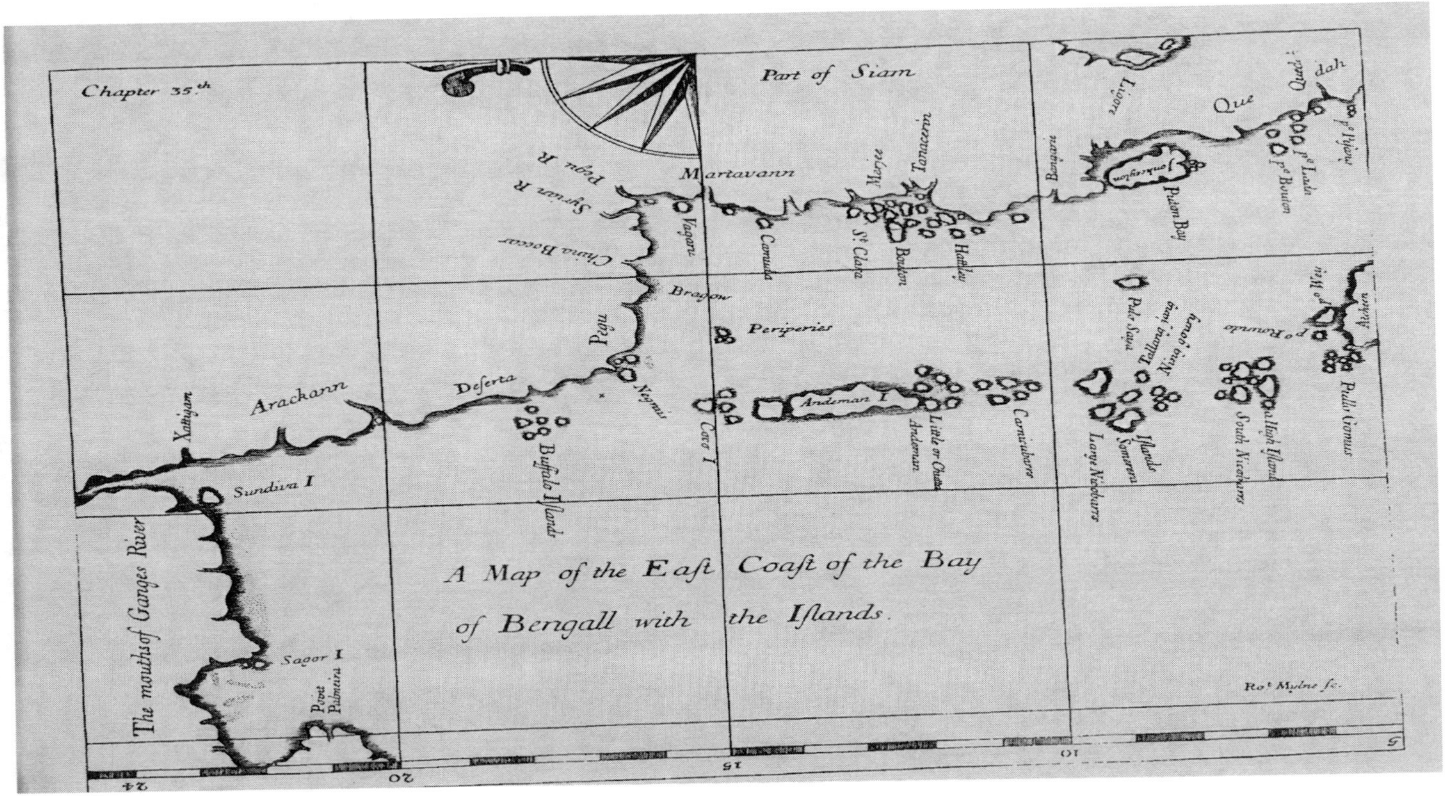
Chapter 35th
Part of Siam
A Map of the East Coast of the Bay
of Bengall with the Islands.
Martavann
Pegu R
Syrian R
China Boccar
Bragow
Pegu
Deserta
Negrais
Arackann
Xattigan
Sundiva I
The mouth of Ganges River
Sagor I
Point Palmira
Vagaru
Camuda
St. Clara
Bouton
Hattley
Mergee
Tanacerin
Bongarie
Puton Bay
Junkseylon
Ligore
Quedah
Pº Bouton
Pº Lada
Pº Pisang
Periperies
Cocos I
Andeman I
Little or Chutta Andeman
Carnicubarre
Buffalo Islands
Pulo Saya
Tallang jang
Nina gouny
Islands Somerera
Large Nicobarrs
South Nicobarrs
High Island
Pº Ronnda
Pº Way
Achen
Pullo Gomus
Roᵗ Mylne sc.
5
10
15
20
24

It is not so fertil in Corn as *Bengal*, and has but few Cotton Manufactories, but it affords the best Timber for building, of any Place about it. The River has a deep enough Entrance, but is pestered with Sand Banks, and some Rocks within. I have known some *English* Ships forced from Point *Palmeira* by Stress of Weather thither, and had safe riding till the North-east Monsoons came to relieve them. The Government is so anarchical, that every one goes armed with Sword, Pistol, and Blunderbush, nay, even the Priests are obliged to go armed, and often use their Arms to as bad Ends as the licentious Laity, and some of the Priests have died Martyrs to villainous Actions.

Arackan is the next maritim Country to the Southward of *Bengal*, and in former Times made some Figure in Trade. It was into this Country that the unfortunate *Sultan Sujah* came a Supplicant for Protection, when *Emirjemal* chased him out of *Bengal*. He carried his Wives and Children with him, and about Two hundred of his Retinue, who were resolved to follow his Fortune, and he carried six or eight Camels Load of Gold and Jewels which proved his Ruin, and in the End, the Ruin of the Kingdom of *Arackan*.

When *Sultan Sujah* first visited the King of *Arackan*, he made him Presents suitable to the Quality of the Donor and Receiver, the *Arackaner* promising him all the Civilities due to so great a Prince, with a safe

Asylum

Asylum for himself and Family: When *Emirjemal* knew where *Sultan Sujah* had taken Sanctuary, he sent a Letter to the King of *Arackan*, wherein he demanded the poor distrest Prince to be delivered up to him, otherwise he threatned to bring his Army into his Country to take him by Force. The threatning Letter wrought so far on the base *Arackaner*, that he contrived Ways and Means to pick a Quarrel with his Guest, to have a Pretext to oblige *Emirjemal*, at last he found a very fair one.

Sultan Sujah having a very beautiful Daughter, the King of *Arackan* desired her in Marriage, but knew well enough that *Sultan Sujah* would never consent to the Match, he being a *Pagan* and she a *Mahometan*. Her Father used all reasonable Arguments to disswade the *Arackaner* from prosecuting his Suit, but in vain, for the *Arackaner* grew daily more pressing, and *Sultan Sujah* at last gave him a flat Denial, on which the base King sent him Orders to go out of his Dominions in Three Days, and forbad the Markets to furnish him any more with Provisions for his Money. *Sultan Sujah* knowing it would be Death for him to go back to *Bengal*, resolved to pass over some Mountains overgrown with Woods, into the King of *Pegu*'s Dominions, which were not above 100 Miles off, and so next Day after Summons, with his Family, Treasure, and Attendants, *Sultan Sujah* began his March, but the barbarous *Arackaner* sent a strong Party after him,

him, who overtook him before he had advanced far into the Woods, and killed most of *Sultan Sujah*'s Company, and seized the Treasure, and brought it back in an inglorious Triumph. What became of *Sultan Sujah* and his fair Daughter, none could ever give a certain Account; whether they were killed in the Skirmish, or whether they were destroyed by wild Elephants and Tigers in the Woods, none ever knew, but the *Arackaners* alledge they were destroyed by the wild Beasts of the Woods, and not by the more savage Beasts in human Shape.

So much Treasure never had been seen in *Arackan* before, but to whom it should belong caused some Disturbance. The King thought that all belonged to him, those that fought for it claimed a Share, and the Princes of the Blood wanted some fine large Diamonds for their Ladies, but the Tribe of *Levi* found a Way to make up the Difference, and perswaded the King and the other Pretenders, to dedicate it to the God *Dagun*, who was the titular God of the Kingdom, and to depositate it in his Temple, which all agreed to; now whether this be the same *Dagon* of *Ashdod*, mentioned in the first Book and fifth Chapter of *Samuel*, I do not certainly know, but *Dagun* has a large Temple in *Arackan*, that I have heard of, and another in *Pegu* that I have seen.

In 1690. a King of *Arackan* dying without Issue, two Princes of the Blood quarrelled about filling up of the Vacancy, they both took

took Arms, and both had an Eye upon the Treaſure, which ſo frightned the Prieſthood, that they removed *Sultan Sujah*'s Treaſure to another Place only known to themſelves; and thoſe two hot Blades purſued their Quarrel ſo warmly, that in one Year themſelves and Families were intirely cut off, and the Kingdom has continued in Anarchy ever ſince.

Arackan has the Conveniency of a noble ſpacious River, and its Mouth is both large and deep enough to accommodate Ships of the greateſt Burden into a ſpacious Harbour, large enough to hold all the Ships in *Europe*.

WHEN the *Engliſh* left *Bengal in Anno* 1686. Mr. *Channock* came thither with Half a Dozen of great Ships, to paſs the South-weſt Monſoons away, the Country aſſiſted them plentifully with Proviſions, but they had no other Commerce; they had no leſs than ſix Fathoms Water going in to the River, and in ſome Places within, above twenty. The Country produces Timber for building, ſome Lead, Tin, Stick-lack, and Elephants Teeth.

THE Sea Coaſt of *Arackan* reaches from *Xatigam* to Cape *Negrais*, about 400 Miles in Length, but few Places inhabited, becauſe there are ſuch vaſt Numbers of wild Elephants and Buffaloes, that would deſtroy the Productions of the Ground, and Tigers to deſtroy the tame Animals, that they think it impracticable to inhabit it, only ſome Iſlands in the Sea are peopled with ſome poor miſerable

ſerable Fiſhers, who get their Bread out of the Water, to keep them from ſtarving, and they live out of the Way of Oppreſſion.

THERE are ſome of the *Mogul's* Subjects who trade to *Arackan* for the Commodities above mentioned, and ſometimes they meet with good Bargains of Diamonds, Rubies, *&c.* precious Stones, and Gold Rupees, which are to be ſuppoſed are ſome of *Sultan Sujah's* Treaſure, pilfered by the avaricious Prieſts.

THERE are abundance of Iſlands on the *Arackan* Coaſt, but they lie cloſe to the Shore, only the *Buffalo* Iſlands lie about four Leagues off, and there is a Rock that ſhews its Head above Water about the Middle of the Chanel, between thoſe Iſlands and the Continent. The Chanels among the *Buffalo* Iſlands ſeem to be clear of Danger, and above 20 Fathoms Water in them, but about 8 Leagues off the North End of the great Iſland of *Negrais*, is a dangerous Rock that only appears above Water in the low Ebbs of ſpring Tides, it lies in 15 Fathoms Water, and twenty Yards off are 13 Fathoms. The other Iſland of *Negrais*, which makes the Point called the Cape, is a ſmall, low, barren rocky Iſland, it is often called *Diamond* Iſland, becauſe its Shape is a Rhombus. About the Year 1704. four *French* Ships went to careen at the great *Negrais*, and turning in between the Iſlands, one Ship of 70 Guns called *L' Indien*, run aground on ſome Rocks lying on the

the Inside of *Diamond* Island, and was lost, but the rest saved the Men, and all her portable Furniture.

THREE Leagues to the Southward of *Diamond* Island, lies a Reef of Rocks a League long, but they do not appear above Water, tho' they are conspicuous at all Times by the Sea breaking on them. There is a good Chanel between the Island and them, above a League broad, and 11 or 12 Fathoms deep; the Rocks are called the *Legarti*, or, in *English*, the *Lizard*.

CHAP. XXXVI.

Gives an Account of the famous Kingdom of Pegu, *its Situation and Product, with its Laws, Customs, and Religion, and some historical Accounts of their Temples and Gods, of Occurrences and Revolutions in the State, and how it became a Province of the Kingdom of* Barma.

THE Sea-coast from *Negrais* to *Syrian* Bar, is in the Dominions of *Pegu*, there are some of the Mouths of *Pegu* River open on that Coast into the Sea. *Dolla* is the first, about fifty Miles to the Eastward of *Negrais*. *China Backaar* is another about forty Miles to the Eastward of *Dolla*, and between these Openings there is a dangerous Bank of black Sand, that runs four or five Leagues out into the Sea, and so far off there are

are but 14 Foot Water. About 60 Miles to the Eastward of *China Backaar*, is the Bar of *Syrian*, the only Port now open for Trade in all the *Pegu* Dominions.

If by Accident a Ship bound to *Syrian*, be driven a League or two to the Eastward of that River's Mouth, a strong Tide carries her on hard Sands till she sits fast on them, for Anchors are of no Use to stop them, because of the Rapidity of the Current; at low Water the Ships are dry when on those Sands, and the Sea leaves them, and retires 5 or 6 Leagues, at which Time the shipwrackt Men walk on the Sands toward the Shore for their Safety, for the Sea comes back with so much Noise, that the roring of the Billows may be heard ten Miles off, for a Body of Waters comes rolling in on the Sand, whose Front is above two Fathoms high, and whatever Body lies in its Way it overturns, and no Ship can evade its Force, but in a Moment is overturned, this violent Boer the Natives call a *Mackrea*.

About six Leagues from the Bar of *Pegu* River, is the City of *Syrian*, it is built near the River's Side on a rising Ground, and walled round with a Stone-wall without Morter. The Governor, who is generally of the Blood-royal, has his Lodgings in it, but the Suburbs are four Times bigger than the City. It was many Years in Possession of the *Portugueze*, till by their Insolence and Pride they were obliged to quit it.

 The

THE ancient City of *Pegu* ſtands about forty Miles to the Eaſtward of *Syrian*, the Ditches that ſurrounded the City, which are now dry, and bear good Corn, teſtifie that few Cities in the World exceeded it in Magnitude, for they are reckoned ſix or ſeven Leagues round their outward Polygon.

IT was the Seat of many great and puiſſant Kings, who made as great a Figure as any in the Eaſt, but now its Glory is in the Duſt, for not one twentieth Part of it is inhabited, and thoſe are but the lower Claſs of People who inhabit it. The Cauſe of the Ruin of the Kingdoms of *Pegu*, *Martavan*, and ſome others under the Dominions of *Pegu*, I had from ſome *Peguers*, in ſeveral Diſcourſes with them about that Revolution, which was thus.

THERE was great Love and Friendſhip between the Kings and Subjects of *Pegu* and *Siam*, being next Neighbours to one another, and they had a good Intercourſe of Trade, both by Land and Sea, till in the fifteenth Century, a *Pegu* Veſſel being at *Odia* the chief City of *Siam*, and when ready to depart for *Pegu*, anchored one Evening near a little Temple a few Miles below the City, and the Maſter of the Veſſel, with ſome of his Crew, going to worſhip in that Temple, ſeeing a pretty well carv'd Image of the God *Samſay*, about a Covet high, fell in Love with it, and finding his Prieſts negligent in watching, ſtole him away, and carried him on board Priſoner for *Pegu*. When the negligent

gligent Priests mist their little God they were in a deplorable Condition, lamenting their Loss to all their neighbouring Priests, who advised them to complain to the King of *Siam* of the Theft, which accordingly they did, imploring his good Offices with the King of *Pegu*, to have their God sent back; and it happened that by the unseasonable Floods in the River that Year, there came to be a great Scarcity of Corn, which Calamity was imputed by the Priests to the Loss of *Samsay*, upon which the pious Prince sent an Embassy to his Brother of *Pegu*, desiring the Restitution of the Image, whose Absence had caused so great Loss and Clamour in his Country.

THE King of *Pegu* being as great a Bigot as his Brother of *Siam*, would by no Means deliver back a God who had fled from the Impieties of his native Land to him for Protection, and with that Answer sent back the *Siam* Ambassador, who was not a little mortified with the Disappointment.

SINCE fair Means could not perswade the *Peguer* to send back the little God, the *Siamer* was resolved to try what Force would do, and accordingly raised an Army of two or three hundred thousand Men to invade the King of *Pegu*'s Dominions, and the first Fury of the War fell on the Province of *Martavan*, being contiguous to the Territories of *Siam*, and with Fire and Sword destroyed the open Country almost to the Gates of the City of *Martavan*, where often the King of *Pegu* kept his Court, and was formerly the Metropolis of an independent Kingdom, before *Pegu* reduced that Country by Conqueſt to be a Province of theirs.

AFTER the *Siamer* had ſatiated his Cruelty and Rage, by the Deſtruction of many poor Innocents, he retired back to his own Country very much elevated with Pride and Vain-glory for his great Atchievements, but next Year he was pretty well humbled, for the *Peguer* raiſed a much greater Army, and embarking them in ſmall Boats on the River *Memnon*, on which the City of *Odia* ſtands in one of its Iſlands, his Army was brought with ſo much Celerity and Secrecy, that the *Peguer* brought the firſt News of his Invaſion, and pitching his Tents round the City, ſoon brought it into great Straits, by ſtopping the daily Proviſions that ſupported it; but unexpectedly the River bringing down great Floods of Waters, ſooner than their ordinary Time, the Country about the City overflowed, and ſpoilt all the *Peguer*'s Proviſions of Corn, and drowned near the Half of his Army, which obliged him to raiſe the Siege, and retire to his own Dominions.

NEXT Year, the *Siamer*, to be revenged, levied another great Army, with which he over-ran all the inland Countries of *Pegu* that lay near him, and annext them to his own Dominions. The *Peguer* finding that he could not recover his Lands without foreign Aid and Aſſiſtance, invited the *Portugueze*, whoſe Name began to be dreadful

in

in *India*, and by the great Encouragement he gave them, got about 1000 Volunteers into his Service. Neither the *Siamers* nor the *Peguers* at that Time underſtood the Uſe of Fire Arms, and their Noiſe and Execution at ſo great a Diſtance terrified them. With the *Portugueze* Aſſiſtance, the *Peguer* went with his Army, which was very numerous, to find out the *Siamer*, and having found him, gave him Battle, the *Portugueze* being in the Front with their Fire Arms, ſoon put the *Siamer* to Flight before they could come to Handy-blows, on which he left the *Peguer's* Country in greater Haſte than he came into it.

THE King of *Pegu* was ſo ſenſible of the *Portugueze* Service in gaining the Battle, and driving the *Siamers* out of his conquered Country, that he made one *Senhor Thoma Pereyra* (who commanded the *Portugueze* in the War) Generaliſſimo of all his Forces, which Preferment made the *Portugueze* ſo inſolent, that in a few Years they became intolerable to all Ranks and Degrees of Perſons in *Pegu*.

BOTH Kings grew tired of War, but both too proud to make Advances toward Peace, ſo that for many Years they had skirmiſhing with ſmall Parties, tho' no ſet Battles, and where-ever the *Portugueze* Arms went, they had Victory to accompany them.

THE King of *Pegu*, to have his Forces nearer the Borders of *Siam*, ſettled his Court at *Martavan*, and kept the *Portugueze* near him,

him, to be ready on all Occaſions, either to repel or aſſault the *Siam* Forces, as Opportunity ſerved, and *Thoma Pereyra* was the darling Favourite at Court, he had his Elephants of State, and a Guard of his own Countrymen to attend him. One Day as he was coming from Court in State, on a large Elephant, towards his own Palace, he chanced to hear Muſick in a Burgher's Houſe, whoſe Daughter being a very beautiful Virgin, had been married that Morning to a young Man of the Neighbourhood. The General went to the Houſe and wiſhed them Joy, and deſired to ſee the Bride. The Parents took the General's Viſit for a great Honour done them, and brought their Daughter to his Elephant's Side; he being ſmitten with her Beauty, ordered his Guard to ſeize her and carry her to his Houſe.

His Orders were but too readily obeyed, and the poor Bridegroom not being able to bear his Loſs, cut his own Throat, and the diſconſolate Parents of their injured Children, rent their Clothes, and went crying and complaining through the Streets towards the King's Palace, imploring their Gods and Country-men to avenge them on the inſolent *Portugueze*, the common Oppreſſors of their Country. Crowds of People came from all Parts of the City to hear and ſee the Tragedy, their Numbers grew ſo great, that the Streets were hardly big enough for them, and their Noiſe ſo loud that it reached the King's Ears, who ſent to know the Cauſe of their

their Uprore. The Meſſenger returning, acquainted the King what had been tranſacted, and he, to appeaſe the Tumult, ſent them Word that he would puniſh the Criminal, and accordingly ſent for his General, but he being much taken up with the Enjoyment of his new Purchaſe, made an Excuſe that he was ſo much out of Order, that he could not then wait on his Majeſty till he was better, which Anſwer ſo provoked the King, that he ordered the whole City to take Arms, and to make a general Maſſacre on all the *Portugueze* whereſoever they could be found in City or Country. The King's Orders were put in Execution ſo ſpeedily, that in a few Hours all the *Portugueze* were ſlaughtered, and the guilty Criminal was taken alive, and made faſt by the Heels to an Elephant's Foot, who dragged him through the Streets till there was no Skin nor Fleſh left to cover his Bones, which Spectacle appeaſed the enraged Populace. There were only three *Portugueze* ſaved, who were accidentally in the Suburbs next the River, who hid themſelves till Night favoured their Eſcape in a ſmall Boat, in which they coaſted along the Shore, feeding on what the Woods and Rocks afforded them, and at length arrived at *Malacca*, to give an Account of the melancholy Scene.

Both Kingdoms being much weakned with bloody Wars, took Reſt for many Years, but never entred on Treaties of Peace So about the Middle of the ſeventeenth Century

tury, the *Siamer* invaded the Dominions of *Pegu*, and conquered all to the Southward of *Martavan*, taking in the Provinces of *Tanacerin* and *Ligore*, who were Tributaries to *Pegu*, and retains them ſtill in his Poſſeſſion.

THE King of *Pegu* finding that the Incroachments of *Siam* daily leſſened his Dominions, and his own Forces were not able to protect what he had left, ſent an Embaſſy to the King of *Barma*, a potent Prince, whoſe Dominions lay about 500 Miles up the River from *Pegu*, to beg his Aſſiſtance to ſtop the *Siamers*, in their Courſe of Conqueſts, and he promiſed to give good Encouragement to the *Barmaes*. The Embaſſy was graciouſly received, and an Army of an hundred thouſand was levied for that Service, and ſent on tranſport Veſſels to *Pegu*, and joyned the *Pegu* Army, who conjunctly marched againſt the *Siamer*, and drove him quite out of his new Conqueſts; and when the *Barmaes* obſerved the Feebleneſs and bad Diſcipline of the *Pegu* Army, they even killed the King of *Pegu*, and broke the *Pegu* Army, and ſeized the Kingdoms of *Pegu* and *Martavan* for their Maſter, and in that Family it continues to this Time. The *Barmaes* ruined both the Cities of *Pegu* and *Martavan*, and ſunk Veſſels in the Mouth of the River of *Martavan*, to make it unnavigable, and ſo it continues. This Account I had at *Pegu in Anno* 1709. both from *Peguers* and *Portugueze*, who agreed in the Hiſtory as I have related it.

THE

THE Dominions of *Barma* are at present very large, reaching from *Moravi* near *Tanacerin*, to the Province of *Yunan* in *China*, about 800 Miles from North to South, and 250 Miles broad from West to East. It has no Sea-port but *Syrian*, and that River is capable to receive a Ship of 600 Tuns. The Town drives a good Trade with *Armenians*, *Portugueze*, *Moors* and *Gentows*, and some *English*; their Import is several Sorts of *Indian* Goods, such as *Beteellas*, *Mulmuls*, *Cossas*, *Sannis*, *Orangshays*, *Tangebs*, *European* Hats coarse and fine, and Silver. The Customs are eight and an half *per Cent.* which, with other Charges, amount to about twelve in the Hundred. The Product of the Country is Timber for building, Elephants, Elephants Teeth, Bees-wax, Stick-lack, Iron, Tin, Oyl of Earth, Wood-oyl, Rubies the best in the World, Diamonds, but they are small, and are only found in the Craws of Poultry and Pheasants, and one Family has only the Indulgence to sell them, and none dare open the Ground to dig for them. Saltpetre they have in Abundance, but it is Death to export it, Plenty of *Ganse* or Lead, which passeth all over the *Pegu* Dominions for Money. About twenty Sail of Ships find their Account in Trade for the limited Commodities, but the *Armenians* have got the Monopoly of the Rubies, which turns to a good Account in their Trade; and I have seen some blue Sapphires there, that I was told were found on some Mountains of this Country.

THE

THE Country is very fruitful in Corn, Fruits, and Roots, and excellent Legumen of ſeveral Species, Abundance of wild Game either quadrupeds or winged. In the Months of *September* and *October*, wild Deer are ſo plentiful that I have bought one for three or four Pence; they are very fleſhy, but no Fat about them. They have many Sorts of good Fiſh, and Swines Fleſh and Poultry are both plentiful and good.

THEY wear none of our *European* Commodities but Hats and Ribbons, and the Gentry will give extravagant Prices for fine Beaver Hats, and rich Ribbons flower'd with Silver and Gold, and if it be never ſo broad it is ſtretcht up the Crownof the Hat as far as it can go, and they uſe no Sort of Cock to their Hats. Cotton Cloths from *Bengal* and *Chormondel*, with ſome ſtripped Silks, are beſt for their Market, and Silver of any Sort is welcome to them. It pays the King eight and an Half *per Cent*. Cuſtom, but in lieu of that high Duty, he indulges the Merchants to melt it down, and put what Alloy they pleaſe in it, and then to paſs it off in Payments as high as they can.

Rupee Silver, which has no Alloy in it, will bear twenty eight *per Cent*. of Copper-alloy, and keep the *Pegu* Touch, which they call flower'd Silver, and if it flowers, it paſſes current.

THEIR Way to make flower'd Silver is, when the Silver and Copper are mixt and melted together, and while the Metal is liquid,

liquid, they put it into a ſhallow Mould, of what Figure or Magnitude they pleaſe, and before the Liquidity is gone, they blow on it through a ſmall wooden Pipe, which makes the Face, or Part blown upon, appear with the Figures of Flowers or Stars, but I never ſaw any *European* or other Foreigner at *Pegu*, have the Art to make thoſe Figures appear, and if there is too great a Mixture of Alloy, no Figures will appear.

THE King generally adds ten *per Cent.* on all Silver that comes into his Treaſury, beſides what was put on at firſt, and tho' it be not flower'd, it muſt go off in all his Payments, but from any Body elſe it may be refuſed if it is not flower'd.

HIS Government is arbitrary. All his Commands are Laws, but the Reins of Government are kept ſteady and gently in the King's own Hand. He ſeverely puniſhes his Governors of Provinces or Towns, if Oppreſſions or other illegal Practices are proven upon them; and to know how Affairs paſs in the State, every Province or City has a *Mandereen* or Deputy reſiding at Court, which is generally in the City of *Ava*, the preſent Metropolis.

EVERY Morning theſe *Mandereens* are obliged to attend at Court, and after his Majeſty has dreſt and breakfaſted, which is generally on a Diſh of Rice boiled in fair Water, and his Sauce is ſome Shrimps dried and powder'd, and ſome Salt and Cod-pepper mixt with thoſe two Ingredients, and that

that Mixture makes a very pungent Sauce, which they call *Prock*, and is in great Eſteem and Uſe among the *Peguers*.

WHEN his Breakfaſt is over, he retires into a Room ſo contrived that he can ſee all the Attendants, but none can ſee him, and a Page ſtands without to call whom the King would have give Account of the current News of his Province or City, which is performed with profound Reverence toward the Room where the King ſtays, and with a diſtinct audible Voice; and if any particular Matters of Conſequence is forgot or omitted, and the King comes to hear of it by another Hand, ſevere Puniſhments follow, and ſo he paſſes his Mornings in hearing the neceſſary Caſes of his own Affairs as well as thoſe of his Subjects.

IF he is informed of Treaſon, Murder, or ſuch like hainous Crimes, he orders the Matter to be judicially tried before Judges of his own chooſing, for that Time and Affair, and on Conviction he ſigns the dead Warrant, wherein he orders, that the Wretch convicted ſhall trade no more on his Ground, and Execution preſently follows, either by beheading, or ordering them to be Sport for his Elephants, which is the cruelleſt Death. Sometimes he baniſhes them for a certain Time to the Woods, and if they are not devoured by Tigers, or killed by wild Elephants, they may return when their Term is expired, and paſs the Remainder of their Days in ſerving a tame Elephant; and for ſmaller

ſmaller Crimes they are only condemned to clean his Elephants Stables for Life.

HIS Subjects, if they may be ſo called, treat him with fulſom Adulation. When they ſpeak or write to him they call him their God (or in their Language *Kiack*) and in his Letters to foreign Princes, he aſſumes the Title of King of Kings, to whom all other Kings ought to be ſubject, as being near Kinſman and Friend to all the Gods in Heaven and on Earth, and by their Friendſhip to him all Animals are fed and preſerved, and the Seaſons of the Year are regularly kept: The Sun is his Brother, and the Moon and Stars are his near Relations, Lord over the Floods and Ebbing of the Sea; and after all his lofty Epithets and Hyperboles, he deſcends to be King of the white Elephant, and of the twenty four white *Somereroes* or *Umbrellaes*. Theſe two laſt he may indeed claim with ſome Shew of Juſtice, for I have ſeen Elephants of a light yellow Colour both in *Pegu* and *Siam*, but who ought to be called their Lord is a Queſtion not yet decided; and as King of the twenty four white *Somereroes*, I believe few Kings will much care to diſpute that glorious Title with him, for thoſe *Somereroes* are only common *China Umbrellaes*, covered over with thin *Chormondel Beteellaes*, and their Canes lackt and gilded, and becauſe his own Subjects dare not uſe any ſuch *Umbrellaes*, he wiſely lays his imperial Commands on all other Kings to forbear wearing of them when they go abroad.

AF-

After his Majeſty has dined, there is a Trumpet blown, to ſignifie to all his Slaves, as he terms other Kings, that they may go to Dinner, becauſe their Lord has already dined. And when any foreign Ships arrive at *Syrian*, the Number of People on board, with their Age and Sex, are ſent to him, to let him know that ſo many of his Slaves are arrived to partake of the Glory and Happineſs of his Reign and Favour, and the higheſt Title his own Subjects aſſume, is the King's firſt Slave.

The King's Palace at *Ava* is very large, built of Stone, and has four Gates for its Conveniencies. Ambaſſadors enter at the Eaſt Gate, which is called the golden Gate, becauſe all Ambaſſadors make their Way to him by Preſents. The South Gate is called the Gate of Juſtice, where all People that bring Petitions, Accuſations, or Complaints, enter. The Weſt is the Gate of Grace, where all that have received Favours, or have been acquitted of Crimes, paſs out in State, and all condemned Perſons carried out in Fetters; and the North Gate fronting the River, is the Gate of State where his Majeſty paſſes through, when he thinks fit to bleſs his People with his Preſence, and all his Proviſions and Water are carried in at that Gate.

When Pots of Water, or Baskets of Fruits are carried through the Streets for the King's Uſe, an Officer attends them, and all the People that fortune to be near, muſt fall on their Knees, and let it paſs

paſs by, as a good *Catholick* does when he ſees the Hoſt.

WHEN an Ambaſſador is admitted to Audience in the Palace, he is attended with a large Troop of Guards, with Trumpets ſounding, and Heralds proclaiming the Honour the Ambaſſador is about to receive, in going to ſee the Glory of the Earth, his Majeſty's own ſweet Face, and between the Gate and the Head of the Stairs that lead to the Chamber of Audience, the Ambaſſador is attended with the Maſter of the Ceremonies, who inſtructs him to kneel three Times in his Way thither, and continue ſo with his Hands over his Head, till a Proclamation is read before he dare riſe. Some of his Elephants are inſtructed to fall on their Belly when the King paſſes by them.

THIS Relation I had from one Mr. *Roger Aliſon*, who had been twice Ambaſſador from the Governor of Fort St. *George*, or his Agents at *Syrian*, to the Court of *Ava*; and tho' the Palace is very large, yet the Buildings are but mean, and the City tho' great and populous, is only built of *Bambow* Canes, thatcht with Straw or Reeds, and the Floors of Teak Plank, or ſplit *Bambows*, becauſe if Treaſon or other capital Crimes be detected, the Criminals may have no Place of Shelter, for if they do not appear on the firſt Summons, Fire will fetch them out of their combuſtible Habitations.

HIS Sword-officers have no Salary, nor his Soldiers for their Support, but there is

a

a Province or a City given to ſome Minion, who is to give Suſtenance to ſuch a Number of Soldiers, and find the Palace at *Ava* with ſuch a Quota of Proviſions as the Providore thinks fit to appoint.

WHEN there is a War, and Parties are ſent on Expeditions, then the King allows them Pay, Clothes, Arms, and provides Magazines of Proviſions for them; but aſſoon as the War is at an End, then the Clothes and Arms are returned, by which Means Diſcipline is little known among them, and a Man of a tolerable Stock of Courage may paſs there for an Hero.

THE Quality of an Officer is known by his Tobacco Pipe having an earthen or metallick Head, with a Socket to let in a joynted Reed, that on its upper End has a Mouth-piece of Gold, joynted as the Reed or Cane is, and by the Number of Joynts in the golden Mouth-piece, the Quality of the Officer is known, and Reſpect paid him accordingly.

ALL Cities and Towns under this King's Dominions, are like *ariſtocratical* Commonwealths. The Prince or Governor ſeldom ſits in Council, but appoints his Deputy, and twelve Counſellers or Judges, and they ſit once in ten Days at leaſt, but oftner when Buſineſs calls them. They convene in a large Hall, mounted about three Foot high, and double Benches round the Floor for People to ſit or kneel on, and to hear the free Debates of Council. The Hall being built on Pillars of Wood, is open on all Sides, and the Judges

Judges ſet in the Middle on Matts, and ſitting in a Ring there is no Place of Precedence; there are no Advocates to plead at the Bar, but every one has the Privilege to plead his own Cauſe, or ſend it in Writing to be read publickly, and it is determined judicially within the Term of three Sittings of Council, but if any one queſtions his own Eloquence, or Knowledge of the Laws of Equity, he may impower a Friend to plead for him, but there are no Fees but what the Town contributes for the Maintenance of that Court, which in their Language is called the *Rounday*, and thoſe Contributions are very ſmall: There are Clerks ſet at the Backs of the Judges, ready to write down whatever the Complainant and Defendant has to ſay, and the Caſe is determined by the Prince and that Council, very equitably; for if the leaſt Partiality is found awarded to either Party, and the King is made acquainted with it by the Deputies at Court, the whole Sentence is revoked, and the whole Board are corrected for it, ſo that very few have Occaſion to appeal to Court, which they may do if they are aggrieved, and if an Appeal is made upon ill Grounds, the Appellant is chaſtiſed, which juſt Rigour hinders many tedious Suits that ariſe where there are no Penalties annext to ſuch Faults.

The Judges have a particular Garb of their own. Their Hair being permitted to grow long, is tied on the Top of their Heads with Cotton Ribbon wrapt about it, and it ſtands upright in the Form of a ſharp Pyramid. Their Coat is of a thin *Betella*, ſo that their Skin is eaſily ſeen through it. About their Loyns they have a large *Lungee* or Scarf, as all other *Peguers* have, that reaches to their Ancles, and againſt the Navel a round Bundle made of their *Lungee*, as big as a Child's Head, but Stockings and Shoes are not uſed in *Pegu*.

THE *Barmaes* wear the ſame Habit, and imprint ſeveral Devices in their Skins, prickt with a Bodkin, and Powder of Charcoal rubbed over the little Wounds, while the Blood continues wet in them, and the black Marks remain ever after. The *Peguers* dare not paint their Skins, ſo that the Natives of each Nation are eaſily known by the diſtinguiſhing Mark of Painting or Plainneſs. There are few of their Men fat, but plump, well ſhap'd, of an Olive Colour, and well featur'd.

THE Women are much whiter than the Men, and have generally pretty plump Faces, but of ſmall Stature, yet very well ſhap'd, their Hands and Feet ſmall, and their Arms and Legs well proportioned. Their Headdreſs is their own black Hair tied up behind, and when they go abroad, they wear a *Shaul* folded up, or a Piece of white Cotton Cloth lying looſe on the Top of their Heads. Their bodily Garb is a Frock of Cotton Cloth or Silk, made meet for their Bodies, and the Arms of their Frock ſtretcht cloſe on the Arm, the lower Part of the Frock reaching Half-thigh down. Under the Frock they have

a

a Scarf or *Lungee* doubled fourfold, made fast about their Middle, which reaches almost to the Ancle, so contrived, that at every Step they make, as they walk, it opens before, and shews the right Leg and Part of the Thigh.

THIS Fashion of Petticoats, they say, is very ancient, and was first contrived by a certain Queen of that Country, who was grieved to see the Men so much addicted to *Sodomy*, that they neglected the pretty Ladies. She thought that by the Sight of a pretty Leg and plump Thigh, the Men might be allured from that abominable Custom, and place their Affections on proper Objects, and according to the ingeiuous Queen's Conjecture, that Dress of the *Lungee* had its desired End, and now the Name of *Sodomy* is hardly known in that Country.

THE Women are very courteous and kind to Strangers, and are very fond of marrying with *Europeans*, and most Part of the Strangers who trade thither, marry a Wife for the Term they stay. The Ceremony is, (after the Parties are agreed) for the Bride's Parents or nearest Friends or Relations, to make a Feast, and invite her Friends and the Bridegroom's, and at the End of the Feast, the Parent or Bride-man, asketh them both before the Company, if they are content to cohabit together as Man and Wife, and both declaring their Consent, they are declared by the Parent or Friend to be lawfully married, and if the Bridegroom has an House, he carries her thither, but if not, they have a Bed provided in the Houſe where they are married, and are left to their own Diſcretion how to paſs away the Night.

THEY prove obedient and obliging Wives, and take the Management of Affairs within Doors wholly in their own Hands. She goes to Market for Food, and acts the Cook in dreſſing his Victuals, takes Care of his Clothes, in waſhing and mending them ; if their Huſbands have any Goods to ſell, they ſet up a Shop and ſell them by Retail, to a much better Account than they could be ſold for by Wholeſale, and ſome of them carry a Cargo of Goods to the inland Towns, and barter for Goods proper for the foreign Markets that their Husbands are bound to, and generally bring fair Accounts of their Negotiations. If ſhe proves falſe to her Husband's Bed, and on fair Proof convicted, her Huſband may carry her to the *Rounday*, and have her Hair cut, and ſold for a Slave, and he may have the Money ; but if the Husband goes aſtray, ſhe'll be apt to give him a gentle Doſe, to ſend him into the other World a Sacrifice to her Reſentment.

IF ſhe proves prolifick, the Children cannot be carried out of the Kingdom without the King's Permiſſion, but that may be purchaſed for 40 or 50 *L. Sterl.* and if an irreconcilable Quarrel happen where there are Children, the Father is obliged to take Care of the Boys, and the Mother of the Girls. If a Husband is content to continue the Marriage,

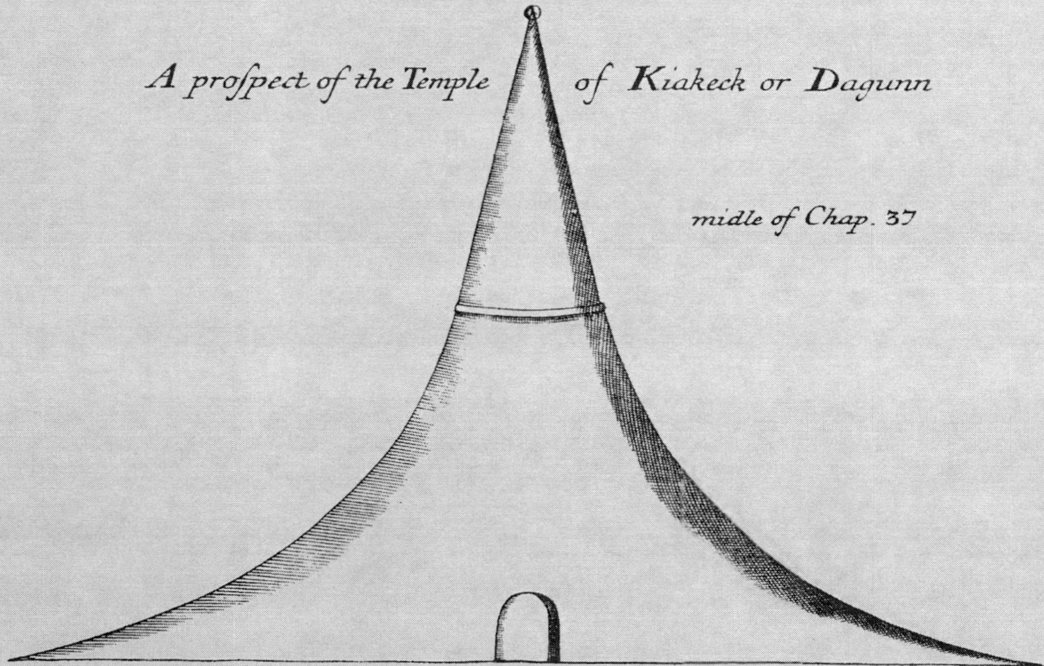

A prospect of the Temple of Kiakeck or Dagunn

midle of Chap. 37

riage, whilst he goes to foreign Countries about his Affairs, he must leave some Fund to pay her about six Shillings eight Pence *per* Month, otherwise at the Year's End she may marry again, but if that Sum is paid her on his Account, she is obliged to stay the Term of three Years, and she is never the worse, but rather the better lookt on, that she has been married to several *European* Husbands.

CHAP. XXXVII.

Gives an Account of the Pegu *Clergy their Charity,* &c. *their Temples, and the Reason why they are so numerous, and their Trials by* Ordeal, *the Fertility of the Country, and the Ceremony in burning the Corps of an high Priest.*

THE *Pegu* Clergy are the best Observers of the Rules of Morality and Charity, that I have met with in my Travels, and the People are pious and hospitable. There are vast Numbers of Temples built in this Country, but most of Wood, because that Material is plentifullest and cheapest, and takes Varnish and Gilding best, being gawdily painted both within and without. Every one has free Liberty to build a *Baw* or Temple, and when it is finished, purchases or bestows a few Acres of Ground to maintain a certain Number of Priests and Novices, who manure and cultivate the Ground for their own Suſtenance, and in the Garden the Prieſts and Novices have a Convent built for their Conveniency of Lodgings and Study, and thoſe are their ſettled Benefices, for they are no Charge to the Laity, but by their induſtrious Labour in managing their Garden, they have enough for themſelves, and ſomething to ſpare to the poor Indigent of the Laity; but if their Garden is too ſmall or ſteril for the Subſiſtence of their Family, then they ſend ſome Novices abroad with a large Orange-coloured Mantle about their Bodies, with a Basket hanging on their left Arm, a little Drum in the left Hand, and a little Stick in the right, and when they come to the People's Doors they beat three Strokes with the Stick on the Drum, and if none come to anſwer, they beat again, and ſo on to the third Time, and then if none anſwer, they proceed to the next Houſe without ſpeaking a Word, but they are ſeldom ſent away without an Alms of Rice, Pulſe, Fruits, or Roots, which is their only Food, and what they receive more than they have preſent Occaſion for, they diſtribute to the Poor, for they never take Care for to Morrow, living all their Days in Celebacy, they have none of the Anxiety of thinking about Proviſion for a Widow and Children. Their innocent exemplary Lives procure them many Free-will-offerings from the well diſpoſed Laity, and what is ſaved after providing their Convents, of Eatables and Clothing, re-

returns to the Maintenance of the distrest Laity, who, through Age, Sickness, or other Accidents, cannot maintain themselves by Labour, but none who are able to work, partake of their Charity.

THEY preach or lecture frequently, and have a numerous Auditory. Their Religion is *Paganism*, and their System of Divinity *Polytheism*. They have Images in all their Temples or *Baws*, of inferior Gods, such as *Somma Cuddom*, *Samsay*, and *Prawpout*, but they cannot form an Idea of the Image of the great God, whose Adoration is left to their *Tallapoies* or Priests.

THOSE *Tallapoies* or Priests, teach, that Charity is the most sublime Virtue, and therefore ought to be extensive enough to reach not only to human Species, but even to Animals, wherefore they neither kill nor eat any, and they are so benevolent to Mankind, that they cherish all alike without Distinction, for the sake of Religion. They hold all Religions to be good that teach Men to be good, and that the Deities are pleased with Variety of Worship, but with none that is hurtful to Men, because Cruelty must be disagreeable to the Nature of a Deity: So being all agreed in that Fundamental, they have but few *Polemicks*, and no Persecutions, for they say that our Minds are free Agents, and ought neither to be forc'd nor fetter'd.

THE Images in their Temples are placed in *Domes*, in a sitting Posture, with their Legs across, their Toes all alike long, their

Arms and Hands very ſmall in Proportion to their Bodies, their Faces longer than human, and their Ears large, and the Lappets very thick. The Congregation bows to them when they come in and go out, and that is all the Oblation they receive.

THEY never repair an old *Baw*, nor is there any Occaſion for that Piety or Expence; for in every *September* there is an old Cuſtom for Gentlemen of Fortune, to make Sky Rockets, and ſet them a flying in the Air, and if any fly any great Height, that is a certain Sign that the Owner is in favour with the Gods, but if it comes to the Ground, and ſpends its Fire without riſing, the Owner is much dejected, and believes that the Gods are angry with him, but the happy Man, whoſe Rocket makes him in the Gods Favour, never fails of building a new *Baw*, and dedicates it to the God he adores, and ſome Prieſts, whoſe Temples are gone to Decay, bring their Images to adorn it, who have the Benefice for their Pains.

I have ſeen ſome of thoſe Rockets ſo large, that one of them could contain above five hundred Weight of Powder Duſt and Coal, which is their common Compoſition. The Carcaſe is the Trunk of a great Tree made hollow, leaving about two Inches of ſolid Wood without the Cylinder, to ſtrengthen it, the Hollow they fill with the Compoſition well ramm'd in, and after that is done, they make Thongs of green Buffaloes Hides, and hale tight round the Carcaſe to keep it from ſplitting,

ting, and those Thongs are put from one End to the other, in the Place of Hoops, and when they grow dry, they are as close on the Carcase as so many Hoops. Then they secure the Ends, that the Composition may come gradually out, when fired. The Carcase they place on a Branch of a large high Tree, which grows plentifully in their Fields, and fix it in the Position they would have it mount in when fired, and then they take a large *Bambow* for a Tail to balance it. Some I have seen above 120 Foot long. When the Tail is made fast according to Art, then the Day of Solemnity is proclaimed, and great Numbers of People of all Ranks, Degrees and Ages, assemble to see the Rocket fly. When all are convened, the Lashings that fastned it to the Tree, are cut, except so many as can support it from falling, and there are Men with Hatchets ready to cut them, when the Fire is put to it, which is done by the Owner, and then the Rocket takes Flight, and some fly a prodigious Height, others come to the Ground, and fly 5 or 600 Paces in an irregular Motion, wounding or scorching all that come in its Way. The Consequences of the high Flier and the low, I have described at Length above.

A little While after the Rockets flying they have another Feast, called the *Collock*, and some Women are chosen out of the People assembled, to dance a Dance to the Gods of the Earth. Hermophradites, who are numerous in this Country, are generally chosen,

if

if there are enow preſent to make a Set for the Dance. I ſaw nine dance like mad Folks, for above half an Hour, and then ſome of them fell in Fits, foming at the Mouth for the Space of half an Hour; and, when their Senſes are reſtored, they pretend to foretel Plenty or Scarcity of Corn for that Year, if the Year will prove ſickly or ſalutary to the People, and ſeveral other Things of Moment, and all by that half Hour's Converſation that the furious Dancer had with the Gods while ſhe was in a Trance.

THEY have various Sorts of Muſick, but the Pipe and Tabor are eſteemed the beſt, tho their ſtringed Inſtruments pleaſed my Ears beſt. They have one Sort in Shape of a Galley, with about twenty Bells of ſeveral Sizes and Sounds, placed faſt on the upper Part, as it lies along. The Inſtrument is about three Foot long, and eight or ten Inches broad, and ſix Inches deep. They beat thoſe Bells with a Stick made of heavy Wood, and they make no bad Muſick.

THERE are two large Temples near *Syrian*, ſo like one another in Structure, that they ſeem to be built by one Model. One ſtands about ſix Miles to the Southward, called *Kiakiack*, or, the *God of Gods Temple*. In it is an Image of twenty Yards long, lying in a ſleeping Poſture, and, by their Tradition, has lien in that Poſture 6000 Years. His Doors and Windows are always open, and every one has the Liberty to ſee him; and, when he awakes, this World is to be annihilated.

lated. The Temple ſtands on an high champain Ground, and may eaſily be ſeen, in a clear Day, eight Leagues off. The other ſtands in a low Plain, North of *Syrian*, about the ſame Diſtance, called *Dagun*. His Doors and Windows are always ſhut, and none enters his Temple but his Prieſts, and they won't tell what Shape he is of, only he is not of human Shape. Aſſoon as *Kiakiack* diſſolves the Being and Frame of the World, *Dagon* or *Dagun* will gather up the Fragments, and make a new one. There are yearly Fairs held near thoſe Temples, and the Free-will Offerings ariſing at thoſe Fairs, are for the Uſe of the Temples.

FOR finding out ſecret Murder, Theft or Perjury, the Trial of Ordeal is much in Cuſtom in *Pegu*. One Way is to make the Accuſer and the Accuſed take ſome raw Rice in their Mouths, and chew, and ſwallow it, but he that is guilty of the Crime alledged, or of falſe Accuſation, cannot ſwallow his Morſel, but the innocent chews and ſwallows his eaſily.

ANOTHER Way they have by driving a Stake of Wood into a River, and making the Accuſer and Accuſed take hold of the Stake, and keep their Heads and Bodies under Water, and he who ſtays longeſt under Water, is the Perſon to be credited, and whoſoever is convicted by this Trial, either for the Crime alledged, or for malicious Slander, by Accuſation, muſt ly on his Back three Days and Nights, with his Neck in a Pair of Stocks, without

without Meat or Drink, and fined to boot They have alſo the Cuſtom of dipping the naked Hand in boyling Oyl, or liquid Lead, to clear them from atrocious Crimes, if accuſed, and if the Accuſer ſcalds himſelf in the Trial, he muſt undergo the Puniſhment due to the Crime, which makes People very cautious how they calumniate one another. And, if any one aſperſe a Woman with the Name of Whore, and cannot prove the Aſperſion to be true, they are fined ſeverely.

THE Country is fruitful and healthful, and the Air ſo good, that when Strangers come hither in a bad State of Health, they ſeldom fail of a ſpeedy Recovery; but the ſmall Pox is dreaded as peſtiferous, and in the Province of *Kirian* that Diſtemper is moſt dangerous and moſt infectious, ſo that if any one is ſeized by that Diſeaſe, all the Neighbourhood removes to two or three Miles Diſtance, and builds new Houſes, which are eaſily done with *Bambows* and Reeds, which they have in great Plenty. They leave with the diſeaſed Perſon a Jar of Water, a Basket of raw Rice, and ſome earthen Pots to boyl it in, then they bid him farewel for twenty one Days. If the Patient has Strength enough to riſe and boyl Rice, he may then recover, if not, he muſt even die alone. And it is obſervable, that, while a Perſon has that Diſtemper, the Tiger, for all his Voraciouſneſs, will not touch him. If the Patient dies within the Term of twenty one Days, then the Smell certifies them on their approachproaching the House, and if he live, they carry him to their new built City, and make him a free Burgess.

I saw the Ceremony of an high Priest's Funeral, and was not a little pleased with the Solemnity. After the Corps had been kept three or four Months by Spirits or Gums from Putrefaction, there was a great Mast fixt in the Ground, so fast, that it could be moved no Way from its perpendicular Position. Then, about fifty or sixty Yards on each Side of that Mast, four smaller Masts were placed, and fixed perpendicularly in the Ground. Around the great Mast, in the Middle, were erected three Scaffolds above one another, the lowermost bigger than the second, and the third smaller than that, so that it lookt like a Pyramid four Stories high. The Scaffolds were railed in on each Side, except an open Place of three or four Foot wide on each Side. All the Scaffolds, and the Ground below them, were filled with Combustibles. From the Mast in the Middle four Ropes were carried to the other four Masts, and hal'd tight, and a Fire-rocket on each Rope was placed at the respective small Masts. Then the Corps was carried to the upper Story of the Pyramid, and laid flat on the Scaffold, and, after a great Shew of Sorrow among the People there present, a Trumpet was sounded, which was a Signal to set Fire to the Rockets, which, in an Instant, flew with a quick Motion along the Ropes, and set Fire to the Combustibles, and

and in a Moment they were all in a Flame, ſo that in an Hour or two all was conſumed.

THIS high Prieſt was held in ſo great Veneration, that he was reckoned a Saint among the People. He was in great Eſteem with the King, and when any Nobleman fell into Diſgrace, he uſed his Intereſt with the King to have him reſtored again to Favour, unleſs they were guilty of atrocious Crimes, and, in that Caſe, he uſed his Endeavours to have the Rigour of the Puniſhment extenuated.

ALL the *Pegu* Clergy are Mediators in making up Caſes of Debate and Contention that happen among Neighbours. They never leave mediating till there be a Reconciliation, and, in Token of Friendſhip, according to an ancient Cuſtom there, they eat *Champock* from one another's Hand, and that ſeals the Friendſhip. This *Champock* is Tea of a very unſavoury Taſte, it grows, as other Tea does, on Buſhes, and is in Uſe on ſuch Occaſions all over *Pegu*.

AND now, ſince I muſt leave *Pegu*, I muſt not omit giving the Clergy their due Praiſes in another particular Practice of their Charity. If a Stranger has the Misfortune to be ſhip-wrack'd on their Coaſt, by the Laws of the Country, the Men are the King's Slaves, but, by the Mediation of the Church, the Governors overlook that Law; and when the unfortunate Strangers come to their *Baws*, they find a great Deal of Hoſpitality, both in Food and Raiment, and have Let-

ters

ters of Recommendation from the Priests of one Convent to those of another on the Road they design to travel, where they may expect Vessels to transport them to *Syrian*; and if any be sick or maim'd, the Priests, who are the *Peguers* chief Physicians, keep them in their Convent, till they are cured, and then furnish them with Letters, as is above observed, for they never enquire which Way a Stranger worships God, but if he is human, he is the Object of their Charity.

THERE are some *Christians* in *Syrian* of the *Portugueze* Offspring, aud some *Armenians*. The *Portugueze* have a Church, but the scandalous Lives of the Priests and People make them contemptible to all People in general.

I have only to add to my Observations of *Pegu*, that, in former Times, *Martavan* was one of the most flourishing Towns for Trade in the East, having the Benefit of a noble River, which afforded a good Harbour for Ships of the greatest Burden; but, after the *Barmaes* conquered it, they sunk a Number of Vessels full of Stones, in the Mouth of the River, so that now it is unnavigable, except for small Vessels. They make earthen Ware there still, and glaze them with Lead-oar. I have seen some Jars made there, that could contain two Hogsheads of Liquor. They have also still a small Trade in Fish. Their Mullet dried is the best dry Fish I ever tasted, either in *India* or *Europe*.

THE

The Islands off the Coast of *Pegu*, are the *Cocoes*, uninhabited, but full of Cocoa-nut Trees. They ly about 20 Leagues West-south-west from Cape *Negrais:* And the Islands *Perperies* ly 36 Leagues South of the said Cape. They are high Islands uninhabited, and so environed with Rocks under Water, that there is Danger in landing on them. They seem to be overgrown with Woods, and that is all that I could observe of them. There is another small Island called *Commoda*, that lies about 10 Leagues off the Coast of *Pegu*, but is not inhabited.

CHAP. XXXVIII.

Treats of Merjee *and* Tanacerin, *and of the Sea-coast in the King of* Siam's *Dominions, of the Massacre there of the* English in Anno 1687. *also of* Quedah, *and the other maritim Countries and Islands as far as* Malacca.

THE next Place on the Continent, to the Southward, is *Merjee*, a Town belonging to the King of *Siam*, situated on the Banks of the River of *Tanacerin*, lying within a great Number of small uninhabited Islands. The Harbour is safe, and the Country produces Rice, Timber for building, Tin, Elephants, Elephants Teeth and *Agala* Wood. In former Times a good Number of *English* free Merchants were settled at *Merjee*, and drove

a

a good Trade, living under a mild indulgent Government; but the old *East-india* Company envying their Happiness, by an arbitrary Command, ordered them to leave their Industry, and repair to Fort St. *George*, to serve them, and threatned the King of *Siam* with a Sea War, if he did not deliver those *English* up, or force them out of his Country, and, *in Anno* 1687. sent one Captain *Weldon* in a small Ship called the *Curtany*, to *Merjee* with that Message. He behaved himself very insolently to the Government, and killed some *Siamers*, without any just Cause. One Night when *Weldon* was ashore, the *Siamers* thinking to do themselves Justice on him, got a Company together, designing to seize or kill the Aggressor, but *Weldon* having Notice of their Design, made his Escape on board his Ship, and the *Siamers* missing him, tho' very narrowly, vented their Rage and Revenge on all the *English* they could find. The poor Victims being only guarded by their Innocence, did not so mach as arm themselves, to withstand the Fury of the enraged Mob, so that seventy six were massacred, and hardly twenty escaped on bord of the *Curtany*; so there was the tragical Consequence of one Man's Insolence.

Before that fatal Time, the *English* were so beloved and favoured at the Court of *Siam*, that they had Places of Trust conferred upon them, both in the civil and military Branches of the Government. Mr. *Samuel White* was made *Shawbandaar* or Customſtom-maſter at *Merjee* and *Tanacerin*, and Captain *Williams* was Admiral of the King's Navy ; but the troubleſom Company, and a great Revolution that happened in the State of *Siam*, made ſome repair to Fort St. *George*, others o *Bengal*, and ſome to *Atcheen*.

THE Iſlands oppoſite to the Coaſt of *Tanacerin*, are the *Andemans*. They ly about 80 Leagues off, and are ſurrounded with many dangerous Banks and Rocks ; they are all inhabited with *Canibals*, who are ſo fearleſs, that they will ſwim off to a Boat if ſhe approach near the Shore, and attack her with their wooden Weapons, notwithſtanding the Superiority of Numbers in the Boat, and the Advantage of miſſive and defenſive Arms of Iron, Steel and Fire.

I knew one *Ferguſſon*, who commanded a Ship from Fort St. *George*, bound from *Malacca* to *Bengal*, in Company with another Ship, going too near one of the *Andeman* Iſlands, was driven, by the Force of a ſtrong Current, on ſome Rocks, and the Ship was loſt. The other Ship was driven thro' a Chanel between two of the ſame Iſlands, and was not able to aſſiſt the ſhip-wrack'd Men, but neither *Ferguſſon* nor any of his People were ever more heard of, which gave Ground to conjecture that they were all devoured by thoſe ſavage *Canibals*.

I ſaw one of the Natives of thoſe Iſlands at *Atcheen in Anno* 1694. He was then about 40 Years of Age. The *Andemaners* had a yearly Cuſtom to come to the *Nicobar* Iſlands,

ſlands, with a great Number of ſmall *Praws*, and kill or take Priſoners as many of the poor *Nicobareans* as they could overcome. The *Nicobareans* again joyned their Forces, and gave the *Canibals* Battle, when they met with them, and one Time defeated them, and gave no Quarter to the *Andemaners*. This Man above mentioned, when a Boy of 10 or 12 Years of Age, accompanied his Father in the Wars, and was taken Priſoner, and his Youth recommending him to Mercy, they ſaved his Life, and made him a Slave. After he had continued ſo three or four Years, he was carried to *Atcheen* to be ſold for Cloth, Knives and Tobacco, which are the Commodities moſt wanting on the *Nicobars*. The *Atcheeners* being *Mahometans*, this Boy's Patron bred him up in that Religion, and ſome Years after his Maſter dying, gave him his Freeedom; he having a great Deſire to ſee his native Country, took a *Praw*, and the Months of *December*, *January* and *February* being fair Weather, and the Sea ſmooth, he ventured to the Sea, in order to go to his own Country, from the Iſlands of *Gomus* and *Pullo-wey*, which ly near *Atcheen*. Here the Southermoſt of the *Nicobars* may be ſeen, and ſo one Iſland may be ſeen from another, from the Southermoſt of thoſe to *Chitty-andeman*, which is the Southermoſt of the *Andemans*, which are diſtant from *Atcheen* about an hundred Leagues. Arriving among his Relations he was made welcome, with great Demonſtrations of Joy to ſee him alive, whom they expected to have been long dead.

HAVING retained his native Language, he gave them an Account of his Adventures; and, as the *Andemaners* have no Notions of a Deity, he acquainted them with the Knowledge he had of a God, and would have perswaded his Country-men to learn of him the Way to adore God, and to obey his Laws, but he could make no Converts. When he had stay'd a Month or two, he took leave to be gone again, which they permitted, on Condition that he would return. He brought along with him four or five hundred Weight of Quick-silver, and he said, that some of the *Andeman* Islands abound in that Commodity He had made several Trips thither before I saw him, and always brought some Quick-silver along with him. Some *Mahometan Fakires* would fain have accompanied him in his Voyages, but he would never suffer them, because he said, he could not engage for their Safety among his Country-men. When I saw him, he was in Company with a *Seid*, whom I carried a Passenger to *Surat*, and from him I had this Account of his Adventures.

THE next Place of any Commerce on this Coast, is the Island of *Jonkceyloan*, it lies in the Dominions of the King of *Siam*. Between *Merjee* and *Jonkceyloan* there are several good Harbours for Shipping, but the Sea-coast is very thin of Inhabitants, because there are great Numbers of Freebooters, called *Salleiters*, who inhabit Islands along the Sea-coast, and they both rob, and take People for Slaves,

and

and tranſport them for *Atcheen*, and there make Sale of them, and *Jonkceyloan* often feels the Weight of their Depredations.

THE North End of *Jonkceyloan* lies within a Mile of the Continent, but the South End is above three Leagues from it. Between the Iſland and the Continent is a good Harbour for Shipping in the South-weſt Monſoons, and on the Weſt Side of the Iſland *Puton* Bay is a ſafe Harbour in the North-eaſt Winds. The Iſlands afford good Maſts for Shipping, and abundance of Tin, but few People to dig for it, by reaſon of the aforementioned Outlaws, and the Governors being generally *Chineſe*, who buy their Places at the Court of *Siam*, and, to reimburſe themſelves, oppreſs the People, in ſo much that Riches would be but a Plague to them, and their Poverty makes them live an eaſie indolent Life.

YET the Villages on the Continent drive a ſmall Trade with Shipping that come from the *Chormondel* Coaſt, and *Bengal*, but both the Buyer and Seller trade by Retail, ſo that a Ship's Cargo is a long Time in ſelling, and the Product of the Country is as long in purchaſing.

THE Iſlands off this Part of the Coaſt are the *Nicobars*, and are about 90 Leagues diſtant from the Continent. The Northmoſt Cluſter is low, and are called the *Carnicubars*, and by their Vicinity to the *Andemans*, are but thinly inhabited. The middle Cluſter is fine champain Ground, and all but one, well inhabited. They are called the *So-*

merera Iſlands, becauſe on the South End of the largeſt Iſland, is an Hill that reſembles the Top of an *Umbrella* or *Somerera.* About ſix Leagues to the Southward of *Somerera* Iſland, lies *Tallang-jang* the uninhabited Iſland, where one Captain *Owen* loſt his Ship in *Anno* 1708. but the Men were all ſaved, and finding no Inhabitants, they made Fires in the Night, and next Day there came 5 or 6 Canoaes from *Ning* and *Goury*, two fine Iſlands that ly about four Leagues to the Weſtward of the deſert Iſland, and very courteouſly carried the ſhipwrackt Men to their Iſlands of *Ning* and *Goury*, with what little Things they had ſaved of their Apparel and other Neceſſaries.

THE Captain had ſaved a broken Knife about four Inches long in the Blade, and he having laid it careleſly by, one of the Natives made bold to take it, but did not offer to hide it. The Captain ſeeing his Knife in the poor Native's Hand, took it from him, and beſtowed ſome Kicks and Blows on him for his ill Manners, which was very ill taken, for all in general ſhewed they were diſſatisfied with the Action; and the ſhipwrackt Men could obſerve Contentions ariſing between thoſe who were their Benefactors in bringing them to their Iſland, and others who were not concerned in it: However, next Day as the Captain was ſitting under a Tree at Dinner, there came about a Dozen of Natives towards him, and ſaluted him on every Side with a Shower of Darts made of heavy hard Wood, with their Points hardned in the Fire, and

and so he expir'd in a Moment. How far they had a Mind to pursue their Resentment, I know not, but their Benefactors kept Guard about their House till next Day, and then presented them with two Canoaes, and fitted them with Out-leagers to keep them from overturning, and put some Water in Pots, some Cocoa-nuts and dry Fish, and pointed to them to be immediately gone, which they did. Being sixteen in Company, they divided equally, and steered their Course for *Jonk-ceyloan*, but in the Way one of the Boats lost her Out-leager, and drowned all her Crew, the rest arrived safe, and I carried them afterwards to *Matchulipatam*.

Ning and *Goury* are two fine smooth Islands, well inhabited, and plentifully furnished with several Sorts of good Fish, Hogs and Poultry, but they have no Horses, Cows, Sheep, nor Goats, nor wild Beasts of any Sort, but Monkies. They have no Rice nor Pulse, so that the Kernel of Cocoa-nuts, *Yams*, and Potatoes serves them for Bread.

ALONG the North End of the eastmost of the two Islands, are good Soundings from ten to eight Fathoms Sand, about two Miles off the Shore. The People come thronging on board in their Canoaes, and bring Hogs, Fowl, Cocks, Fish, fresh, salted and dried *Yams*, the best I ever tasted, Potatoes, Parots and Monkies, to barter for old Hatchets, Sword-blades, and thick Pieces of Iron-hoops, to make defensive Weapons against their common Disturbers and implacabale Enemies the

Andemaners; and Tobacco they are very greedy of, for a Leaf of Tobacco, if pretty large, they will give a Cock, for three Foot of an Iron Hoop, a large Hog, and for one Foot in Length, a Pig. They all ſpeak a little broken *Portugueze*, but what religious Worſhip they uſe, I could not learn.

THE Iſland *Somerera* lies about 8 Leagues to the Northward of *Ning* and *Goury*, and is well inhabited by the Number of Villages that ſhew themſelves as we ſail along its Shores. The People, like thoſe of *Ning* and *Goury*, are very courteous, and bring the Product of their Iſland aboard of Ships to exchange for the aforementioned Commodities. Silver nor Gold they neither have nor care for, ſo the Root of all Evil can never ſend out Branches of Miſery, or bear Fruit to poiſon their Happineſs. The Mens Clothing is a Bit of String round their Middle, and about a Foot and an Half of Cloth ſix Inches broad, tuckt before and behind within that Line. The Women have a Petticoat from the Navel to the Knee, and their Hair cloſe ſhaved, but the Men have the Hair left on the upper Part of the Head, and below the Crown, but cut ſo ſhort that it hardly comes to their Ears.

THE Southward Cluſter of the *Nicobars*, is mountainous, and the People partake of its unpoliſhed Nature, being more uncivil and ſurly than thoſe to the Northward. Their Iſlands produce the ſame Neceſſaries as the others do.

Quedah

Quedah is the next Place of Note on the Continent to the Southward, and is honoured with the Title of a Kingdom, tho' both ſmall and poor. The Town which bears the ſame Name, ſtands on the Banks of a ſmall navigable River, deep, but narrow, about 50 Miles from the Sea, and the King reſides in it, but ſhews no Marks of Grandeur, beſides arbitrary governing.

THEIR Religion is *Mahometan*, much mixt with *Paganiſm*. The People are deceitful, covetous, and cruel. It was many Years tributary to *Siam*, but in their long *Pegu* War, it threw off the Yoke. Its Product is Tin, Pepper, Elephants, and Elephants Teeth, Canes, and *Damar*, a Gum that is uſed for making Pitch and Tar for the Uſe of Shipping. The King is poor, proud, and beggarly, he never fails of viſiting ſtranger Merchants at their coming to his Port, and then, according to Cuſtom, he muſt have a Preſent. When the Stranger returns the Viſit, or has any Buſineſs with him, he muſt make him a Preſent, otherwiſe he thinks due Reſpect is not paid to him, and in Return of theſe Preſents his Majeſty will honour the Stranger with a Seat near his ſacred Perſon, and will chew a little *Betel*, and put it out of his royal Mouth on a little gold Saucer, and ſends it by his Page to the Stranger, who muſt take it with all the Signs of Humility and Satisfaction, and chew it after him, and it is very dangerous to refuſe the royal Morſel.

SOME

SOME Ages ago, *Ligore* was a Kingdom of it ſelf, and the Kings of *Quedah* and *Ligore* fell at Variance. He of *Quedah* invaded the Territories of *Ligore*, and left his Queen and his Son, an hopeful Youth about twenty Years of Age, to govern in his Abſence. The Mother and Son grew enamour'd of each other, and ſhe found her ſelf with Child by the reciprocal Eſteem they bore one another. She being juſtly afraid of the King's Reſentment on his Return, laid the Danger before her Son, that threatned them both, and adviſed the dutiful Child to prevent their Death by killing his Father. Whereupon he wrote to the King for Leave to give him a Viſit in the Camp, which Favour he obtained, and proceeded accordingly to the Place where his Father was with his Army. At his Arrival he was received by all with great Demonſtrations of Joy, particularly by his Father, who made him lodge in his own Tent. The Villain let his Father fall aſleep, and then ſtabbed him to the Heart, and immediately left the Army, and haſted to his loving Mother, to give her an Account of his noble Action. In the Morning the King being found dead, and the Son gone, the Regicide was ſoon known; and becauſe the Queen ſhould not continue long a Widow, the obedient Child married her himſelf, becauſe none in the Country had royal Blood in their Veins but himſelf, and ſhe could not ſtoop to match below the Dignity of a ſovereign Prince. Such libidinous Marriages are very frequent in this Country to this preſent Time.

Perah

Perah is the next Country to *Quedah*. It is properly a Part of the Kingdom of *Johore*, but the People are untractable and rebellious, and the Government *anarchical*. Their Religion is heterodox *Mahometism*. The Country produces more Tin than any in *India*, but the Inhabitants are so treacherous, faithless, and bloody, that no *European* Nation can keep Factories there with Safety. The *Dutch* tried it once, and the first Year had their Factory cut off. They then settled on *Pullodingding*, an Island at the Mouth of the River *Perah*, but about the Year 1690. that Factory was also cut off, and I never heard that any Body else ever attempted to settle there since.

THERE are several other Places along that Coast of *Malaya*, that produce great Quantities of Tin, but *Salangore* and *Parsalore* are the most noted, tho' little frequented by *Europeans*, because they have too many of the *Perah* Qualities, to be trusted with honest Mens Lives and Money. Their Religion is also a Sort of scoundrel *Mahometism*.

CHAP.

CHAP. XXXIX.

Gives an Account of Malacca, *how the* Portugueze *got Footing there, and fortified it, and how the* Dutch *supplanted the* Portugueze, *and made it a Colony of theirs, with some Occurrences happening to the* Scots *Company's Affairs there, and other Places in* India.

MALACCA is the next Place in Course along this Coast of *Malaya*. Before the *Portugueze* came to *India*, it had been the Place of Residence of the Kings of *Johore*, but they denying the *Portugueze* Commerce in their Country, associated themselves with the King of *Aarow* (a potent Prince in those Times) on the Island of *Sumatra*, who was engaged in a War with the King of *Johore*, and with their joynt Forces obliged him to quit that Place, and retire to *Johore-lami*, which lies at the very Point of that Promontory, within one Degree of the Æquator. There is a noble spacious River that accommodates *Johore-lami*.

As soon as the King of *Johore* was gone, the *Portugueze* began to fortifie, and encompassed a little Hill with a Stone Wall, about a Mile round, in which they built a City, and called it *Malacca*, and by the Conveniency of its Situation, in a few Years it became the greatest Mart in *India*; however, the King of *Johore* was fain to make a Peace with the *Portugueze*, allowing them their Fort, and as as much Ground round it as their Cannon could fling a Shot, and so they became Friends; but the King of *Johore* invaded the King of *Aarow's* Dominions, with a numerous Fleet of Gallies, and in a short Time forced him to crave Aid from the *Portugueze*, who never us'd to deceive their Allies but when they trusted to them, and so the King of *Aarow* lost his Country.

Malacca, a Place of small Accouut, in a short Time became famous all over *India* and *Europe*, lying almost in the Centre of Trade, brought thither by Shipping from the rich Kingdoms of *Japon*, *China*, *Formosa*, *Luconia*, *Tonquin*, *Couchin-china*, *Cambodia*, and *Siam*, besides what *Johore* produced, and *Sumatra*, *Java*, *Borneo*, *Macasser*, *Banda*, *Amboina*, and *Ternate* Islands, that produce many valuable Commodities.

As the *Portugueze* grew great and rich, they grew also insolent, and so continued abusing and affronting their Neighbours till about the Year 1660. the *Dutch* had a War with *Portugal*, on account of some Losses the *Dutch* sustained in *Brazil*.

The *Dutch* sent many Ships and good Forces to *India*, to be equal with the *Portugueze*, for their driving the *Dutch* out of *Brazil*; and how their Arms flourisht on the Coasts of *Malabar* and *Zeloan*, I have observed already in my first Volume, and so I begin again at *Malacca*..

The *Dutch* coming into the Streights of *Malacca* from *Batavia*, with a strong Fleet and

and a Land-army on board of it, ſtruck up an Alliance with the King of *Johore*, offenſive and defenſive, as long as the Sun and Moon gave Light to this World; for I ſaw the Treaty, and heard it read, with thoſe Expreſſions in it: On which the King of *Johore* aſſiſted the *Dutch* with 20000 Men, and laid Siege to the Fort by Land, while the *Dutch* diſtreſſed it by Sea; and yet for all that the Fleet and Army could do, they could not have taken it by Force, but by reducing them by Famine, which would have taken up a great Deal of Time, ſo what they could not effect by Force, they did by Fraud.

THEY heard that the *Portugueze* Governor was a ſordid avaricious Fellow, and ill beloved by the Gariſon, ſo the *Dutch*, by ſecret Conveyances, tampered with him by Letters, promiſing him Mountains of Gold if he would contribute towards their gaining the Fort. At length the Price was ſet of 80000 Pieces of Eight, to be the Reward of his Treachery, and to be ſafely tranſported to *Batavia* in their Fleet, and be made a free Denizon there. So he ſent ſecret Orders to the *Dutch* to make an Attack on the Eaſt-ſide of the Fort, and he would act his Part, which was accordingly done.

HE thereupon called a Council, and told them he had a Mind to circumvent the *Dutch*, by letting them come cloſe to the Fort Walls, and then to fire briskly on them from all Quarters, and deſtroy them at once, ſo the *Dutch* made their Approaches without Molelestation, and placed their Ladders. The Garison sent Message after Message, to acquaint the Governor of the Danger they were in, for want of Orders to fire and sally out on the *Dutch*, as was agreed on in Council, but he delayed so long till the *Dutch* got into the Fort, and drove the Guard from the East-gate, which they soon opened to receive the rest of their Army, who, assoon as they were entred, gave Quarters to none that were in Arms, and marching towards the Governor's House, where he thought himself secure by the Treaty, they forthwith dispatcht him to save the fourscore thousand Dollars.

THE Master Gunner being posted on a large Bastion, whose Walls are washed by the Sea at high Water, with about 100 *Portugueze* along with him, would by no Means yield till he had capitulated with the *Dutch* for fair Quarter for himself and his Company, which the *Dutch* would not adhere to, so that for two Days he gallantly maintained his Post. At last, by continual Fatigue, and Loss of his Men, he was obliged to yield to Fate, and great Superiority of Numbers, and died like an Hero, with his Sword in his Hand; and there is a common Report at *Malacca* still, that the Night after the aniversary Day of his Death, his *Genius* is seen on that Bastion: And I was informed by a *Dutch* Governor at *Malacca*, that on that Night no Sentinels are set there, for that severals have found the Effects of his Fury, by being thrown

thrown over the Wall, and have been either killed or maimed by the Fall.

The *Portugueze*, to ſhew their Zeal to Religion, while they were Maſters of *Malacca*, had no leſs than three Churches and a Chapel within the Fort, and one without, but now there is but one Church and a Chapel within, and none without. That which the *Dutch* now uſe for their Worſhip, ſtands conſpicuouſly on the Top of the Hill, and may be ſeen up or down the Streights at a good Diſtance, and a Flag-ſtaff is placed on the Steeple, on which a Flag is hoiſted on the Sight of any Ship.

The Fort is both large and ſtrong, the Sea waſhing the Walls of one third Part of it, and a deep rapid, but narrow River, the Weſt-ſide of it, and a broad deep Ditch the reſt of it. The Governor's Houſe is both beautiful and convenient, and there are ſeveral other good Houſes in the Fort, and in the Town without the Fort, but the Road for Shipping is at too great a Diſtance to be defended by the Fort, the Shallowneſs of the Sea obliging them to ly above a League off, which is a very great Inconveniency. For in 1709. the *French* coming into the Streights with a Squadron of three or four Sail, ſeeing a large Ship in the Road, newly arrived from *Japon*, ſtood in to the Road, and had certainly carried her out, if the Wind had not failed them about Musket Shot from her.

At *Malacca* the Streights are not above 4 Leagues broad; for tho' the oppoſite Shore on on *Sumatra* is very low, yet it may easily be seen in a clear Day, which is the Reason that the Sea is always as smooth as a Mill-pond, except when it is ruffled with Squalls of Wind, which seldom come without Lightnings, Thunder, and Rain; and tho' they come with great Violence, yet they are soon over, not often exceeding an Hour.

THE Country produces nothing for a foreign Market, but a little Tin and Elephants Teeth, but several excellent Fruits and Roots for the Use of the Inhabitants, and Strangers who call there for Refreshments. The *Malacca* Pine-apple is accounted the best in the World, for in other Parts, if they are eaten to a small Excess, they are apt to give Surfeits, but those of *Malacca* never offend the Stomach. The *Mangostane* is a delicious Fruit, almost in the Shape of an Apple, the Skin is thick and red, being dried it is a good Astringent. The Kernels (if I may so call them) are like Cloves of Garlick, of a very agreeable Taste, but very cold. The *Rambostan* is a Fruit about the Bigness of a Walnut, with a tough Skin, beset with Capillaments, within the Skin is a very savoury Pulp. The *Durean* is another excellent Fruit, but offensive to some Peoples Noses, for it smells very like human Excrements, but when once tasted, the Smell vanishes. The Skin is thick and yellow, and within is a Pulp like thick Cream in Colour and Consistence, but more delicious in Taste. The Pulp or Meat is very hot and nourishing, and instead of surfeiting, they

they fortifie the Stomach, and are a great Incentive to Wantonneſs. They have Cocoanuts in Plenty, and ſome grow in Mariſhes that are overflown with the Sea in Springtides. Their Liquor and Kernel partake of the Qualities of the Ground they grow in, being exceeding Salt. I never ſaw any Cocoanuts grow in Salt Grounds but there, and ſome are ſo large that the Shell will hold more than an *Engliſh* Quart Pot. They have alſo Plenty of Lemons, Oranges, Limes, Sugarcanes, and *Mangoes*. They have a Species of *Mango*, called by the *Dutch* a *Stinker*, which is very offenſive both to the Smell and Taſte, and conſequently of little Uſe. There is little Corn or Pulſe grows in this Country but what is nouriſht in Gardens.

SHEEP and Bullocks are ſcarce and dear, but Swines Fleſh, Poultry, and Fiſh pretty plentiful, and reaſonably cheap, conſidering it is a *Dutch* Colony, whoſe exceſſive Taxes make every Thing dear, and diſcourage the Poor from improving, ſince Poverty ſecures them from farther Oppreſſion. Their Corn comes all from *Java*, *Siam*, or *Cambodia*, but the Freight makes it come out dear to what it is in other Places, whoſe native Ground produces it.

I will paſs by their Court of Juſtice, becauſe it hardly deſerves the Name, ſince Strangers are excluded from the common Laws of Humanity, wherein I am able to give many Inſtances, but I voluntarily paſs by Particularities till another Time.

THERE

THERE is a very high Mountain to the North-eastward of *Malacca*, that sends forth several Rivers, of which that of *Malacca* is one, and all of them have small Quantities of Gold Dust found in their Chanels. The inland Inhabitants called *Monacaboes*, are a barbarous savage People, whose greatest Pleasure is in doing Mischief to their Neighbours, which is the greatest Reason why the Peasants about *Malacca* sow no Grain but what is inclosed in Gardens with thick set prickly Hedges, or deep Ditches; for when their Grain is ripe in the open Plains, the *Monacaboes* never fail of putting Fire to it, in order to consume it. They are much whiter than their neighbouring *Malayas* who inhabit the low Grounds, and the Kings of *Johore*, whose Subjects they are, or at least ought to be, could never civilize them.

THEIR Religion is a Complex of *Mahometism* and *Paganism*, and they have the Character of great Sorcerers, who by their Spells can tame wild Tigers, and make them carry them whither they order them, on their Backs. Once they had a Mind to try their Art on the Town of *Malacca*, but were unsuccessful in their Enterprize, according to common Report there. For one of their chief Wizards assured them that neither Gun, Sword, nor Lance should have Power to hurt them, if they should attempt the Town, whose Defence consists only in a slight Gate, with a little round Bastion, with five or six great Guns mounted on it. So on the Opinion of their Doctors Art, a great Number drew together, and being armed with Lance and Cross, their common Weapons, marched without Order or Fear towards the Gate. When they came near enough, the Gunner of the Bastion pointed some Guns, and set Fire to the Priming, but that flashed, and the Guns would not discharge, which discouraged the Guard of the Gate, but a *Malaya* Soldier, who understood some of the *Monacaboes* Art, called for a Piece of Pork, with which he besmear'd the Mouths of the Cannon, while the Gunner renewed the Priming, and Fire being put to them, the Cannon went off, and did good Execution, which so frightned the *Monacaboes*, that they betook themselves to Flight, and never attempted to disturb the Town since.

I saw strange Cures performed by a *Malaya* Doctor at *Malacca*. One of them was on a Gentleman of my Acquaintance, who was second Supercargo of a *Scots* Ship called the *Speed-well*, which was lost near *Malacca*. After the Ship was lost, the first Supercargo took an House near the Town, by the Seaside, to put their Cargo and Stores in, that were saved, but eleven Chests of Treasure and some fine Goods were lodged in one of the *Dutch* Company's Ware-houses in the Fort, which had three Locks on its Door. The Governor had one Key, and each of the Supercargoes one. A common Strumpet called Mris. *Kennedy*, who at that Time was married to an *Irish* Pirate of that Name, and

kept

kept an Ordinary in *Malacca*, gave the first Supercargo a Philtre that made him dote on her almost to Distraction. He was never easie out of her Company while awake, and in his Sleep he called her by Name. When she had got him so far in the Noose, she pretended she had great Need of Money, and would fain have borrowed a Chest of one thousand Pounds *Sterling* of the *Scots* Company's Money. The bewitched Supercargo could deny her nothing she asked for, and promised, that if he could bring his Second to consent, she should have it, but that Consent could be got on no Terms, tho' the first proferred to be accountable to their Masters for that Sum, and he acquainting her with the Impossibility of getting that Consent, she contrived a Way to remove the Second by Poison, and going to a female Friend of hers, who was well acquainted with the Mystery of Poisoning, procured a Dose so small that she could drop it in his Broth or Drink without his perceiving it; and accordingly she took an Opportunity to dine with them one Day when they had Broth at Table, and in serving the Broth about, she dropt it among his. The same Night it began to operate by Grippings and Sweating, and he being bred a Surgeon, took some Medicines to correct the Grippings, which in some Measure the Medicine did, but he lost his Appetite, and his Excrements came from him as black as Ink. In the Interim a Ship came from *Surat*, bound to *China*, wherein the chief Supercargo was obliged to embarque with the Company's Stock, and left the Second at *Malacca*, to take Care of what was left there. A few Days after the *Surat* Ship ſailed, I arrived at *Malacca*, and found the ſecond Supercargo in a deplorable Condition.

HE finding all Medicines ineffectual, began to fear Poiſon, and ſent for the *Dutch* Doctor of Phyſick to conſult him, who, on Sight of his Excrements, told him plainly that he was poiſoned, and adviſed him to ſend for a noted *Malaya* Doctor, who lived at a Place called *Batantiga*, about four Miles to the North-weſt of *Malacca*, which he forthwith did, and when the Doctor came, he felt his Pulſe, and immediately told that he was poiſoned, and that if he could not tell what Poiſon he had taken, his Cure was very deſperate and uncertain. I adviſed my Friend to let old *Beelzebub* (for he was a Man, or walking Shadow, of a diſmal Aſpect, near an hundred Years old) take him into his Care. My Friend took my Advice, and complimented the Doctor with five *Japon Cupangs*, or fifty *Dutch* Dollars. Old *Eſculapius* laught when he received the Preſent, but could not ſhew one Tooth, but promiſed his utmoſt Endeavours to cure him. He asked my Friend if he ſuſpected any Body particularly, who might ow him a Grudge. He anſwered, none but Mris. *Kennedy*, or ſome of her Companions. The Doctor called for a Tea Cup, and ſome freſh Limes, which were brought to him. He turned all out of the Room but

my

my ſelf and his Patient, and cut ſome Limes, and ſqueezed their Juice into the Tea-cup till it was full. He then mutter'd ſome unintelligible Words, keeping his right Hand moving over the Cup for the Space of three or four Minutes, and finding his Conjuration was not ſatisfactory, he ſhak'd his old Head, and lookt dejected. He then mutter'd ſome other Words with an higher Voice, keeping his Hand in Motion as before, and in two Minutes the Juice in the Cup ſeemed to boil as if Fire had been under it. Then he began to ſmile. I had the Curioſity to put my Finger into the Juice, but it retained its ordinary Coldneſs. He then told his Patient that his Cure was certain, on which he had a Promiſe of five *Cupangs* more when the Cure was effected. He ordered the Patient to ſend a Servant to Mris. *Kennedy*'s Door, and watch between the Hours of Ten and Twelve, and to obſerve well if there was any unuſual Noiſe in her Houſe between thoſe Hours, and ſo took his Leave with a contented Countenance. At Ten my Friend ſent a Servant according to Direction, and he and I ſat diſcourſing about what we had obſerved in the Doctor's Actions towards effecting the Cure. About Eleven the Spy came and told us that Mris. *Kennedy* had run ſtark mad, making an hideous Noiſe, and ſaid, She had ſeen the Devil in the little Houſe in the Garden, in a monſtrous Shape and terrible Aſpect. She ſoon after grew furiouſly mad, ſcratching and biting every Body ſhe could come at, and ſo the Family was forced to throw her on a Bed, and tie her down to it.

In that Fit ſhe continued till about eight in the Morning, that the old Conjurer came to Town, who, upon the Advice given him, went directly to viſit her. Upon Sight of him ſhe became calm and ſenſible. He ordered every Body out of the Room, and askt her what Poiſon ſhe had given to his Patient: She was very loth to tell, and proferred him 500 Dollars to forſake his Patient, and let the Poiſon operate; but he honeſtly refuſed, and aſſured her that the ſame Devil that ſhe ſaw in the Garden, ſhould be her continual Companion all her Days, and would often make her feel the Effects of his Power, if ſhe did not inſtantly declare what the Poiſon was, and from whom ſhe had it. She ſeeing no other Remedy, confeſt where ſhe had the Poiſon, but could not tell what it was. The Doctor ſent for the old Schoolmiſtriſs of Wickedneſs, and when ſhe came, he threatned to torment her alſo, by his humble Servant the Devil, if ſhe did not forthwith declare what Poiſon had been given, which ſhe did, and he took away Mris. *Kennedy*'s Companion the Devil, and the Patient was well enough in eight or ten Days, to follow his Affairs, but Mris. *Kennedy* lookt ever after diſturb'd, as if continually frightned.

Another ſtrange Cure I ſaw him perform on an Officer belonging to my Ship. He was going to ſleep about Midnight, and lying down on his Bed, was bit in the Calf of of the Leg by a *Centipee*, an Insect with many Feet, and very venomous. The Pain that the Bite caused would allow him no Rest. Next Day he expected that the Venom might have been exhausted, but in that he was mistaken, for it grew first red by Inflamation, and then blue and nummed. I sent for the Doctor aforesaid, who came on the first Summons. I told him of the Accident that had happened, and he said there was no Danger. He saw the inflamed Leg, and kept his Hand moving over it, but did not touch it. He muttered some unintelligible Words, and spit on the Place affected, and in five Minutes he could walk without Pain, tho' before the Cure, he could not stand without something to support him.

AND since I have been mentioning the *Scots East-india* Ship and her Supercargoes, I will give a small Account of the Management of their Affairs in *India*. They arrived at *Batavia* about the Beginning of *July* 1701. but being taken up with the Pleasures of the Place, loitred away near a Month of their Time, which had been much better spent in prosecuting their Voyage to *China*: However, by the Beginning of *September*, they reacht the Coast of *China*, where meeting with a *Tuffoon*, or a North-east Storm, that often blows violently about that Season, they were forced to bear away for *Johore*, where they staid about two Months, and then came to *Malacca*, where they had a Mind to clean their

their Ship's Bottom, and to proceed next *April* or *May* for *China*.

THE *Dutch* received them civilly, and gave them Leave to lay their Ship ashore on an Island to the Westward of the Town, about two or three Miles from the Fort, and allowed them to land their Cargo and Stores on the Island, till their Ship was made clean, which they had perfected in two Springs, and bringing the Ship towards the Road again, the Captain being on board, ordered to steer the Ship on some Rocks that lay on the Shore, and were dry at Low-water. The third Mate, who was the only commanding Officer on board, except the Captain, told him of the Danger he was running into, and begged him to alter his Course, but the Captain cursed him for his impertinent Advice, and run the Ship on the Rocks, but the People got a small Anchor and an Halser out, and brought her aflote again, but, assoon as the Anchor was weighed, they run her once more on the Rocks, and she having a little Motion, a Rock work'd itself through her Bottom, and there she was lost without Hopes or Design of being recovered, and with her ended the *Scots East-india* Company's Interest in *India*. Whether the Ship was lost by Ignorance or Design, I will not judge, but, in my Opinion, it was by Design, for, as I heard afterwards, the Captain and Supercargoes had taken up round Sums on the Bottom of the Ship, and took that Method to pay their Debts. I came to *Ma-*

Malacca about the Beginning of *August*, and found the second Supercargo in the ill State I have already mentioned, with the Purser and the Supercargo's Writer, and eleven Men more, who could not get Passages to Countries where they might get Employment. I had then a great Ship and a small one under my Command, so I entred them all on board my Ships in the same Posts they had on board the *Speedwel*, and I entred on a Scheme with the second Supercargo to carry the *Scots* Company's Effects on board my great Ship to *Scotland*, but the first Supercargo, who was, before my Arrival, gone to *China*, and had no Mind ever to see his native Country again, broke our Measures by rambling thro' *India* with his Masters Stock. What the *Scots* Company's Cargo was, I did not see; but the Supercargoes had a Chest of Glass-ware in their own private Adventure, the most obscenely shameful that ever I saw or heard of among Merchants. They were *Priapuses* of a large Size, with a *Scrotum* big enough to hold an *English* Pint of Liquor, either to address the God *Bacchus*, or the Goddess *Venus*, as seemed best to their Votaries.

I prosecuted my Voyage to *Surat*, and left the *Scots* Supercargoes to pursue their Masters Interest in getting their Affairs in a Readiness to get a Cargo for *Europe*, to be carried on board my Ship according to an Agreement made between the second Supercargo and me; but, instead of putting Affairs

fairs in a Readineſs, he embaraſſed them, ſent ſome of his Maſters Stock to ſome inſolvent Merchants in *Amoy* in *China*, and let out ſome on the Bottom of the Ship he took his Paſſage on board of, and tho' that Ship was ordered, by the Owners and Freighters, back to *Surat* directly, a young Gentleman a Supercargo went with her to *Bengal*, and from thence to *Perſia*, where the Ship was ſeized by the Owners Orders, and ſent to *Surat*, where I met with the firſt Supercargo half-dead with Vexation for his Folly, in keeping ſuch a Stock two Years and an half without the leaſt Improvement: And what was left in *China*, was in Danger of ever being recovered, tho' it was afterwards.

At *Surat* the chief Supercargo grew very weak, and finding he had not long to ſtay in this World, had a Mind to ſettle his Affairs here, before he went to the other, ſo one Day he ſent for me, to adviſe him what he ſhould do with his Maſters Effects, if he ſhould die. I asked him if his Accounts were brought forward, and he told me they were, and deſired, that I would take all into my Poſſeſſion, and be accountable to the *Scots* Company, and to remit it Home to them, according to the Orders they would ſend me about it, but I excuſed myſelf, and would not meddle in their Affairs on ſuch weak Terms; but I adviſed him to lodge his Books and Effects in the Hands of one Mr. *Bernard Weyche*, whom I took to be an honeſt and

and induſtrious Gentleman, and ſo he did, and then he died.

He was a Gentleman of a very courteous Behaviour, and underſtood a ſmall Sword excellently well, but not much verſed in Merchandize or foreign Commerce. The ſecond was a very good Surgeon, and was Maſter of the *French* Language, but underſtood nothing in Accounts. The Captain, who ſtaid on board of my Ship above twelve Months, had been bred in his Youth a Driver of Cattle from the Highlands of *Scotland* into *England*. He had very mean Education, and could not tell what he meant either in ſpeaking or writing. He had a brutal Courage, and was the Husband of three Wives all alive together. He knew nothing either of the Theory or practical Parts of Navigation, and yet had been honoured with a Commiſſion for Lieutenant in the royal Navy of *England*.

I muſt now leave my long Digreſſion, and proceed from *Malacca* along the Coaſt of *Malaya*, tho' there are no Places of Commerce between it and *Johore Lami*, which is ſometimes the Place of that King's Reſidence, and has the Benefit of a fine deep large River, which admits of two Entrances into it. The ſmalleſt is from the Weſtward, called by *Europeans* the Streights of *Sincapure*, but by the Natives *Salleta de Brew*. It runs along the Side of *Sincapure* Iſland for 5 or 6 Leagues together, and ends at the great River of *Johore*.

CHAP

CHAP. XL.

Treats of the Dominions of Johore, *its ancient and preſent State occaſioned by a Revolution.*

THE Territories of *Johore* reached from *Perah* to Point *Romano*, which is the ſouthermoſt Promontory on the Continent of *Aſia*, it lying but one Degree to the Northward of the Æquator, about three Leagues from *Johore* River, in Length about 100 Leagues, and in the broadeſt Place about 80.

THE Inhabitants are lazy, indolent, perfidious and cruel. The Country is very woody, being daily refreſht with Showers and Breezes of Wind. It abounds in Tin, Pepper, Elephants Teeth, Gold, *Agala* Wood and Canes, but the Inhabitants are ſuch Drones, that they ſow very little Rice or other Grain. And the inland People ſubſiſt moſtly on *Sagow*, the Pith of a ſmall Twig ſplit and dried in the Sun, and on their Fruits which grow all Seaſons of the Year, and Roots, which they always have in great Plenty, and Poultry, which they rear up.

ABOUT the Sea-coaſt they feed moſtly on Fiſh and Rice brought to them from *Java*, *Siam* and *Cambodia*. The People of Induſtry are the *Chineſe* who inhabit among them in their Towns; and there may be about 1000 Families of them ſettled in the *Johore* Dominions, beſides a much greater Number who drive a foreign Trade among them.

IN

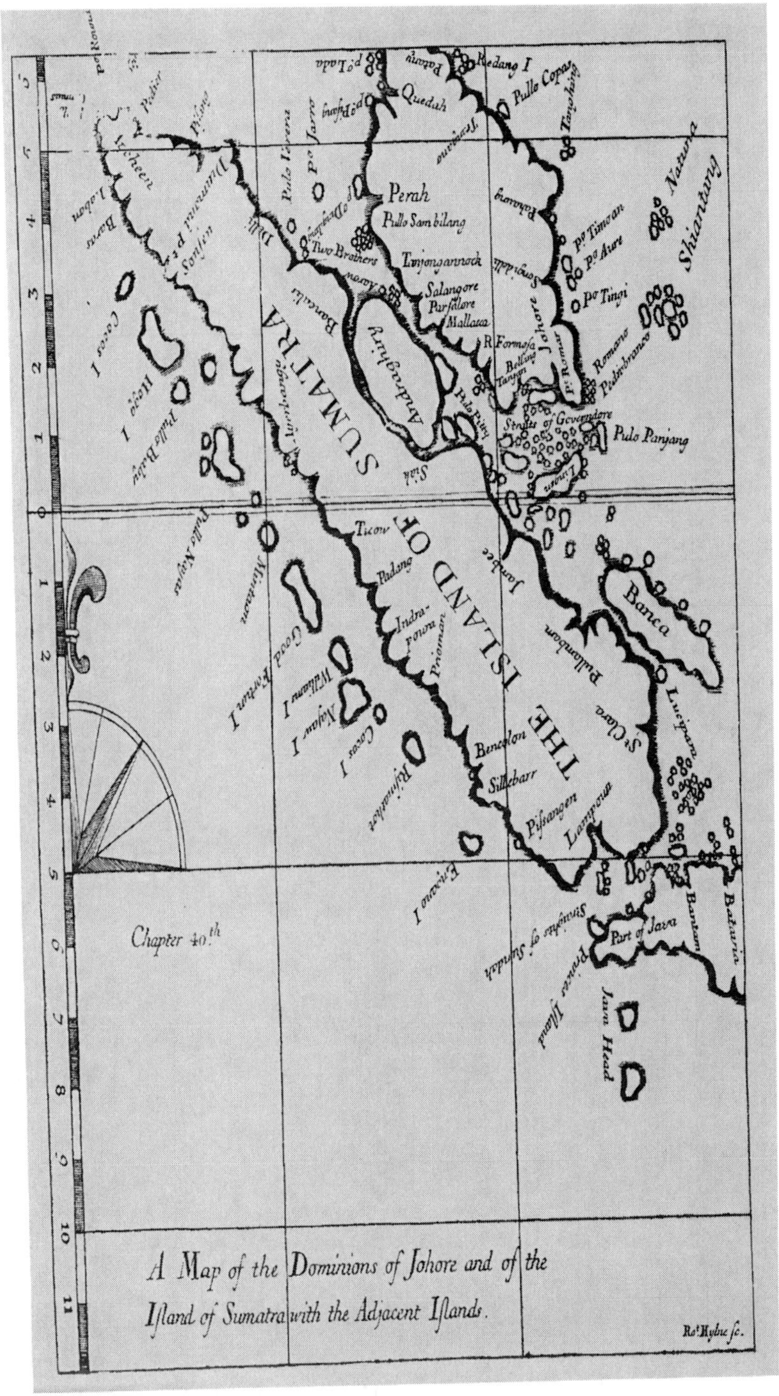

A Map of the Dominions of Johore and of the Island of Sumatra with the Adjacent Islands.

In Religion they are heretical *Mahometans*, and are supplied with Priests from *Surat*; but the *Seids* are in most Esteem among them. They are great Lovers of Praying and Preaching, and frequent their Mosques very often, and look very devout; but their Practices are the most irreligious and immoral of any People I know.

In Anno 1695. their King was a Youth of twenty Years of Age, and being vitiously inclined, was so corrupted by Adulation and flagitious Company, that he became intolerable. I went to *Johore Lami* at that Time, to traffick with his Subjects, and some *China* Men, with a Cargo proper for their Turn, and, according to Custom, went to compliment his Majesty with a Present, in which was a Pair of screw-barrelled Pistols. He desired me to prove them with a Shot, to try how far it would penetrate a Post that was at the Gate, which I did, and he much admired how so little Powder should have Strength to force a Ball so far in the Wood, and begged some Powder and Ball, which I gave him, and the next Time he went abroad, he tried, on a poor Fellow on the Street, how far they could carry a Ball into his Flesh, and shot him through the Shoulder.

He was a great *Sodomite*, and had taken many of his *Orankays* or Nobles Sons, by Force into his Palace for that abominable Service. A *Moorish* Merchant, who was a Freighter on board my Ship, had an handsom Boy to his Son, whom the King one Day

Day ſaw, and would needs have him for a *Catamite*. He threatned the Father, that if he did not ſend him with good Will, he would have him by Force. The poor Man had taken an Houſe cloſe by our Ship, and immediately came with his Son on board, imploring my Protection, which I promiſed him. He had not been half an Hour on board, till a Guard came in a Boat to demand him. I would ſuffer none to enter but the Officer, and an Interpreter for the *Portugueze* Language. The Officer told me his Errand, and, in an huffing Manner, threatned me, if I protected him. I made him no Anſwer, but taught him to leap into the River, and bid the Interpreter tell the King, that, if he offered the leaſt Violence to any that belonged to me, I would fire down his Palace about his Ears. He had never been contradicted before, much leſs threatned, and he ſent for his *Orankays* to know if I was a King or no. They told him that I was on board of my Ship, and that I would prove a dangerous Enemy, if provoked; and begg'd, that his Majeſty would remove to a Village about twenty Miles up the River, and ſtay till our Ship was gone, which Favour he willingly granted us, and ſo we traded with ſome more Security, but were continually in Arms for fear of a Surprize.

HE continued his inſupportable Tyranny and Brutality for a Year or two after I was gone, and his Mother, to try if he could be broke off that unnatural Cuſtom of Converſe

with

with Males, perſwaded a beautiful young Woman to viſit him, when he was a Bed, which ſhe did, and allured him with her Embraces, but he was ſo far from being pleaſed with her Converſation, that he called his black Guard, and made them break both her Arms, for offering to embrace his royal Perſon. She cried, and ſaid it was by his Mother's Order ſhe came, but that was no Excuſe.

NEXT Morning he ſent a Guard to bring her Father's Head, but he being an *Orankay* did not care to part with it, ſo the Tyrant took a Lance in his Hand, and ſware he would have it; but, as he was entring at the Door, the *Orankay* paſt a long Lance through his Heart, and ſo made an End of the Beaſt.

THE Kingdom was three Years without a King, but inteſtine Diſcords daily ariſing, *in Anno* 1700. they chooſed another, a Couſin-german to him that was killed. His Name was *Sultan Abdulla Gialil*, a Prince of great Moderation and Juſtice, and governed well for eight or nine Years, that he held the Reins of Government in his own Hands Trade flouriſhed all over his Dominions, and he was beloved by all his Subjects, but being of a quiet Diſpoſition, and a great Bigot to the *Mahometan* Religion, diſpoſed himſelf to Prayer and hearing Sermons, and left the Management of his Government to a younger Brother, called *Rajah Moudah*, a covetous tyrannical Prince. The King never came out of of his Palace, but devoted himſelf wholly to the Company of Prieſts, who fed his Mind with their Nonſenſe and Cant, and his Brother keeping fair with the Prieſts, came to oppreſs the People, and keep the King ignorant. I had the Honour to be acquainted with him before he was King, and had free Acceſs to him when he was King; but his Brother never ſuffered me to be alone with him, leſt I ſhould have diſcovered ſome of his evil Practices, which I certainly had done, if I could have found an Opportunity, and to have forewarned him of the Danger he was falling into. *In Anno* 1703. I called at *Johore* in my Way to *China*, and he treated me very kindly, and made me a Preſent of the Iſland of *Sincapure*, but I told him it could be of no Uſe to a private Perſon, tho' a proper Place for a Company to ſettle a Colony on, lying in the Center of Trade, and being accommodated with good Rivers and ſafe Harbours, ſo conveniently ſituated, that all Winds ſerved Shipping both to go out and come into thoſe Rivers. The Soil is black and fat: And the Woods abound in good Maſts for Shipping, and Timber for building. I have ſeen large Beans growing wild in the Woods, not inferior to the beſt in *Europe* for Taſte and Beauty; and Sugar-cane five or ſix Inches round growing wild alſo.

In 1708. the King's Brother perſwaded him to leave *Johore Lami*, and reſide at *Rhio* on the Iſland of *Bintang*, about three Leagues off the River of *Johore*, becauſe he thought he he could act his Tyranny with more Security than on the main Continent, and so at *Rhio* he engrossed all Trade in his own Hands, buying and selling at his own Prices, and punishing those who dared to speak against his arbitrary Dealings. At last, in 1712. a Rebellion broke out, that nothing could stop but a Revolution, which dissolved the State into Anarchy.

UPON the Rising of the People, the Tyrant got on board of a Galley, with his Wives and Children, and carried with him above a Tun Weight of Gold, and, without taking Leave of his Brother, fled to *Johore Lami*, but finding a small Army of *Monacaboes* (whom the People had invited to their Assistance) had taken their Quarters there, he betook himself to the Woods with his Family, and left his Galley and Gold a Prey to them. He knew that there could be no long Safety in the Woods, and despairing of Mercy from the injured People, made Desperation supply the Place of Courage. He first killed his Wives and Children, but began to hesitate about killing himself, but a Page of twelve Years of Age asked him if he was afraid to die a Prince rather than be butcher'd like a Slave by some Villain or Slave's Hand, and that he, tho' innocent, and who might expect Mercy, would shew him the Way to die, and with that took a Cress, and run himself through the Body. The Tyrant presently followed the Youth's Example, and immediately expired; but the *Monacaboes* coming ſoon after to the tragical Place, ſaw what had been done, and found the Boy alive; and in his Senſes. They ſtopt his blooding Wound, and carried him to *Johore Lami* till his Strength returned.

WHEN the King heard of the People's Mutiny, and his Brother's Flight, he came out of his Palace, and proferred to ſettle the State in its former Tranquillity, and if that could not appeaſe them, he thought nothing elſe could bring them to Reaſon, but his Life, which he would willingly ſacrifice to atone for his Mal-adminiſtration.

THE People told him, that he was too religious to make a good King, and that he might retire to *Pahaung* or *Trangano*, and ſpend his Time, but as for *Johore* and the Iſlands between *Sumatra* and it, they would conſider what to do with them, and ſo gave him ſome Veſſels to carry him and his Family, with others who would follow his Fortune, to *Trangano*.

ON his Way thither, he called at *Puloaure*, *Tingi*, *Piſſang* and *Timoon*, and the Inhabitants of thoſe Iſlands received him with Demonſtrations of Love, and promiſed to continue in their Duty as his Subjects. He put his eldeſt Son, a Youth about twenty Years of Age, aſhore at *Pahaung*, to keep that Country from revolting, and went himſelf to *Trangano*, where I afterwards had the Honour to ſee him, and there I leave him at preſent, and return to thoſe Iſlands that ly round his Dominions.

CHAP.

CHAP. XLI.

Gives an Account of the Island of Sumatra *its Places of Note in Trade.*

SUMATRA fronts all the Coast of *Malaya*, from *Quedah* to the Promontory of *Johore*, and reaches above 150 Leagues farther. It is one of the greatest Islands in the World. *Atcheen* being the most conspicuous Place for Trade, I will begin with it, and coast along the West Side of it, till I come round again to *Andraguiry*, to the Northwestward of which River there is little or no Commerce.

Atcheen, for many Ages, has been a noted Port for Trade from *Surat*, *Malabar*, *Chormondel*, *Bengal*, *Pegu* and *China*. It lies at the North-west End of the famous *Sumatra*, and, for many Years, was blest with a Woman's Government. Queen *Elizabeth* of *England* sent the Queen of *Atcheen* a Compliment of some *English* Rarities, among which were some Brass Guns, with the Arms of *England* on them, and the Friendship cultivated by the two Queens, procured great Indulgences from the Queen of *Atcheen*, to the *English* who traded to her Country. About the Year 1675. the *Dutch* made War on her, because she would not permit them to settle a Factory at *Atcheen*, or rather, to make her their Vassal. They shut up the Port of *Atcheen* by their Shipping, and straitned the Town for Want of Provisions and other Neceſſaries, that came yearly from *Bengal*, but an *Engliſh* Ship came from thence with Rice and Cloth proper for the Market; but the *Dutch*, after their uſual Manner, forbad the *Engliſh* Traffick, while they had a War. The Maſter of the *Engliſh* Ship being afraid of Ruin by the Loſs of his Voyage, ſent Advices to the *Atcheeners* to be ready near the Shore on a Night that he appointed, and he would run his Ship aſhore in the Bay, loaded as ſhe was, and they might have both the Corn and Cloth, whether the *Dutch* would or no, which Project was put in Practice, and had the deſired Effect, with the Loſs of the Ship only. This Piece of Service ſo pleaſed the Queen, that ſhe called a Council of her *Orankays*, and magnifying the *Engliſh* Friendſhip, in a full Council declared all *Engliſh* free of *Atcheen*, to pay for a Ship with three Maſts, 100 *Tayels*, or about 80 *L. Sterl.* as a Preſent to the Queen, in Lieu of all Cuſtoms, let the Cargo be never ſo rich, and for a Brigantine or Sloop 40 *Tayels*, and that no *Engliſh* Goods ſhould be carried to the Cuſtom-houſe, or ſurveyed in their own Houſes, and that all *Engliſh* Merchants Houſes were to be reckoned as Sanctuaries to ſuch as could not pay their Debts, or had committed any ſlight Fault.

THIS Harmony continued till the Year 1700. that the Queen died, and a *Seid* or Preacher getting a ſtrong Party, was made King, promiſing to do Wonders; but, in all my Travels, I never found a civil Government

ment, with a Prieſt at the Head of it, proſper long, and ſo it fell out here. The firſt Thing of Moment he contrived, was to make the *Engliſh* pay 10 *per Cent.* Cuſtoms on the Goods they imported, which they would not come into, nor would they unlade their Goods, but on the old Footing.

In *May* 1702. I arrived there with a great Ship, and good Force, for it was dangerous to traffick by Sea, becauſe of the Impediment that the *French* and the Pirates gave to Trade in *India*. I had on board a rich Cargo from *Surat*, and, on my Arrival I took the *Chap* at the great River's Mouth, according to Cuſtom. This *Chap* is a Piece of Silver about 8 Ounces Weight, made in Form of a Croſs, but the croſs Part is very ſhort, that we take with both Hands, and put to our Fore-head, and declare to the Officer that brings the *Chap*, that we come on an honeſt Deſign to trade, and after that Ceremony is over, we go in our Boats freely to the Town, which ſtands about four Miles up the River; but, before we take the *Chap*, no Boat muſt go on Penalty of a Fine.

When I came to Town, I went to pay my Viſit to the *Shawbundaar*, who is Cuſtom-maſter, and common Arbitrator of Differences ariſing among Merchants. Some Gentlemen that reſided there, and ſome Maſters of Ships belonging to the *Engliſh*, accompanied me. I carried my Boat's Crew, armed with Fuzee and Bayonet, for my Guard. After ſome Compliments had paſt between the

Shawbundaar and me, he told me, that if I had a Mind to trade there, I muſt carry my Goods to the Cuſtom-houſe, and there to be opened, and 10 *per Cent.* laid by for the King, whether we ſold the reſt there or no. I told him that was a new Method that I did not underſtand, and could not come into, but withal adviſed him to take Care how their King quarrelled with the *Engliſh*, who were as capable to reduce them to Straits as the *Dutch* were, when the *Engliſh* relieved them. He anſwered me, that they were not afraid of what the *Engliſh* could do, for their Power being divided, they could do nothing but threaten.

I took my Leave of him abruptly, and told him, that we knew how to fight in Defence of our Rights and Privileges better than how to threaten. There were three *Engliſh* Veſſels lying in the River, which had paid their Cuſtoms and ſold their Cargoes at under Rates, and two Merchants that reſided at *Atcheen*. We all dined together, and, after Dinner, held a Conſultation how to behave in this Affair, that affected our Merchants in general, who traded thither. At laſt it was agreed, that I ſhould aſſiſt the Merchants in getting their Effects off on board of my Ship, and to get their Veſſels out of the River, by the Aſſiſtance of my Boats and Men, and then to ſhut up the Port, all which was done in one Day and a Night. I then ſent a Linguiſt to tell the *Shawbundaar*, that ſince the *Engliſh* were denied Trade at their Port, we for-

forbad Trade to any other Nation, and deſired that no Boats might paſs out of their Rivers, either to trade or fiſh, on their Peril. They continued quiet two Days, and on the Third they ſent ſome Boats off, from a ſandy Bay about three Miles from our Ship. I ſent two Boats well mann'd to ſeize their Nets, but aſſoon as they perceived my Boats, they ran theirs aſhore, and took out what was in them; and as my Boats were rowing near the Shore within a Mile of my Ship, about 40 or 50 Muskets were fired on them out of ſome Buſhes that grow thick, a little Way from the Strand. My Boats fired in their Turn at the Place where they ſaw the Smoke, and I made a Signal to bring them aboard again, and found only two of my Men ſlightly wounded.

THE ſame Evening we had Advice, that they were about mounting three Culverins that lay in a little Fort on the River's Side, as we go to Town. I immediately ordered my Armourer to get about 100 ſhort Spikes of ſeveral Sizes, and harden them well, and carried them in my Boat, which I double manned, and coming into the River, we eſpied a great Number of Men in the Fort. I rowed directly towards it, and they within expecting to have a Meſſage to carry to the King, ſtood gazing till we came cloſe to the Wall, and then we ſaluted them with a Shower of twenty or thirty Granadoes, that ſo frightned them, that happy was he who got firſt away. We then entred the Fort, and found

found ſome wounded Men in it. We preſently ſpik'd up the Vents of the Guns, and left them, and came at our Leiſure aboard again.

A Day or two after, as my Boat was rowing along the Shore, towards a *Praw* that was coming in towards the ſmall River, they again fired out of their Buſhes. I had forty two Guns mounted on my Ship, and bringing my Broadſide to bear, I got five and twenty on that Side, and pointing them well among the Trees and Buſhes where we obſerved the Smoke to ariſe, we gave them a Volley of great Shot in return of their Volley of ſmall. By Report our great Shot did ſome Execution, but particularly on the poor Fiſhers, who had a Village a little within the Woods, that we did not ſee.

THIS Stoppage of Trade and Fiſhing, and killing and wounding the People, made a great Noiſe among the poorer Sort, having in nine Days Time found more of the Effects of Hoſtility, than ever they did in their Lives before, and ſo gathering together in great Numbers, went in a Body to the Palace, threatning Vengeance on the Cauſers of their Calamity, and if the *Engliſh* were not reſtored to their ancient Privileges, they would have a Woman to reign again.

A Nephew of the deceaſed Queen lived then privately at *Pedier*, a Town about ſeven Leagues off. Some *Orankayas* who were diſcontented with the new King's Government, firſt becauſe he was a Foreigner, and that

that the Affairs of State were ill managed and that a War with the *Engliſh* was impending, wrote to that Gentleman, that if he would come to them with a ſmall Force, they would raiſe a Party to dethrone him that reigned, and he might have a fair Chance to ſucceed him.

HOWEVER, the reigning King not expecting that his new Cuſtoms would meet with ſuch Oppoſition, ſent an *Orankaya* aboard of my Ship, with the Linguiſt, to know why we made War on him. We replied that he was the Aggreſſor, by robbing us of our juſt Rights and Privileges, acquired by our Services, and in firing at our Boats, ſo we wondred that the King could ask a Reaſon of us. The *Orankaya* told us, that he had brought a Power to make up all Differences on the King's Part, but that we muſt conſent to ſome new Things, as that we ſhould pay no Cuſtoms, but a Preſent as before, but that our Goods muſt go to the Cuſtom-houſe, and there to be opened, and was going on, but I interrupted him, and told him he had demanded more than could be granted already, ſo he might ſave himſelf the Trouble of making farther Demands. When he found that nothing new could be obtained, he ſaid he would carry our Anſwer to the King, which he did; and the ſame Evening Proclamation was cried through the Streets, that the *Engliſh* might again repair to their reſpective Houſes, and trade on the old Foundation.

NEXT

NEXT Day I went to wait on the *Shaw-bundaar*, but carried a Guard of twenty *Europeans*. He askt me why I carried ſo many arm'd Men in my Company. I told him that I underſtood there were like to be Commotions in the Country, and I was reſolved to be neuter, and would not be inſulted by either Party. He begg'd that I would land ſome Bales of Goods, to ſhew that we were reconciled, which I did, to the no ſmall Joy of the Town's People, who were quite tired with their new King's Experiments.

BUT the Clamours of the People did not ceaſe. For when they had News of their deceaſed Queen's Nephews raiſing Forces to come to *Atcheen*, the Diſorders of the State increaſed, but I left them, and purſued my Voyage to *Malacca* and *Johore*, where I met with the *Scots* ſecond Supercargo, as is before mentioned.

Atcheen affords nothing of its own Product fit for Export, but Gold Duſt, which they have pretty plentiful, and of the fineſt Touch of any in thoſe Parts, it being two *per Cent.* better than *Andra-ghiry* or *Pahaung* Gold, and is equal in Touch to our *Guinea*. They do not dig for it, but catch it in *Gullies*, or little Rivulets, as it waſhes off the Mountains, and one particularly, a very high Mountain in Form of a Pyramid, called Gold Mount, which by Report furniſhes them yearly with above 1000 Pound Weight.

ELEPHANTS are very plentiful at *Atcheen*, and conſequently their Teeth, which the *Su-rat*

rat Merchants buy up for their Markets. In 1702. I ſaw one who had been kept there above 100 Years, but by Report was then 300 Years old, he was about 11 Foot high, and had a vaſt Deal of Sagacity.

WHEN any young male Elephant grows unruly, which they uſually do in rutting Time, and break their Fetters and go aſtay, this old Elephant is immediately ſent out, and following the Track of his Foot, will find him out, and bring him back to his Stable, either by fair or foul Means.

AT *Atcheen* they have a ſmall Coin of Leaden Money called Caſh, from twelve to ſixteen Hundred of them goes to one *Mace*, or *Maſſcie*. The *Maſſcie* is a ſmall Gold Coin of fourteen Pence current, but in Value about twelve Pence *Engliſh*. I have taken a Gold *Maſſcie*, and put it with a *Maſſcie* of Caſh, and thrown them into a Puddle of Water, and the Elephant would find out the Gold among the Lead, by the nice Feeling of his Proboſcis.

THERE is a very comical Piece of Revenge he took on a Taylor in *Anno* 1692. A Ship called the *Dorothy*, commanded by Captain *Thwaits*, called at *Atcheen* for Refreſhments in her Way from *England* to *Bengal*, and two *Engliſh* Gentlemen reſiding then at *Atcheen*, went aboard to furniſh themſelves with what *European* Neceſſaries they had Occaſion for; and, amongſt other Things, they bought ſome *Norwich* Stuffs for Clothes, and there being no *Engliſh* Taylor to be had, they employed

ployed a *Surat* Taylor, who kept a Shop on the *Bazaar*, or great Market-place, and had generally half a Dozen, or half a Score Workmen to ſew in his Shop. It was the old Elephant's Cuſtom to reach in his Trunk at Doors or Windows as he paſſed along the Side of a Street, begging decayed Fruits or Roots, which the Inhabitants generally gave him.

As he was one Morning going to the River to be waſhed, with his *Carnack*, or Rider on his Back, he chanced to put his Trunk in at the Taylor's Window, and the Taylor prickt him with his Needle, inſtead of giving an Alms. The Elephant ſeem'd to take no Notice of the Affront, but went calmly on to the River, and was waſhed, and being done with waſhing, troubled the Water with one of his fore Feet, and then ſucked up a good Quantity of that dirty Water into his Trunk, and paſſing unconcernedly along the ſame Side of the Street where the Taylor's Shop was, he put in his Trunk at the Window, and blew his Noſe on the Taylor with ſuch a Force and Quantity of Water, that the poor Taylor and his Life-guard, were blown off the Table they wrought on, almoſt frightned out of their Senſes, but the *Engliſh* Gentlemen had their Clothes ſpoiled by the Elephant's comical, but innocent Revenge.

No Place in the World puniſhes Theft with greater Severity than *Atcheen*, and yet Robberies and Murders are more frequent there than in any other Place. For the firſt

Fault,

Fault, if the Theft do not amount to a *Tayel* Value, it is but the Loſs of an Hand, or a Foot, and the Criminal may chooſe which he'll part with; and if caught a ſecond Time, the ſame Puniſhment and Loſs is uſed, but the third Time, or if they ſteal five *Tayel* in Value, that Crime entitles them to *Souling*, or impaling alive. When their Hand or Foot is to be cut off, they have a Block with a broad Hatchet fixt in it with the Edge upwards, on which the Limb is laid, and ſtruck on with a wooden Mallet, till the Amputation is made, and they have an hollow *Bambow*, or *Indian* Cane, ready to put the Stump in, and ſtopt about with Rags or Moſs, to keep the Blood from coming out, and are ſet in a conſpicuous Place, for Travellers to gaze on, who generally beſtow a little Spittle in a Pot, being what is produced by the Maſtication of Beetle, and that ſerves them inſtead of Salve to cure their Wounds.

Those who ſuffer the Penalty of the Law, who have no Families in the Town, are baniſhed to *Pullo-wey*, an Iſland about four Leagues to the North-eaſtward of *Atcheen*, and there they cultivate the Ground, and breed Poultry for the Uſe of the Town; and I have heard that there are above five hundred of thoſe *Banditti* Inhabitants on it. There is another Iſland that lies about three Leagues to the Northward of *Pullo-wey*, called *Pullo-rondo*. It is uninhabited, and ſends forth a Reef of Rocks towards *Pullo-wey*, above one third Part of the Chanel. Between them and

and *Pullo-gomus* is Cluſter of high mountainous and rocky Iſlands, to the North-weſtward of *Atcheen*, and their End runs to ſeven Leagues Diſtance from the Road. There is no Danger lying above a Mile off them; and between *Atcheen* Head an high ſteep Promontory, and the South End of *Gomus* Iſlands, there are two Chanels to come from the Weſtward into the Road. The ſmalleſt, which is not a Quarter of a Mile broad, has no Danger in it, but the broadeſt, which is above two Miles broad, is peſtered with Rocks half Way over from *Gomus* Iſlands.

THE Vallies about *Atcheen* produce excellent Fruits, and the beſt *Mangoſtanes* in the World grow there. The Air is very ſalutary, and the River Waters are excellent for bathing. Waſhing in it before Sun-riſing, and after ſetting, has cured inveterate Fluxes; and I have been told, that frequent Bathing has cur'd the Pox.

CHAP. XLII.

Gives an Account of the Iſlands and trading Ports on the Weſt Coaſt of Sumatra.

AND now I leave *Atcheen*, and purſue my Travels along the Weſt Coaſt of *Sumatra*. *Labon* is the firſt Place noted for Gold Duſt and Camphire, but has no Commerce with Strangers. *Hog* Iſland lies oppoſite to it, about ten Leagues off. This Iſland takes

takes it Name from the great Numbers of wild Hogs on it, who are the only Inhabitants, as *Cocoa* Iſland, cloſe to it, takes its Name from the great Numbers of Cocoa-nut Trees growing on it.

Baros is the next Place that abounds in Gold, Camphire, and *Benzoin*, but admits of no foreign Commerce. It lies within the South End of *Hog's* Iſland, about the ſame Diſtance from it that *Labou* is. This Place ſets a Boundary to the Kingdom of *Atcheen.*

Ayerbangie is the next Place of Notice. It produces Gold and Pepper, it lies about one Degree to the Northward of the Æquator, and has the Advantage of a good ſafe Harbour, but it is little frequented, becauſe of the Treachery of the Natives, who make ſmall Account of murdering Strangers, if they can but get the leaſt Advantage by it. The Harbour lies in a ſmall but deep Bay, and three ſmall Iſlands lying before it, make it a moſt excellent Harbour; and the Chanels between the Iſlands, and between the Shore and the Iſlands, are clear of Danger. The North End of *Pullo-nayas* lies about twenty Leagues without it. The Inhabitants of that Iſland prove the beſt Slaves in *India*, and are ſold at an higher Price in the *Atcheen* Market than any others.

Padang is about twenty Leagues to the Southward of the Æquator, where the *Dutch* have a Colony, and a ſtrong Fort to defend it from the Inſults of the Natives. It coſt the *Dutch* many Men, and much Treaſure before they could force a Settlement there, tho' at laſt they gained their Point, but being a Country that produces only Gold and Pepper, the Profits can hardly bear the Charge. The Iſland of *Good Fortune* lies about 20 Leagues without it.

Indrapura is the next, and lies about fifty Leagues to the Southward of the Æquator. It was formerly an *Engliſh* Factory, but the *Dutch* inſulted it in King *William*'s War with *France*, and it has made but a ſorry Figure in Trade ſince. Its Commodity is only Pepper, but it affords great Plenty of it, and very cheap. The Iſland of *Naſaw* lies about 15 Leagues without it.

Bencolon is an *Engliſh* Colony, but the *European* Inhabitants not very numerous. About the Year 1690. the *Eaſt-india* Company built a Fort there, and called it *York* Fort, but Brick or Stone Walls in that Country cannot long continue firm, becauſe Concuſſions of the Earth are ſo frequent by Earthquakes, that ſolid Walls are rent by the ſhaking of their Foundations. It has the Conveniency of a River to bring their Pepper out of the inland Countries, but great Inconveniencies in ſhipping it off on board the Ships, for there is a dangerous Bar at the River's Mouth, which has proved fatal to many poor *Engliſh* Men. The Road for Shipping is alſo inconvenient; for in the South-weſt Monſoons, there being nothing to keep the great Swell of rolling Seas off them, but a ſmall Iſland called *Rat* Iſland, the Ships are ever in a vio-

violent Motion while that Monsoon lasts.

The inland Princes are often at Variance among themselves, and sometimes are troublesom to the Trade of our Colony, but as their Wars are short, the *English* are in little Danger by them. In the Year 1693. there was a great Mortality in the Colony, the Governor and his Council all died in a short Time after one another, and one Mr. *Sowdon* being the eldest Factor, had his Residence at *Prayman*, or *Priaman*, a subordinate Factory to *Bencolon*, being called to the Government of the Colony, but not very fit for that Charge, because of his intemperate drinking, it fortuned in his short Reign, that four Princes differed, and rather than run into Acts of Hostility, referred their Differences to the Arbitriment of the *English* Governor, and came to the Fort with their Plea. Mr. *Sowdon* soon determined their Differences in favours of the two that complained; and because the others seem'd dissatisfied with his Determination, ordered both their Heads to be struck off, which ended their Disputes effectually, and made them afterwards to make up Differences among themselves, without troubling the *English* with their Contentions and impertinent Quurrels, but Governor *Sowdon* was sent for to Fort St. *George*, and another sent in his Place less sanguin.

And ever since that Time there has been a Succession of moderate Governors, and some have been guilty of as much Temerity the other Way. For *in Anno* 1719. the then Governor, having ſome Diſputes with ſome of the Natives, was ſomewhat fearful of them. On a feſtival Day, in firing Guns, a Wad from one of them ſet Fire to an Houſe thatcht with Reeds, and ſeveral others contiguous to it took Fire from it, ſo that it ſpread through the Market Place. The Governor believing it to be done maliciouſly by the Natives, left the Fort precipitantly, and got on board of a Ship in the Road, leaving ſome Cheſts of Money, and all the Artillery, Arms, Ammunition, and other Effects of his Maſters, behind him, and his Gariſon, following their Leader, left their Poſts, and got aboard alſo.

THE Natives being ſurpriſed with the ſudden Departure of the *Engliſh*, went into the Fort, and took what they had moſt Occaſion for; but ſome *Chineſe* Merchants, who had ſettled at *Bencolon*, being alſo frightned, embarked on their Veſſels, and diſperſed themſelves in Places where they thought they might be moſt ſecure.

THE chief Merchant of the *Chineſe*, who is generally called the *China* Captain, in the Places where the *Chineſe* have Trade, went to *Batavia* to ſome Relations he had there, but the *Dutch*, according to their wonted Hoſpitality in *India*, puniſhed him as a Criminal, and taught him to make Lime and carry Stones the Remnant of his Days, for daring to ſettle among the *Engliſh*. Some of the *Chineſe* I ſaw the ſame Year at *Trangano* in *Johore*, who gave me this Account. Whereever

ever these poor *Chinese* came, in Places where the *Dutch* had Power, they were as heartily persecuted as a Poor *Protestant* is that takes Sanctuary in a Country where the holy, charitable, zealous *Romish* Clergy have Power.

THE Natives were almost ruined by the *English* Desertion. For as their Trade lay all on their Pepper, none came to buy it, and their Regret being known at Fort St. *George*, there was a new Governor sent back with a new Garison, to take Possession again of their own Fort. What the Company lost by that unaccountable Piece of Temerity, I know not, but they gained very little Credit by it.

THE Country above *Bencolon* is mountainous and woody, and I have heard that there are many *Vulcanoes* in this Island; but whatever may be the Cause, the Air is full of malignant Vapours, and the Mountains are continually clothed with thick heavy Clouds, that break out in Lightning, Thunder, Rain, and short-liv'd Storms. Their Food is not fit for every Stomach. Tame *Buffalo* may be had, but no Cow-beef. Poultry are scarce and dear, and so is Fish, but some Sorts of Fruits are pretty plentiful; however, the Gentlemen there live as merrily, tho' not so long, as in other Places blest with Plenty, and so sociable, that they leave their Estates to the longest Liver.

Sillebar lies but four Leagues to the Southeastward of *Bencolon*, and has a fine convenient Harbour to shelter Shipping from all Dangers caused by Storms, but the fresh Water is bad, and if drunk any confiderable Time, caufes Grippings and Fluxes, but it wants a River to bring Pepper from the inland Countries. There is no Place of Commerce or Note between *Sillebar* and *Lampoun* Point, which is the Southwardmoft Point on *Sumatra*, nor any Thing remarkable on the Sea fhore, but a fmall Village called *Piffangen*, which has a fmall low Ifland lying a little Way off it, and there is above 40 Fathoms deep within an *Englifh* Mile of the Shore. And the Ifland of *Engano* lies in the Offing, about 20 Leagues from it. It is an Ifland about 3 Leagues long, uninhabited, very fmooth, without Mountains, and may be feen nine or ten Leagues off.

Lampoun lies twenty Leagues from the Point within the Streights of *Sunda*, at the Bottom of a deep Bay. The *Englifh* had a good Pepper Factory there, but it being a Part of the King of *Bantam*'s' Dominions, that Factory was loft when the *Dutch* compelled the *Englifh* to leave *Bantam*, *in Anno* 1683. and what *Lampoun* produces, is carried to them at *Bantam*.

CHAP

CHAP. XLIII.

Treats of the East Side of Sumatra, *with the adjacent Islands, their Product, Commerce, and Customs.*

THERE are no other Places of Note on that Part of the *Sumatra* Coast, till we come to *Pullambam*, which lies opposite to the North-west Point of the Island of *Banka*, about four Leagues distant from it. *Pullambam* is a *Dutch* Factory that brings them great Quantities of Pepper, being under Contract with the King of *Pullambam*, and other inland Princes, to take off all their Pepper at a certain Price, I think it is for 10 Pieces of Eight, or 50 Shillings *Ster.* a *Bahaar*, of 400 Pounds *English* suttle Weight, one Half to be paid in Money, and the other Half in Cloth. The Cloth Part the Company pays at 70 *per Cent.* on the prime Cost; but all other Nations are debarr'd Commerce there, except the *Chinese*, and by their Means the *English* come in for a Share of their Pepper, as our Ships pass through the Streights of *Banka*.

Pullambam lies about eight Leagues from the Sea, on the Banks of a large River, which divides it self into several Branches, and they disemboque at four Mouths into the Sea. The *Dutch* keep two small Sloops cruising about those Mouths of the River, to prevent Smuggling, but I and many others have found Ways and Means to lade our Ships full with Pepper, notwithstanding the strict Guard. An hundred Pounds to the King, and as much to the *Dutch* Chief, make a Cargo of a thousand *Bahaars* easily procur'd.

THE *Pullambam* Pepper is very foul, in so much that we seldom find less than 10 or 12 *per Cent.* Garblage, but then we buy it for nine Pieces of Eight a *Bahaar*. The *Dutch* lade off about 3000 Tuns *per Annum*, from this Place, and the *Chinese* and Natives lade off as much more. The Natives are obliged to carry theirs to *Batavia*, and sell to the *Dutch* Company, but if they meet with a Market by the Way, they'll embrace it; for the Company's Payment being most in Cloth at high Rates, they are not fond of trading with them.

THE *Dutch* Company formerly drove a good Trade in *Ophium*, at *Pullambam*, which (like *French* Claret and Brandy) drew much ready Cash out of his Country, as those do out of ours, but *in Anno* 1708. the King ordered only the Importation of three Chests, each containing about 160 Pound Weight, and if Smugglers were detected, they paid their Goods and Lives for their Disobedience.

THE Island of *Banka* lying so near the Coast of *Pullambam*, I'll take a View of it as I pass along. It is about fifty Leagues long, and sixteen broad, some Places being broader, and some narrower. For about 30 Leagues it faces the *Sumatra* Coast, keeping between 3 and 6 Leagues distant. The Entrance from the

the Southward being farthest distant in the Streights of *Banka*, at the Mouth of which is the Island of *Lucipara*, a small barren Island, which sends forth Sand Banks almost three Leagues towards the Coast of *Sumatra*. And within a Mile of that Shore, where the Chanel is deepest, there are but four Fathoms and an half Water, but the Bottom is soft.

About 12 Leagues from the North End is the Place of the King's Residence. In 1710. a Son of the King of *Pullambam* was King, and a Fire accidentally happening in a Village, when the Fire was extinguished, they chanced to find much melted Metal under the Rubbish, which proved to be Tin. The King ordered his People to dig a little into the Ground, and they found Plenty of Ore, which he now reaps a good Advantage by. The *Dutch* sent from *Batavia* for Leave to settle a Factory there, but could not obtain that Favour, the King declaring that his Country should be free for all Nations to trade in.

The Natives of the Island are, as most other *Malayas*, very treacherous, inhumane and inhospitable to Strangers, who have the Misfortune to be ship-wrackt on that Coast. I knew one Captain *Pelling*, who belonged to some Gentlemen of *Atcheen*, and had the Misfortune to be ship-wrackt there, and they cut him off and all his Crew, except two Boys who were made Slaves: But I know a very honest ingenious Gentleman now alive in in *England*, who had better Fortune, for, after his Ship was loſt in the Streights of *Banka*, he and his Men directed their Courſe to *Pullambam*, where a very hoſpitable *Dutch* Gentleman, who fortuned to be Chief of the *Dutch* Affairs at that Time, gave them a kind Reception, and procured them Paſſage for *Batavia*, where, ſome Years after, I was in Company with the Hoſt and Gueſt together.

Banka has a very foul Coaſt for 6 Leagues within *Monapin* Point, which is the North-weſt Cape-land on the Iſland; and over that Cape there is an high Mountain called *Monapin* Hill. On the North-eaſt Coaſt of the Iſland there are ſo many Banks and Rocks under Water, that Navigation is very precarious, and none but *Panjalangs* and *Praws* (ſmall Veſſels) venture to go that Tract; beſides, there are no Places of Commerce on the North-eaſt Side of *Banka*, to invite a Stranger by the Proſpect of Gain, and ſo I return back to the Coaſt of *Sumatra* again, without taking Notice of the little Pepper and *Dammar* that are the Product of *Banka*.

FROM *Pullambam* there are no Places of Commerce on the Coaſt, till we come to *Jambee*, which is about 100 *Engliſh* Miles. Here formerly the *Engliſh* had a Factory on an Iſland near its River's Mouth, called *Barella*; but the Impediments their Trade met with from the *Dutch*, who had a Factory in the Country up the River, made the *Engliſh* Company withdraw. The *Dutch* kept a little

Factory

Factory at *Jambee* till 1710. and then withdrew also. That Country produces only Pepper and Canes; and, by the Laziness of the Inhabitants, there is hardly any of them procurable.

The Island *Lingen* lies under the Æquator, about 20 Leagues from *Jambee*, and as far from the River of *Johore*, and is a Part of the *Johore* Dominions. It is about twenty Leagues long, and ten broad. It is very mountainous within, and very low towards the Sea. Its Product is some Pepper and Canes, and it abounds in Porcupines, which affords them the valuable Porcupine *Beakoar*. Some of them I have seen as big as a Wall-nut, and of the same Shape, and pretty near in Colour, valued at 600 Pieces of Eight. Between *Lingen* and *Sumatra* are the Streights of *Drions*, where generally Ships pass that go from *Malacca* to *Batavia*.

On the *Sumatra* Shore there are no Places of Commerce, till we come to the South Entrance of *Andraghira* River, and there lies *Pattapan*, a Town belonging to the Dominions of *Johore*, that affords Pepper and Gold. Off the Mouth of that River about ten Leagues ly the two Islands of *Carimon*, and between them and the *Sumatra* Shore, are the Streights of *Labon*. Upon the East Side of the great *Carimon*, is the Entrance of the Streights of *Drions*; and between the small *Carimon* and *Tanjong-bellong* on the Continent, is the Entrance of the Streights of *Sincapure* before mentioned, and also into the Streights

Streights of *Governadore*, the largeſt and eaſieſt Paſſage into the *China* Seas. There are many Iſlands lying thick hereabout, all under the Dominions of *Johore*.

THE *Dutch* have alſo a Factory on the River of *Andraghira*, called *Siack*, but of no great Moment. It is ſo unhealthful, that incorrigible Sots, and other Lumber of the active World, are ſent thither to expiate their Offences againſt Nature, and very ſeldom any return back to give an Account of the Salubrity of the Country. The Reaſon may be, that yearly there are vaſt Numbers of Fiſh called *Shades*, about the Bigneſs of a large Haddock, full of Bones, and Rows about one third of their own Magnitude, which come into that River to ſpawn, and great Numbers of People reſort thither in that Seaſon to catch them, for the ſake of their Rows, and throw away the reſt of the Fiſh, which ſo corrupts the Air, that few can hold out one Year, but are relieved every ſix Months, except thoſe who are ſent for Sacrifices to *Pluto*.

THE *Dutch* have another Factory right oppoſite to *Malacca*, on the Side of a large River, called *Bankalis*. Whether that be a Branch of *Andraghira* River I know not, but I believe it is. The Company vends a great Deal of Cloth and Ophium there, and brings Gold-duſt in Return. That beneficial Trade was not known to the *Dutch* before 1685. that one Mr. *Lucas*, a Factor in the Company's Service at *Malacca*, was adviſed

vised by a *Malaya* to send some *Surat Baftaes* dyed blue, and some *Berams* dyed red, which are both coarse Cotton Cloth much worn in that Country; and Ophium is as much in Request there, as Tea is with us. In 10 Years that he kept that Trade wholly to himself, tho' in other Mens Names, he got an Estate of 10 or 12 Tuns of Gold, or about 100000 Pounds *English*, and then revealed the Secret to the Company, who took that Trade altogether into their own Hands.

THERE are prodigious Numbers of wild Swine about *Bankalis*, and, in the Months of *December* and *January*, their Flesh is very sweet and fat. In those Months great Numbers of People resort thither in small *Praws*. Some go into the Woods, and drive them towards the River, while others are ready with Dogs to drive them into it, and when one goes, all the Herd follows. Others are ready with Lances in their *Praws*, to pursue them in the Water, and lance them, and so many as are lanced, drop down on the other Shore, and they are immediately carried to Places appointed, where there are many Fires made of Brush-wood and Leaves of Trees, which the Woods afford in great Plenty, and, in those light Flames, they singe the Hair off, and take out the Intrails, and cut them up in proper Pieces, and salt them in the *Praws*; and every *Praw* has a Share proportionable to the Number of Men it brings. After it has lien three or four Days in Salt, they wash the Pork, and hang

it

it in Smoke, and then put it into Casks, which they have ready for their Purpoſe, with ſome dry Salt, and ſell it by the Cask to the beſt Bidder. And I think it is the moſt ſavoury ſalt Pork that ever I taſted.

THOSE Fiſh Rows caught at *Siak*, they pickle up in Salt and Tamarinds, and then dry them in Smoke, and when dry enough, put them up in large Leaves of Trees, and tranſport them to all the Countries about, from *Atcheen* to *Siam*. It is called, when dried, *Turbow*, and of Pork and *Turbow* they drive a good Trade, which, I think, far exceeds *Caviar*.

THERE is no other Place on the *Sumatra* Coaſt, between *Bankalis* and *Atcheen*, that admits of Commerce with Strangers, tho' there are ſeveral large Rivers, at leaſt, by their Outlets to the Sea, they appear to be ſo. There is one called *Delley*, that lies 5 Leagues within *Pullo Verera*, a ſmall uninhabited Iſland, that affords nothing but freſh Water and Wood. The Inhabitants on that Part of *Sumatra*, are ſaid to be *Canibals*. *Diamond* Point lies about 20 Leagues to the Northweſt of *Pullo Verera*, that ſends dangerous Rocks above a League off Shore. The Inhabitants are uncivilized, murdering all whom they can ſurpriſe or maſter. And at *Piſſang*, about 10 Leagues to the Weſtward of *Diamond* Point, there is a fine deep River, but not frequented, becauſe of the Treachery and bloody Diſpoſition of the Natives. Twelve Leagues farther Weſt lies *Pedier*.

It

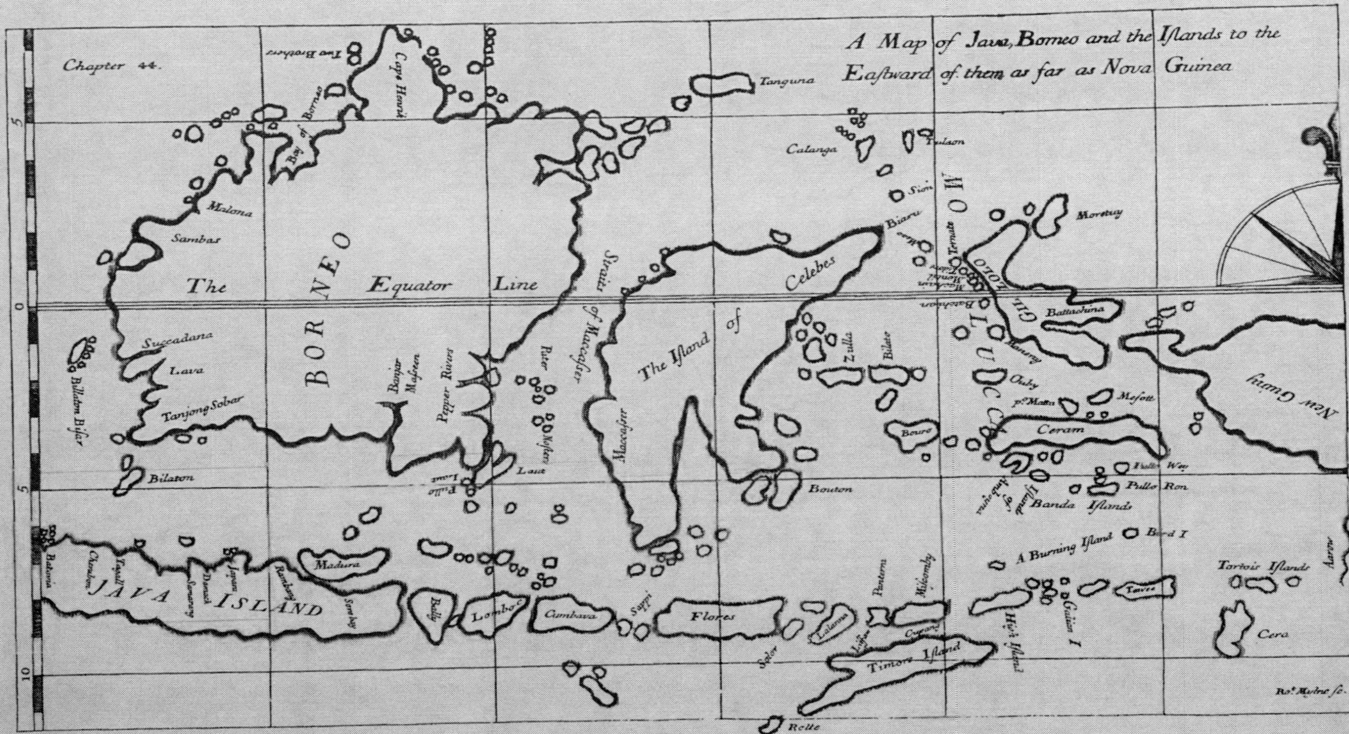
Chapter 44.
A Map of Java, Borneo and the Islands to the Eastward of them as far as Nova Guinea
The BORNEO
Equator Line
Straits of Maccasser
The Island of Celebes
Maccasser
MOLUCCA
GILOLO
New Guiny
JAVA ISLAND
Two Brothers
Cape Henrik
Bay of Borneo
Malona
Sambas
Succadana
Lava
Tanjong Sobar
Billaton Bisar
Bilaton
Banjar Massen
Pepper Rivers
Pulle Laut
Laut
Pater Nosters
Tanguna
Calanga
Tulaon
Sion
Biaru
Ternate
Batchian
Battachina
Moretay
Zulla
Bilate
Bouro
Bouton
Oaby
Ceram
Mesott
Pullo Way
Pullo Ron
Banda Islands
Island of Amboyna
A Burning Island
Bird I
Tortois Islands
Aarow
Cera
Tavre
Galian I
High Island
Timore Island
Rotte
Solor
Flores
Cambava
Sappi
Lombo
Bally
Madura
Batavia
Cheribon
Tagall
Samarang
Damack
Japara
Rambang
Sorebay
Panterra
Misoomby
Rob. Mylne sc.

It has the Benefit of a good River, but being but eight Leagues from *Atcheen*, it has no Trade.

CHAP. XLIV.

Treats of Java, *and the Islands near it, with an Account of the Garisons and Factories settled on that Island by the* Dutch, *the Product and Commerce of* Java, Bally, Lombock, Flores, Solore, Leolana, Panterra, Miscomby, Timore, Banda *and* Molucca *Islands, and the Islands of* Celebes *their Product, Extent and Commerce.*

AND now having ended my Tour round *Sumatra*, I must return to the Southward, and travel to the Eastward of *Sumatra*, and to the Southward of the Æquator, among those famous Islands; and *Java* being the westmost, I begin there, and march Eastward among Islands far from any Continent.

Princes Island is close to the West Point of *Java*. It has a Chanel between it and *Java*, but there is some Danger in it. There are no Inhabitants on it; but there are three Places that afford good Water, and Wood enough for Ships bound out of the Streights of *Sunda* to *Europe*. There are several other Islands in the Streights, as *Caccotoa*, *Duars*, in the Way, the *Button* and *Cape*, and several others without Name.

THE

THE first Place of Commerce on the West End of *Java*, is the famous *Bantam*, where the *English* and *Danes* had their Factories flourishing till *Anno* 1682. at which Time the neighbourly *Dutch* fomented a War between the old King of *Bantam* and his Son, and because the Father would not come into their Measures, and be their humble Slave, they struck in with the Son, who was more covetous of a Crown than of Wisdom. They, with the Assistance of other Rebels, put the Son on the Throne, and took the old King Prisoner, and sent him to *Batavia*; and, in 1683. they pretended a Power from the new King to send the *English* and *Danes* a packing, which they did with a great Deal of Insolence, according to Custom. They next fortified, by building a strong Fort within a Pistol-shot of one that the old King had built before to bridle their Insolence.

THE only Product of *Bantam* is Pepper, wherein it abounds so much, that they can export 10000 Tuns *per Annum*. The Road is good, and secure for the Safety of Shipping. It is in a pleasant Bay, wherein are several small Islands, which retain their *English* Names still; and the Natives still lament the Loss of the *English* Trade among them, but the King has much more Reason than his Subjects to regret the Loss of their Commerce. The Good-will the Natives bear to the *Dutch* may be conjectured from their Treatment, when they find an Opportunity, for if an *Hollander* goes but a Musket-shot from

from their Fort, it is five to one if ever he returns, for they are dextrous in throwing a Lance, or shooting of poisoned Darts thro' a wooden Pipe or Trunk; and the King never redresses them, pretending the Criminal cannot be found.

Batavia is about 20 Leagues to the Eastward of *Bantam*, and a great Number of small Islands ly scattered in the Way, too tedious to mention. *Pullo-panjang* off *Bantam*, and *Edam* off *Batavia* are the most conspicuous, and the Road of *Batavia* is almost surrounded with Islands, some of them inhabited, and some not. Its Topography I'll refer to another Time, with some historical Accounts of it, both ancient and modern.

Cheraboan is the next Colony on the Coast, to the Eastward of *Batavia*, belonging to the *Dutch*, where they have a Fort and a small Garison.

Tagal is also a *Dutch* Settlement, with a small Fort for its Defence; and there is no other remarkable Place till we come to *Samarang*, a good Colony, with a Fort of Mud and Wood to defend it. *Damack* and *Coutus*, two Places that ly between *Samarang* and *Japara*, are noted, one for the Abundance of Rice that it exports, and the other for great Quantities of good Sugars that it produces. They are peopled mostly with *Chinese*, and so is

Japara, which formerly had an *English* Factory, but now is altogether in the *Dutch* Hands. It is defended by two Forts, one

 on

on an Hill, and the other in a Plain, where the Town ſtands, and has a ſmall River to waſh its Walls. The Road is ſecured by two Iſlands that ly about a League off the Town. I bought good white Sugar in Cakes here for two *Dutch* Dollars *per Pecul*, being 140 *lb. Engliſh* ſuttle Weight.

Tampeira is the next Place to the Eaſtward, and to the Eaſtward of it is *Rambang*, about 2 Leagues from it, where the *Dutch* have a ſmall wooden Fort, and a little Gariſon of ſixteen Men. Thoſe two afford nothing but excellent Teak Timber for building. And to the Eaſtward of *Rambang* is *Sorobay*, which lies within the Iſland *Madura*, and, I believe, is the eaſtmoſt Settlement the *Dutch* have on the Iſland of *Java*. It produces much Pepper, ſome Bees-wax and Iron. *Sorobay* is about 125 Leagues to the Eaſtward of *Batavia*, and the Country, along Shore, as pleaſant and fruitful in Grain and Fruits as any in the World. Tame Cattle and wild Game are very plentiful, good and cheap. At *Rambang* I bought a Cow, fleſhy and fat, for two Pieces of Eight, that weighed above 300 Weight; and wild Hog and Deer we killed daily with our Fowling-pieces, as we did alſo Peacocks and wild Poultry. The Cocks are all like one another, with red Necks and Bodies, and black Wings and Tail; and the Hens are exactly like large Partridges. The Cocks are pretty large, and when they take Wing, they make a Noiſe that may be heard half a Mile. Their Fleſh is both

ſa-

savoury and juicy; and the wild Hog is excellent. In the Woods are many flying Squirrels. Some of them I have seen tame in Cages. They also have little Horses wild in the Woods, and some Tigers, but being not much pinched with Hunger, they seldom attack Men. They have one dangerous little Animal called a *Jackoa*, in Shape almost like a Lizard. It is very malicious, and pisses at every Thing that offends it, and wherever the Liquor lights on an animal Body, it presently cankers the Flesh, unless immediate Cauterizings are used, and if that cannot be had, the Piece must be cut out, for, if once it blisters the Skin, there is no Cure for it afterwards; but he seldom fails of giving Notice where he is, by a loud Noise calling *Jackoa*.

I was once at Supper with some *Dutch* Gentlemen at *Rambang*, in an House thatcht with Cocoa-nut Leaves, and we were no sooner set, but one of those *Jackoas* opened its Throat almost over our Heads. The *Dutch* Gentlemen took the Alarm, and arose from the Table in great Haste, and ran out of the Room, calling to me, who sat still (not a little surprised to see their sudden Flight) to follow them, for my Life was in Danger, and, on hearing that Admonition, I was not long after them; but its Noise spoiled our Supper.

As there are many Species of wild Animals in those Woods, there is one particular, called the *Oran Outang*. It is nearest to human, both in Shape and Sagacity, among all the Herd of Animals. I ſaw one about four Foot high, groſs bodied, long Arms from the Shoulders to the Elbows. His Finger Ends reacht juſt to his Knees, as he ſtood upright. His Thighs and Legs plump, but too ſmall in Proportion to his Body. His Feet long, and broad at the Toes, but a little too narrow at the Heel. His Belly prominent, covered with a light-coloured Fur, the reſt of his Body being brown, and the Fur thicker and longer than the Belly Fur. His Head ſomewhat large. His Face broad, and full. His Eyes gray and ſmall. His Noſe little and flat. His Upper-lip and Under-jaw very large. He blows his Noſe, and throws away the Snot with his Fingers, can kindle a Fire, and blow it with his Mouth. And I ſaw one broyl a Fiſh to eat with his boyled Rice. The Females have their regular *Menſtrua.* They have no Tail, and walk upright. They are of a melancholy Diſpoſition, and have a grave dejected Countenance, and even when they are young, they are never inclined to play, as moſt other Animals are. There is a ſmaller Sort, but of a different Species, called *Oumpaes*; but their Legs and Arms are very ſmall.

THEY have many large Crocodiles or Allegators in their Rivers and Mariſhes, and ſometimes they go a Mile or two off to Sea, and get foul of the Fiſhers Nets. I was cleaning a Veſſel (that I bought at *Samarang*) on a Bed of *Ooze*, and had Stages fitted for my People

People to stand on, when the Water came round the Vessel, and we were plagued with five or six Allegators, which wanted to be on the Stage, and every Moment disturbed our Men, so I, and two of my Men, sat on the Vessel's Deck, and fired Muskets at them, but our Ball did them no Harm, because their hard scaly Coat was Shot-proof. At last we contrived to shoot at their Eyes, and we shot at one so. Assoon as he found himself wounded, he turned Tail on us, and, with great Flouncings, made towards the Shore about half a Mile from us, and the rest following him, we were pretty quiet after that. A Day or two after, some Fishers told us, that they had seen a dead Allegator lying on the Shore, and pointed whereabout they saw him. I went, in a Boat, ashore, and found him lying at full Length. I measured his Length, and found, from his Nose to his Tail, twenty seven Foot and an half, and he was about one third Part of his Length in Circumference about the Belly.

I was in *Samarang* in 1704. in the Months of *July* and *August*, when Navigation on that Coast is accounted dangerous. A War happened then to break out between the Natives of that Part of *Java* and the *Dutch*, about the Succession of a new *Sun Suonan* or Emperor, the old one demising about that Time. The *Dutch* would impose the old Emperor's Brother on them against the general Bent of the Nation, and the Nobility were for his eldest Son, being the eſtabliſhed Law and Cuſtom of the Country.

I being then bound for *Batavia*, the Commodore deſired me to carry a Pacquet of Letters for the General and his Council, which I did, and delivered them, before they were ſix Days old, to the General (*Jan Van Hoorn*) which Piece of Service recommended me to his Favour, which he demonſtrated afterwards in ſome Indulgences I had, and ſome Confidence he repoſed in me.

The War begun then, laſted 20 Years longer than at firſt the *Dutch* imagined. It taught the *Javans* the Art of War, having a great Number of *Maccaſſers* and *Ballies*, who had been trained up in the *Dutch* Company's Wars againſt ſeveral Nations. Many of them came into the eldeſt Son's Intereſt, who having as good Courage and ſubtle Stratagems, with much greater Agility of Body than the *Dutch*, made the War more terrible and dangerous than any the Company had ever entred into, notwithſtanding the Pretender had a large Party of *Javans*, and was aſſiſted by *Maccaſſers*, *Amboineſe*, *Ballies* and *Bougies*; but they wanted the *European* Diſcipline that the others had who ſerved the young Emperor, for they could encamp and mine as well as the *Dutch*.

A *Dutch* Captain, in his March towards the *Dutch* Camp, fell, with his Company, into an Ambuſh of *Javans*. Some of his Men were killed, but he, and moſt of his Men were taken Priſoners. The *Dutch* Camp

Camp was pitched on the Side of a River, and the *Javans* a few Miles above them on the same River's Side. Next Day, to the *Dutch* great Amazement, they saw the Captain and his Men swimming down with the Stream, on Bundles of Reeds, with all their Legs, Thigh-bones and Arms broken, and most of them alive. Their Country-men took them out of the River, and used Means to save their Lives, but very few lived, which put their whole Army in some Dread, by observing what Quarter they might expect if any of them were taken Prisoners.

THE Religion of *Java* is partly *Mahometan* and partly *Pagan*. The *Pagans* choose Women to be Priestesses, and they are generally old, and well skilled in Witchcraft. And it is reported, that they have frequent Conversation with the Devil, who appears to them in an horid monstrous Shape, and the Priestesses sacrifice an Hog to him. The Emperor resides at an inland Town called *Cartasouri*, about three Days Journey from *Samarang*, where I'll leave him, and proceed to

THE Island of *Madura*, that produces nothing for a foreign Market, but Deer Skins. They may be had in great Abundance, and very cheap. This Island confronts *Java* to its very eastermost Point. I have no Knowledge of the Islands to the Eastward of *Java*, but what I have had by Information from the *Dutch*, who are the only Possessors of that Commerce, except two *English* Ships that fell in among some of those Islands, and so I will go on in thoſe lame Obſervations and Remarks.

I obſerved before, that *Sorobay* was the eaſtermoſt Settlement the *Dutch* have on *Java*, neither have they any Footing, that I have heard of, on the South Side of that Iſland, tho' the Natives are pretty well civilized, and as Ships from *Europe* fall in with that Coaſt, they will bring off Proviſions to ſell them, particularly if they ſee *Engliſh* Colours, for very often the *Dutch* buy their Commodities, but pay nothing for them.

THE Iſland of *Bally* lies next *Java* to the Eaſtward. It abounds in Proviſions for the Inhabitants, but affords nothing fit for Exportation. The Natives are daring and bold, even to Deſperation. Many of them enter in the *Dutch* Service, and make good Soldiers. Between *Java* and *Bally* are the Streights of *Bally*.

Lambock is next *Bally* to the Eaſtward, and about the ſame Magnitude. It produces the ſame Neceſſaries as *Bally*, but nothing to export.

Combava is next to *Lambock* to the Eaſtward, an Iſland as big as both the laſt two mentioned. It produces nothing for Export. Between it and *Lambock* are the Streights of *Allaſs*, named from a Town ſtanding on the Shore, about the Middle of the Streights.

THE next Iſlands to the Eaſtward of *Combava*, are the two Iſlands of *Sappi*, of ſmall Account in Commerce, and ſo is

THE

The Island of *Flores* to the Eastward of them, tho' it is an Island above 50 Leagues long, and 18 broad. *In Anno* 1703. Captain *Wright* in the *Leghorn* Galley, lost his Passage from *Banjar* on *Borneo*, to *Batavia*, and by contrary Winds, and strong Currents, was driven to this Island, and anchored at a Town on the West End of it called *Larrentoucka*. Finding the Place convenient and safe to pass three or four Months of the Westerly Monsoons, he took an House ashore, and kept sometime one Part of his Ship's Crew ashore, and sometimes another, to refresh them. He gave Warning to the People of the Town not to trust his Men, but they, minding their own Profit, had trusted the Seamen about 100 *L. Sterl.*. A little before he was ready to sail, the Creditors came and demanded their Money. He refused Payment, alledging that a publick Crier had gone through the Town forbidding any Body to trust his Men, and that Crier was ordered by a Magistrate to proclaim the Prohibition. The Creditors said it was true they could not recover any Thing by Law, but if he valued his own Health he would satisfie them, if not in all, yet in Part, and so he paid one Half, which most of them were content with, but one old Witch was not, but threatned his Destruction, if she had not all her Demand paid.

The Captain knowing that the Natives were very skilful in the Art of Poisoning, resolved to prevent their taking any Opportunity that Way,

Way, and ſo went on board to eat and ſleep, and was ſo cautious, that he would not ſo much as taſte their green Fruits, nor ſmell their Flowers, after the Time that the old Hag threatned him, and yet before he left the Place, he found himſelf much troubled with Grippings and Fluxes. I was at *Batavia* when he came there. He could not reach the Road with his Ship before he anchored, but was forced to anchor without, and ſent his Boat on board of my Ship, to deſire Help to weigh their Anchor. I ſent a Boat with 20 Men and an Officer, to bring their Ship into the Road, which next Morning they did; the poor Man was brought to that Paſs by the Effects of Poiſon, that he could not walk without being ſupported, nor could he lift his Hand to his Head.

I waited on him aſhore, and he deſired to be carried to his uſual Quarters, at the Sign of the red Lion, kept by a Woman called *Black Moll*, a Native of the Iſland of *Flores*, and he giving her an Account of his Condition, and how ignorant he was of the Cauſe of it, ſhe bid him be cheerful, for ſhe knew how he had been poiſoned, not by any Thing taken inwardly, but by a Spell, and bid him recollect himſelf, and try if he could remember if he had not ſtept over a Bit of Paper, or the Leaf of a Flag, in going in or out of any Houſe, which, after a little Pauſe, he could very well remember he had. She aſſured him that he ſhould be perfectly well in a Month's Time, and ſhe performed her Promiſe

mise to Admiration. I left *Batavia* before the Cure was perfected, but afterwards when I came to *Batavia*, she gave me an Account that she had restored him to perfect Health, and several Years after, I saw him at Fort St. *George*.

Solor, *Loolana*, *Panterra*, and *Miscomby*, all ly to the Eastward of *Flores*. They produce a little Sandal-wood, and *Cassia-ligna*. The *Dutch* have a Factory on *Solor*.

THE Island *Timor* lies within 20 Leagues to the South of those four Islands abovementioned. It is a large Island about 90 Leagues long, and 18 broad. The Natives acknowledge the King of *Portugal* their Sovereign, and have embraced the *Romish* Religion. They permitted the *Portugueze* Colony of *Maccao* in *China*, to build a Fort on it, which they called *Leifaw*, and the *Dutch* a Factory called *Coupang*, but would never suffer either to interfere with the Government of their Country. The *Portugueze* of *Maccao* drove a very advantagious Trade to *Timor* for many Years, and finding the Natives inclined to be passive *Catholicks*, tried by fair Means to get the whole Government of the Country into the Church's Hands, but could not beguile them that Way, therefore they tried Force, and commenced a War, but to their Cost they found, that the *Timoreans* would not lose their Liberty for fear of the Loss of Blood. They chose one *Gonsales Gòmez* their General. He was a Native of *Timor*, and had travelled to *Maccao* and *Goa*. He allowed the

the King of *Portugal* to be the Sovereign and Protector of their Country, and they would be his loyal Subjects, providing their Laws and Liberties might be secured to them.

THAT War with the City of *Maccao* lasted about fifteen Years. It began about the Year 1688. and was not quite finished in the 1703. and *Maccao* in the End was ruined by it, for it exhausted both their Stock of Men and Money to such a Degree, that of 1000 Citizens the Town had before the War, there was hardly fifty left at the End of it, and of forty Sail of trading Ships, not above five left.

THE Vice-roy of *Goa* sent an Embassy to *Gonsales Gomez*, in the Year 1698. to perswade him to Peace, and to accept of a Governor General and an Archbishop from *Goa*, but to no Purpose, for they declared, that they would admit of no foreign Governors in their Country, either in Church or State.

THE Product of the Island is Sandal-wood, the best and largest in the World, which is a great Commodity in *China*, also Gold and Bees-wax. The Gold is plentiful, but of a low Touch, not amounting to 20 *Caracts* fine. And all Manner of Provisions are plentiful and cheap, but no anchoring about the Island, except at *Leifaw* and *Coupang*. And the Coast is subject to frequent *Tornadoes*, or Squalls of Wind and Rain, introduced with much Thunder and Lightning.

THE Natives report, that at a certain Season of the Year, after the South-west Mon-

soons

ſoons are ſet in, they can diſcern an high mountainous Land to the Southward of them, and continues in Sight from *December* to the latter End of *February*, or the Beginning of *March*, and then diſappears. If the Report be true, it muſt be ſome floting Iſland, that comes from and goes to *New Holland*, which is the next Tract of Land to the South of *Timor*. Theſe Accounts I had from a *Portugueze* Gentleman called *Alexander Pinto*, who was a Captain at *Leifaw* four Years, and was bound from *Batavia* to *Goa*, *in Anno* 1704. He went Paſſenger with me, and ſeem'd to be a Man of Probity.

I never met with any Body that could give me any tolerable Account of the Iſlands to the eaſtward of *Timor*, or of *New Guinea*, or *New Holland*, and ſo I'll paſs by them, and direct my Courſe to the Iſlands of *Banda*, where Cloves, Nutmegs, and Mace grow, but are now all engroſſed by the *Dutch*, who allow one of them called *Pullo-wey*, to belong to the *Engliſh*, after they had been at 40 Years Pains to cut down all the Clove and Nutmeg Trees that grew on it, and have made it Death for the Natives ever to plant any on it.

THE *Engliſh* had alſo a Factory on *Pulloron*, but were glad to leave it about the Year 1618. The *Dutch* have that Iſland ſtill, with *Loutore* and *Noro*, where they reap plentiful Crops of Spice.

I muſt now ſteer Weſt-north-weſt about 30 Leagues, to the famous Iſland of *Amboina*, where

where as real a Tragedy was acted on the *English*, as ever happened among Friends and Allies. The Story is too well known to need a Place here. However, at present it has altered its Scene, and turned prodigiously religious, having no less than 50 *Dutch Protestant* Churches on that holy Island, and the Natives are very fond and forward to turn Converts, especially since some *Amboinese* Youths have been sent to *Holland*, and trained up in their Universities, and honoured with Church Orders. They coming back to their own native Land, loaded with such fine Qualifications, and receiving great Respect from their Masters the *Dutch*, make the Conversion of the Populace very easie.

THE *Dutch* have so fortified *Amboina*, by their own Report, that they think it impregnable. It is true *Victoria* Bay is fathomless till Shipping come within a Mile of their Forts, and there is no other Place for anchoring on that Side of the Island, but I have heard some *Dutch* Officers, in disputing their Knowledge of *Amboina*, say, that on that Side that fronts the Coast of *Ceram*, there are several Places of anchoring at a Mile or two distant from the Shore, and never a Fort built to impede an Enemy's landing, and that if an Army superior in Force to what the *Dutch* have at *Victoria*, would march but six or seven Leagues by Land, they might come on the Back of the Town, and lodge on Hills so near it, that none could pass the Streets in the Town, nor appear on their Bulwarks or

Bat-

Batteries; but this was a Secret that the *English* or *French* ought not to know.

THE Island *Ceram*, near *Amboina*, has also Cloves and Nutmegs, and the *Dutch* appropriate that Island to themselves, and have a Factory on it called *Ambay*. It is a large Island of 70 Leagues long, and 15 broad.

Buro is also a *Dutch* Island, producing Cloves and Nutmegs. It lies West-north-west of *Amboina*, about 35 Leagues distant. It is about 20 Leagues long, and in the Middle 10 broad.

Pullo-ouby lies in the Way between *Buro* and *Gilolo*, the largest of all the *Molucca* Islands. The South Part of *Gilolo* is called *Batta-china*, and the Æquator cuts the Island in the Middle. On the West Side of *Gilolo*, and at a little Distance from it, ly *Batchian*, *Matchian*, *Montil*, *Tidor*, and *Ternatey*. They are but small Islands, but produce the greatest Quantities of Cloves and Nutmegs, of all the *Molucca* Islands.

ONE Captain *Ethrington*, in a Ship called the *Resolution*, made a Trip to *Gilolo* about the Year 1692. and got 40 Tuns of Spice. He called at *Batavia* in his Way to *England*, and the *Dutch* being very solicitous to know where he had been, he freely told them, to let them see the *English* were not quite ignorant of that Navigation, if they had a Mind to follow it.

I now continue my Course Westward along the Æquator, to the Island *Celebes*, the East-Side of which Island, and a great Number of

smaller

ſmaller ones, are little frequented by Strangers, but on the South-weſt Corner of it is *Maccaſſer*, where the *Dutch* have a Factory, but its chief Product is Corn, which indeed all thoſe eaſtern Iſlands abound in, and conſequently in Poultry. The Natives are of a light Olive Colour, and the Women well ſhaped, and pretty beautiful, for which Reaſon they are in great Eſteem among the *Dutch* and *Chineſe*, who buy them for Bed-fellows, and often marry them. The Men and Women are both ſhort in Stature, but well featured, and well limb'd. They are very loving and faithful if well uſed, but exceeding revengeful if ill uſed. The Country is populous and very large, being almoſt 200 Leagues long, but the Breadth unequal. At the broadeſt it is about 70 Leagues. About 30 Leagues Weſtward lies

CHAP. XLV.

Gives an Account of Borneo.

THE great Iſland of *Bornew*, or *Borneo*, the largeſt except *California*, in the known World. The Weſt Side of it is for the moſt Part deſert. On the South End lies *Pullo-laut*, a moſt excellent Harbour for Shipping. The Iſland is but thinly peopl'd, its Product being nothing but Rice, but the North End of it lies near many Rivers that come out of the Pepper Countries. The Iſland

ſland is about 20 Leagues long, but of an unequal Breadth, tho' in ſome Parts it is 12 Leagues broad.

THERE is a Chanel runs between *Pullo-lout* and the Iſland of *Borneo*, about two Miles broad, ſome Places narrower, and ſome broader, and from ſeven to five Fathoms deep, all the Way through, and there are ſeveral riſing Grounds along that Shore, fit to build Houſes on, which is a Rarity on the Sea Coaſts of *Borneo*, ſeldom to be met with. I heard Mr. *Sylvanus Landen*, who had been Chief of *Borneo*, ſay, that he much wondred why the Company of *England* ſhould have ſettled a Factory at *Banjar-maſſeen*, where they were forced for ſeveral Years to keep their Factory on Flotes of great Trees tied together, and made faſt to Trees growing in the Water, on the Side of a River, with Cables made of *Rottans*, and when they built a Factory, they were forced firſt to drive Poles in the Ground, to make a Foundation, as the *Dutch* do at *Amſterdam*, and raiſe Earth on them to build upon.

CAPTAIN *Barry*, a very ingenious Gentleman, drew the Plan, but died before the Work was brought to any great Forwardneſs, and Mr. *Cunningham*, who came thither from *Pullo-condore*, when that Factory was cut off by their *Maccaſſer* Soldiers, came to the Head of the Company's Affairs. He was bred a Surgeon, and had turn'd *Virtuoſo*, would ſpend whole Days in contemplating on the Nature, Shape, and Qualities of a Butterfly or a Shellfiſh, and left the Management of the Company's Buſineſs to others as little capable as himſelf, ſo every one but he was Maſter.

THEIR Factory was not half finiſhed before they began to domineer over the Natives, who paſt in their Boats up and down the River, and very imprudently would needs ſearch one of the King's Boats, who was carrying a Lady of Quality down the River, which ſo provoked the King, that he ſware Revenge, and accordingly gathered an Army, and ſhipt it on large *Praws*, to execute his Rage on the Factory and Shipping that lay on the River. The Company had two Ships, and there were two others that belonged to private Merchants, and I was pretty deeply concerned in one of them. The Factory receiving Advice of the King's Deſign, and the Preparations he had made, left their Factory, and went on board the Shipping, thinking themſelves more ſecure on board than aſhore. When all Things were in a readineſs, the Army came in the Night, with above 100 *Praws*, and no leſs than 3000 deſperate Fellows. Some landed and burnt the Factory and Fortifications, while others attackt the Ships, which were prepared to receive them. The *Engliſh* had made faſt Nettings from the Mizon to the fore Shrouds, about two Fathoms high above the Gunnel, that they might not be too ſuddenly boarded by the Enemy, and to have the Opportunity of uſing their Blunderbuſhes and Lances, before the Enemy could get on their Decks Aſſoon as as they in the Ships saw the Fleet approaching near them, they plied their Guns with double Round and Partridge, and made a great Carnage, but all did not deter the Assailants from boarding, who when they got as high as the Gun-wall or Gunnel, were at a Loss how to get over the Netting, and so were killed with great Ease. Some got in at the head Door of one of the Ships, and killed some *English* in the Fore-castle, but they were soon destroyed. The two great Ships, tho' in Danger, beat off the Enemy with small Loss, but the little Ships were both burnt, with most of their Men, and one *Dutch* Gentleman who was obliged to flee from *Batavia* on one of the small Vessels, was also burnt in her. His Name was *Hoogh Camber*, and had been Ambassador to the King of *Persia*.

I heard some *China* Men say, who were there at the Time of the Engagement, that the *English* killed, (in two Hours that the Action was hot,) above 1500 Men, besides many wounded and maim'd, but the *English* were forced to be gone from their Settlement. The King thought his Revenge had gone far enough in driving them from their Settlement, and finding the Loss of the *English* Trade affected his Revenue, he let all *English* who traded to *Johore* and other circumjacent Countries, know, that he would still continue a free Trade with the *English* on the old Footing, but would never suffer them, or any other Nation to build Forts in

 his

his Country. Several *English* have been there ſince, and loaded Pepper, and have been civilly treated ; and the *Dutch* ſent a Ship from *Batavia in Anno* 1712. to trade with them, but the Natives refuſed Commerce with them.

THE inland Country is very mountainous, but towards the Sea very low and mariſhy, occaſioned by the great Rains that continue about 8 Months in the Year. It produces Rice, and many Sorts of Fruits in great Abundance. Pepper is peculiar to the Countries about *Banjaar*; and to the weſtward about *Succadaana*, they have ſmall Diamonds, but their Waters being inclined to be yellow, are not ſo much in Eſteem as thoſe of *Golcondah*.

THE *Engliſh* had formerly a Factory at *Succadaana*, but why they left it I know not, unleſs it was for the Unwholſomneſs of the Country; yet *in Anno* 1694. I met with a Ship from Fort St. *George*, bound to *Succadaana*, commanded by one Captain *Gullock*, who had been there the Year before, and praiſed it for a wholſom Country, and the Inhabitants very civil and obliging. He bought ſome *Surat Baſtaes* of me, at 45 *per Cent.* on Invoyce, and expected to make as much himſelf.

IT is reported, that on the Coaſt of *Borneo*, between *Lao* and *Sobar*, there are many *Canibals*, but I never heard it confirmed by any but *Chineſe*. And from *Sobar* to *Succadaana*, the People are civil enough to Strangers.

Sam-

Sambas is the next Country of Commerce to the Northward of *Succadaana*. It produces but very little Pepper, but ſome Gold, Pearls, and Bees-wax, which makes it well frequented by the *Chineſe*, who carry *Surat* Piece-goods from *Malacca* and *Johore*, and barter to very good Purpoſe for the aforeſaid Commodities. Bees-wax is the current Caſh in that Country. It is melted but not refined, and caſt in Moulds of an oblong Square, the Breadth about two Thirds of the Length, and the Thickneſs Half of the Breadth, and a *Rattan Withy* to lift them by, caſt in the Wax. A Piece weighs a Quarter of a *Pecul*, which comes to in *Engliſh* Weight, 34 Pound, and a *Pecul* is valued in Payments at 10 *Maſſcies*, or 40 Shillings *Sterl.* They have alſo for ſmaller Payments Pieces of Eight to a *Pecul* and Sixteenths, and for ſmaller Money they have *Couries*. The Prince and People are very hoſpitable and civil, ſo that Strangers trade there with Security. I knew a *French Armenian*, who coming from *Manilla*, had the Misfortune to loſe his Ship on that Part of the Coaſt that belongs to the King of *Sambas*. They had but little Goods, for generally *Spaniſh* Dollars are the common Return for Goods ſold at *Manilla*. When the People that were ſhipwrackt came aſhore, they were carried to the King, who examined what they were, from whence they came, and whither bound, with what they were loaded, and ſeveral other Interrogatories, and then ordered them Proviſions, and Men and Boats to aſſiſt them in ſaving their Treaſure, for there was but very little loſt beſides the Ship and Stores that were not worth the Trouble of ſaving. The King gave him Pearls and Bees-wax for his Silver, at ſuch reaſonable Rates, that the *Armenian* gained 40 *per Cent.* at *Batavia.* (whither he went on a *China* Veſſel) for the Goods he diſpoſed of there. At *Batavia* he took Paſſage on board a *French* Ship for *China*, and in their Way called at *Trangano*, where I met with him in the 1719. I had the whole Account from himſelf, and ſaw ſome beautiful Pearls that he was carrying to the *China* Market, and among them a Pair of Pears worth 50 *L. Sterl.*

THE *Chineſe* drive a ſmall Trade from *Siam* and *Cambodia*, to the Town called *Borneo*, that lies about 80 Leagues to the Northward of *Sambas*, and theſe are all the trading Places that ly about the North End of this Iſland, that I could hear of. The Religion in *Borneo* is *Pagan*, except in ſome Places on the Sea Coaſt there are ſome *Mahometans*, and ſo I muſt leave *Borneo*, and ſteer my Courſe towards the Coaſt of *Johore* on the Continent, but in my Way there are two Cluſters of Iſlands that ly half-way. One is called *Anamba*, and the other *Natuna*, but by the Natives *Sciantan*, is the common Appellation for both Cluſters. Their Inhabitants are called *Bougies*, a fierce deſperate People, and the only Product of thoſe Iſlands is Betle-nut, and the Religion *Mahometan* The Iſlands are very high, and may be eaſily

easily seen in a clear Day above fifteen Leagues.

CHAP. XLVI.

A Continuation of the Dominions of Johore *on the Continent, and the Islands adjacent.*

THE *Johore* Islands to the North-eastward of the Promontory of *Romano*, (from whence I took my Departure, when I steered among the Islands) are first *Pullo-tingi*, then *Pullo-aure*, then *Pullo-pisang*, and then *Pullo-timoun*, the highest and largest among them. They are all inhabited and produce Poultry, and small Goats, and some Fruits, but no Commodities for Export. Their Religion is *Mahometan*.

Pabaung lies North-west of *Pullo-timoun*, about 20 Leagues distant. *Pullo-varella* lies in the Way, but it is rather a Rock than an Island, therefore hardly worth noticing. *Pabaung* River has a pretty large Island lying in its Mouth, which makes two Chanels into it. The North Entry has no less than four Fathoms and an Half at High-water, and the Chanel is about an hundred and fifty Yards broad. Just within the Bar is good secure Anchoring in six Fathoms, and there are good fresh Water Springs within two hundred Paces of the Sea-shore. The River is a Mile broad, but so full of Banks, that it is with Trouble a small Vessel of thirty Tuns can go to the Town, which lies about twelve Miles up the River, where I left *Rajah Bowncea*, before I took my Ramble among the Iſlands. He was there *in Anno* 1719. with five or ſix hundred Men to keep that Country firm to his Father.

Pahaung River runs far into the Country, and waſhes the Foot of *Malacca* Hill. There is Abundance of Gold Duſt found in it, and I have ſeen ſome Lumps, of five or ſix Ounces each. They do not dive for the Duſt above three Fathoms, tho' there are ſome Places in the River above Ten deep, and generally where the deepeſt Water is, moſt Gold-duſt is found. It has exported ſome Years above eight hundred Weight. Along the Sides of the River Pepper is planted for Export, but not above 300 Tuns in a Year, becauſe they want Vend for more, tho', if they had a Market to carry it off, in five Years Time they could make a Product of 3000 Tuns. Beſides Pepper and Gold, there are Tin and Elephants Teeth, but in no great Plenty, and the beſt Canes in the World grow hereabout. The Country is woody, and is ſtor'd with wild Game and Fruits, their Rivers and Sea with great Plenty and Variety of excellent Fiſh, but the Country is not reckoned very healthful, becauſe of the Abundance of Rains. *Trangano* is the next Place of Note for Commerce, and *in Anno* 1720. the Place of Reſidence of a poor diſtreſt King, who by a ſenſeleſs Devotion to Superſtition, ruin'd his Country and his own Family.

I

I gave an Account before of his Brother's tragical End, and the daring Boldneſs of a Youth that ſhewed him the Way to die by his own Hand. In 1719. I ſaw the Youth waiting on the King, and fanning him with a Peacock's Tail. In my Way to *Siam*, I called at *Trangano*, and went to wait on him, and he remembred that he had been acquainted with me five and twenty Years before. I ſtaid about a Week, and every Day he wanted to ſee me. He often repented his taking the Weight of Sovereignty on his Shoulders, and feared that his End would prove as tragical as his Brother's.

Trangano ſtands pleaſantly near the Sea, on the Side of a River that has a ſhallow Bar, and many Rocks ſcattered to and again within the River, but Room enough in many Places to moore ſmall Ships very ſecurely, to keep them ſafe from the Dangers of the Winds or Floods. There may be about one thouſand Houſes in it, not built in regular Streets, but ſcattered in ten or twenty in a Place diſtant a little Way from another's *Villa* of the ſame Magnitude. The Town is above half-peopled with *Chineſe*, who have a good Trade for three or four *Jonks* yearly, beſides ſome that trade to *Siam*, *Cambodia*, *Tunqueen* and *Sambas*. When I came back from *Siam* with my Cargo unſold, as I mentioned before, I came to *Trangano* to diſpoſe of what I could of my Goods, and to procure a new Cargo for *Surat*, the kind King aſſiſted me in doing both, with

all

all the Readineſs and Cheerfulneſs imaginable.

WHILE my Ship lay in the Road, the *Bougies* came with a Fleet of two hundred Sail of *Praws*, deſigning to plunder the Town of *Trangano*; but they were afraid to paſs ſo near our Guns as they muſt have been neceſſitated to do before they could get into the River. When they came to a Place about 5 Leagues off, they ſent a *Praw* to my Ship, and the Officer told me, that he had a Commiſſion to profer and pay me 3000 *Spaniſh* Dollars, if I would let them paſs quietly into the River. I ordered him away, and threatned, that, if they came, they ſhould feel the Force of my Powder and Shot. When I came aſhore, the King askt me if I would protect him. I told him I would with all the Force I had. He wept, as if he had been diffident, and deſired that I would take him on board of my Ship, and carry him whitherſoever I went, for his Life was burdenſom to him, and he could truſt none of his own People. I perſwaded him that I was ſincere in my Reſolution to protect him, and that it would look too mean to run away from his Kingdom, while there was a Poſſibility to regain it.

HE told me, that he had ſent Ambaſſadors to the *Dutch* at *Malacca* for Aſſiſtance, according to the ancient League between his Anceſtors and them, when they joyned their Forces to expel the *Portugueze* from *Malacca*; but inſtead of finding Relief there, his

his Enemies were assisted with Powder and Shot, and his rebellious Subjects had a safe Retreat at *Malacca*.

I advised him to take Protection from the *Dutch*, and allow them the Monopolization of the Trade of his Country, and to part the Revenues between him and them. He seemed to be offended with the Proposal, but said he would be glad if the *English* would settle in his Dominions, and fortify what Places they pleased, and that he would willingly come under their Protection, and that there were none that ever entertained the *Dutch* in their Countries as Guests but would willingly be quit of them again, if they could.

THERE happened to come a *French* Ship thither at that Time, being bound to *China*. The King gave the Captain and me an Invitation to Dinner, and, after we had regaled ourselves, we entred on a Discourse of the miserable State of a Country under the Malignancy of a civil War. He asked us, if such Calamities had happened to *England* or *France*. We assured him there had been often such Distempers among us, but that when the Disease was cured, our State became as strong and vigorous as ever.

HE had several Times askt me, if I thought the *English* might be perswaded to settle a Colony in his Country, that *Pahaung* might be made a Place of great Trade, if there were Shipping and Stock to carry off the Pepper and Tin which that Country alone could produce.

duce. I told him, I could give him no Encouragement to believe they would.

He then deſpairing of getting an *Engliſh* Colony ſettled, propoſed to Mr. *Pedro-villamont Garden*, who commanded the *French* Ship, if he thought the *French* Nation might be induced to ſettle in his Dominions, and the *French* Gentleman gave him Hopes that the King of *France* might be induced to accept of his Friendſhip, and ſettle a Colony, providing he would certify his Requeſt by a Letter, which the King of *Johore* readily agreed to. It was written in the *Malayan* Language, and tranſlated by a *Chineſe* into *Portugueze*, and I tranſlated it from that Language into *Engliſh*. The Original and the *Engliſh* Tranſlation were delivered to the *French* Captain, but I never heard of it ſince.

He told me, that when I came to *Bombay*, I ſhould acquaint the Governor of the Deſire he had to live under the Protection of the *Engliſh*, and that with 150 Men they might bridle the Inſolence of his own rebellious Subjects, and their Allies the *Bougies* too.

Trangano is a very pleaſant and healthful Country, and affords a fine Land-skip from the Sea. The Hills are low, and covered with ever-green Trees, that accommodate the Inhabitants with Variety of delicious Fruits, ſuch as Lemons, Oranges, Limes, *Mangoes*, *Mangoſtans*, *Ramboſtans*, *Letchees* and *Dureans*: And in the Vallies, Corn, Pulſe and Sugar-

Sugar-canes. The Ground is cultivated by the *Chinese*, for the lazy *Malayas* cannot take that Trouble.

THE Product of the Country is Pepper and Gold, which are mostly exported by the *Chinese*. About 300 Tuns are the common Export of Pepper, and we have it almost for one half of the Price that we pay for *Malabar* Pepper From the Month of *October* till *March*, their River is shut up by the Bar, which fills up by the Impetuosity of the great Seas sent on that Shore by the North-east Monsoons; but in the Months of *July* and *August* their Seas produce the finest Fish that ever I saw or tasted. There is one Sort exactly like a Salmon, both in Shape and Taste, but the Fish is white, as the Salmon is red. Their Poultry are large, plump and sweet, but Beef is scarce, except Buffalo Beef, and that is plentiful enough.

In Anno 1720. the *Bougies* came to *Pullo-capass*, which is but five Leagues from *Trangano*; but there are other Islands that ly 12 Leagues more southerly, called, in the Maps, by the Name of *Pullo-capass*, but their right Name, which the Natives call them by, is *Pullo-tetang*.

HOWEVER, from *Pullo-capass* the *Bougies* sent an Ambassy to *Trangano*, pretending an Accommodation with the King, to see if he would allow them to enjoy the Continent and Islands beyond the Promontory of *Romano*, and they would leave him the quiet Possession of the rest; and, while they were

were in a large Hall conferring, ſome unuſual ſudden Noiſe happened to be heard from without, which the guilty *Bougies* taking to be ſome Deſign in Execution againſt them, one of them runs to the King, and creſt him to the Heart, which made a very great Diſorder, and many were killed on both Sides; and what *Bougies* remained, got on board of their Gallies, and poſted to their Fleet at *Pullo-capaſs*, with the News of what had happened at *Trangano*, and next Day the *Bougies* went into the River, and plundred the Town, except certain Houſes which belonged to the *Dattabandaar*, or firſt Miniſter, whom the King, in his Life-time, ever miſtruſted, but, by the ill Situation of his Affairs, was obliged to hide his Thoughts, and defer his Reſentments till a proper Time.

The next Place, to the Northward, in the *Johore* Territories, is *Patany*. It was formerly the greateſt Port for Trade in all thoſe Seas, but the Inhabitants being too potent to be afraid of the King's Laws, they became ſo inſolent, that Merchants were obliged to remove their Commerce to Countries of more Security. It was the ſtaple Port for *Surat* Shipping, and from *Goa*, *Malabar* and *Chormondel* they had a good Trade, and ſo they had from *China*, *Tunquin*, *Cambodia* and *Siam*; but the Merchants finding no Reſtraint on Robbers and Murderers, were obliged to give their Trade a Turn into another Chanel, which was a great Advantage to *Batavia*, *Siam* and *Malacca*, where they were kindly

uſed,

ufed, and in thofe Ports it has continued ever fince.

THE *Johore* Dominions reach but four or five Leagues farther North, which, like moft Borderers, are inclined to Rapine, and lying fo near another's Dominions, where they may be fcreened from the Power of their own Laws, when they commit Depredations, it makes them exercife their Villanies with Impunity. Between *Trangano* and *Patany* ly the Iflands of *Redang*. They are uninhabited, but fometimes the *Saleeters* or *Malaya* Freebooters frequent them, and when they meet with trading Veffels that they are able to mafter, they make Prize of them, and carry the Men into other Countries than where they belong to, and fell them for Slaves; and when they meet with no Purchafe at Sea, they go afhore in the Nights, and fteal all they can get. Men, Women and Children go all into the Booty; but the *China* Veffels afford them moft Prizes.

THE Kings of *Johore* ever paid Homage to the Kings of *Siam*, by fending them a Rofe made of Gold in a golden Box once in three Years. The Year 1719. happened to be the Year that the Rofe came, for I faw the Meffenger that brought it at *Siam*, where he had Orders from his Mafter to know how my Affairs went, with a Profer of the King's Service, if I came back into his Country.

CHAP.

CHAP. XLVII.

Gives an Account of the Dominions and City of Siam, *with Remarks on the Revolution that happened there.*

SANGORE is the firſt Town on the King of *Siam*'s Dominions. On that Side it is under the Government of *Ligore*, which was once the Metropolis of a Kingdom of the ſame Name, but, by civil Diſſenſions, it became a Prey to the King of *Siam*.

Sangore ſtands on the Side of a large River. It yields ſome Tin, Elephants Teeth, Agala-wood and coarſe Gold, but the Inhabitants meet with ſo great Diſcouragements in digging for Tin, that there is very little to be procured; and what is manufactured, is bought up by the *Dutch* Factory at *Ligore*.

Ligore lies about 12 Leagues to the Northward of *Sangore*, and between them lies a low uninhabited Iſland, called *Papier*. It reaches from *Sangore* within 3 Leagues of *Ligore* River. It is well ſtored with wild Buffaloes, Hog and Deer, which are free for all Perſons to kill at Pleaſure. The Road of *Ligore* lies two Leagues from the River, and about a League within the River's Mouth ſtands the *Dutch* Factory, a pretty commodious Houſe, built of Brick, after the *Dutch* Faſhion. The Town ſtands about two Miles above the Factory. It is built of *Bambows*, and thatcht with Reed. There are many *Pagan* Temples in it, which have Steeples

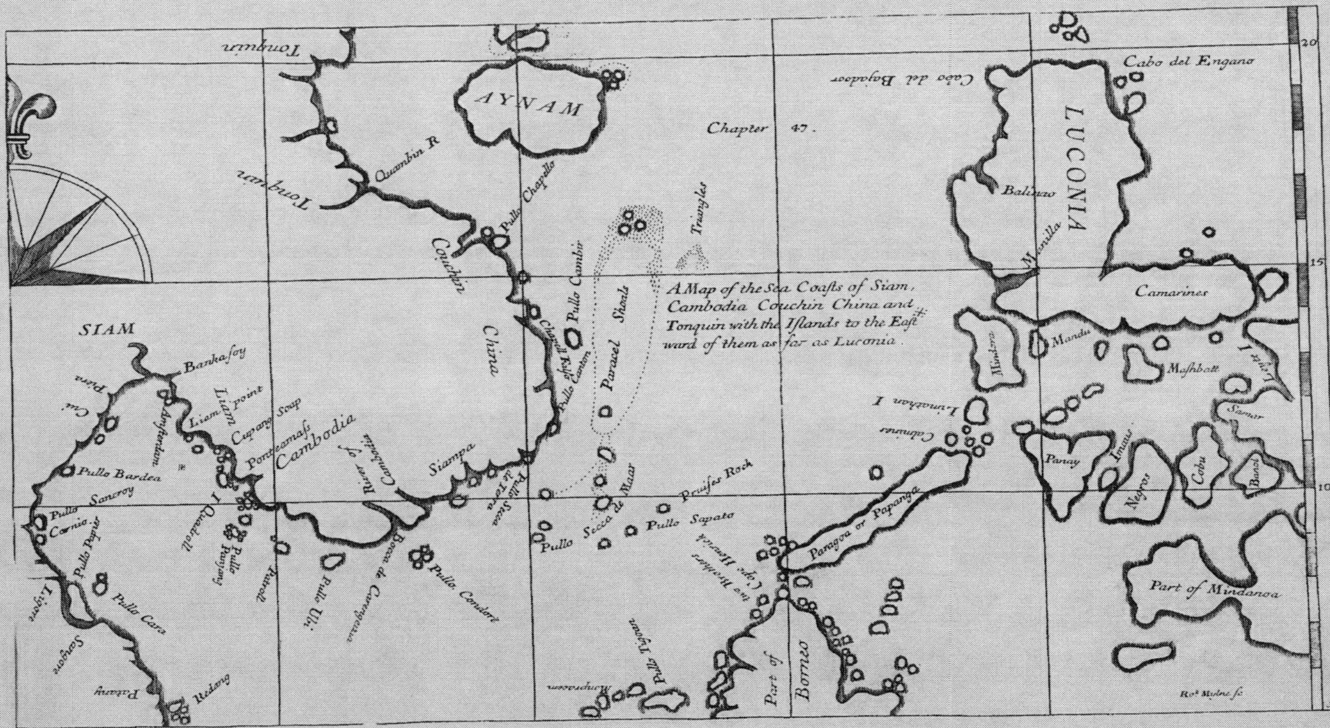
A Map of the Sea Coasts of Siam, Cambodia Couchin China and Tonquin with the Islands to the Eastward of them as far as Luconia.
Chapter 47.
LUCONIA
Cabo del Engano
Cabo del Bajadoor
Balinao
Manilla
Camarines
Mindora
Mandu
Mashbatt
Leyte I
Samar
Limathan I
Calmines
Panay
Imaus
Negros
Cebu
Banol
Paragoa or Papanga
Part of Mindanoa
Part of Borneo
two Brothers
Cape Henrick
Pullo Tygoan
Pruises Rock
Pullo Sapato
Pullo Secca de Maar
Paracel Shoals
Triangles
Pullo Cambir
Pullo Canton
AYNAM
Pullo Chapello
Couchin
China
Quambin R
Tonquin
Tonquin
Siampa
Pullo Secca de Terra
River of Cambodia
Cambodia
Ponteamass
Cupang Soap
Liam point
Liam
Banka-soy
SIAM
Pira
Cui
Amsterdam
Pullo Bardea
Sancroy
Pullo Cornia
Pullo Papir
Pullo Cara
Ligore
Sangore
Patany
Redang
I Quadroll
Pullo Panjang
Patroll
Pullo Ubi
Bocca de Carengeura
Pullo Condore
Rob. Mylne sc.
5
10
15
20

Steeples built very high, in Form of very ſharp Pyramids. They are ſo ſmall, that, in the Road, they look like Ships Maſts. It produces Abundance of Tin, but the *Dutch* engroſs it all.

Pullo Cara, an high Iſland, lies about 12 Leagues off *Ligore*. The next Place of Note is *Cui*, a Place that produces great Quantities of Tin and Elephants Teeth, but all are ſent to the City of *Siam* or *Odia* for the King's Uſe. The reſt of the Coaſt being little frequented, I will paſs by it, and ſteer for the Bar of

Siam. The City ſtands on an Iſland in the River *Memnon*, which, by Turnings and Windings, makes the Diſtance from the Bar about 50 Leagues. The Country is low, and as fruitful as any Spot of Ground in the World, in Rice, Legumen, Fruits and Roots, Cattle wild and tame. And the River abounds in many Species of excellent Fiſh, which plentifully indulge the Inhabitants, and make them indolent and lazy, and conſequently proud, ſuperſtitious and wanton.

The City is reckoned ten Miles round the Walls, and many Canals, from the River, pierce thro' the City from all Quarters. The Walls of the City are high and thick, built of Stone and Brick; but the Houſes of the Natives, tho' large, are low, built on Stakes driven into the Ground, about 10 or 12 Foot high; but the *Mahometans*, *Chineſe* and *Chriſtians* raiſe the Grounds they build on high enough to be ſecure from the yearly Inundations. The Natives Houſes are raiſed on thoſe Stakes on the ſame Account, and as their Walls are built of *Bambow* and Reeds, their Roofs are built of the ſame Materials, and are all thatcht, except what are built on *Terra firma*, and they are generally tiled. There are many arch'd Bridges in the City, built of Brick or Stone, and ſome of Wood. The Floors of the Natives Houſes are made of ſplit *Bambow* or Reeds made faſt together, ſo that one cannot move on them without both Noiſe, and ſhaking them.

THE three Palaces of their Kings, and ſome Temples, are the only magnificent Edifices in the City; and ſome Steeples belonging to the Temples are gilded with Gold on the Outſide, and in a Sun-ſhine they reflect the Rays ſo ſtrongly, that, at two or three Miles Diſtance, they diſturb the Eye, when lookt upon.

THEY have many large Temples well decorated after their Way, and well ſtockt with gilded Images of Gods and Goddeſſes, of the Prieſts Contrivance and Canonizing, and they never want Devotees to adore them, who pay their deceitful Impoſers very well for deceiving them; but they are not the only People that are ſo cunningly deluded, for the fatal Cuſtom has ſpread univerſally in all the Corners of the World.

THE great God, who created the Univerſe, they have no Image of, nor can they make any of him, becauſe he never ſhewed himſelf in any bodily Shape, and therefore they can form no Idea of his Shape, Dimenſions

or

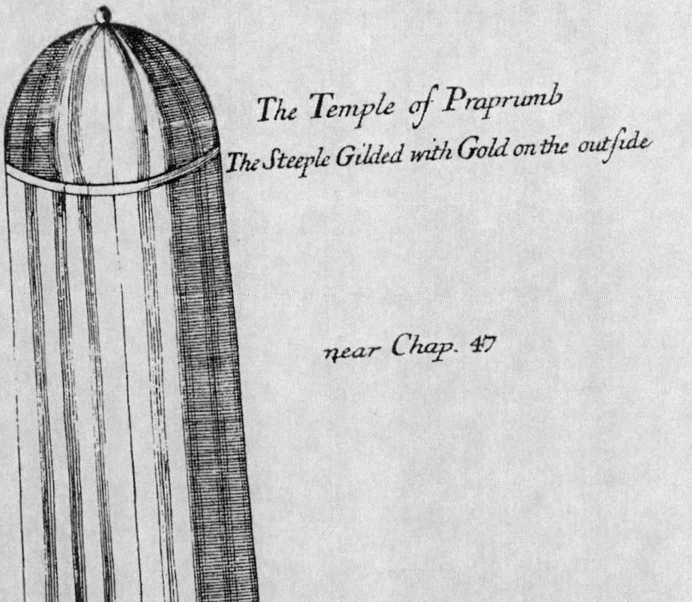

The Temple of Praprumb

The Steeple Gilded with Gold on the outside

near Chap. 47

or Beauty; but *Tipedah*, the great God's Partner has often ſhewed himſelf, and him they worſhip in his Image with the higheſt Adoration. *Praw Prumb* and *Sommo Cuddem* his Friends they adore with the ſecond Degree in Worſhip; and *Prapout* and *Samſay* have the third Sort of Veneration paid to their Images.

THEY have many little Deities inferior to thoſe above mentioned, whom they adore as Patrons or Protectors of ſeveral Tribes of Men, and other Animals of different Countries and Cities, of Health, Proſperity and other Chances and Caſualties, ſo every one is at Liberty to chooſe his own Patron or Protector, and worſhip him according to his own Mind, but none are perſecuted for the Opinion of the Way he is to worſhip, either the great or the little Gods. That heavenly Frenzy is only a raging mad Diſtemper that affects the melancholick Brains of the weſtern World.

I was in one Temple pretty large, built exactly four Square, and each Square contained juſt an Hundred Images. They were placed in Notches or *Domes* about four Foot from the Ground. There were more Goddeſſes than Gods, and all were in a ſitting Poſture croſs-legg'd, as Taylors ſit on their Shop-boards. Their Noſes were low and ſmall, their Viſage long, their Ears large, and the Lappets of them thick and plump. They ſat promiſcuouſly in thoſe Notches, and all clothed in one Livery of Gold-leaf. They were almoſt as big as full-grown Men and Women, but very different in their Subſtances. The Prieſts told us, that ſome were of pure Gold, others of *Tecul* Silver, which has no A loy in it, ſome of Copper and ſome of Braſs, and ſome of bak'd Clay; but, for Want of ſumpture Laws among them, it was hard to know the Gentleman from the Beggar by their Garb, or a Lady from a Lawndreſs.

In one Temple, as I was informed, ſtands the famous *Samſay* twenty Yards in Height. He is in a right lineal Deſcent from little *Samſay*, who cauſed ſo much War between *Siam* and *Pegu*, which never ended but with the Diſſolution of the *Pegu* Empire. In moſt of their Temples there are frightful Dragons ſtanding Sentinels at their Gates, but whether they are placed there to keep in the Gods, or to keep out Devils, I know not.

There are reckoned no leſs than fifty thouſand Clergymen or *Tallapoys* belonging to the Temples in and about the City of *Siam*; but they are eaſy to the State, having no ſtated Benefices or other Revenues, and yet they are plentifully ſupplied with all the Neceſſaries of Life by the Charity and Benevolence of the Laity.

There is one Temple about three Miles below the City, on the oppoſite Side of the River, called the *Fiſhes* Temple, becauſe annually in the Month of *September*, when the Floods overflow the low Ground, (as in *Egypt*) there are good Numbers of Fiſhes almoſt like ſmall Salmon, that frequent a Pond cloſe

close to that Temple, and are to be found in no other Place in the *Siam* Dominions, and they are so tame, that they will come close to our Boats, and frisk and play on the Surface of the Water, if any Body has a Mind to feed them with Bread, Cocoa-nut Meat, or other Food that does not easily separate. 'Tis only to hold some near the Surface of the Water, and they will take it familiarly from the Hand. I have often taken Pleasure to feed them, and see them play, but assoon as we leave off feeding them, they will withdraw, so that hardly one is to be seen till a new Supply of Victuals is offered to them.

BUT none dares offer to take one of them, for fear of raising a zealous sanctified Mob, who punish small Faults with the greatest Severities, and those Fishes being consecrated to the God of that Temple, are securely protected by the Consecration. They continue about the Temple till the Middle of *December*, that the Floods begin to draw off the Ground, and then they depart, and are seen no where in any River or Pond belonging to *Siam*, till *September* brings them back to their Temple.

WHATEVER Animal comes within the Verge of a Temple, it is secured from Pursuit or Violence. I knew a *Portugueze* Inhabitant of *Siam*, who shot a Crow as it sat on the Branch of a Tree that grew near a Temple, on which the Priests raised a Mob, who broke both the poor Man's Legs and Arms, and left him in the Field for dead,

 but

but ſome *Chriſtians* coming accidentally by, carried him in a Boat, in that deplorable State, to a *French* Surgeon, who ſet his Bones, and cured him. I ſaw him alive and well *in Anno* 1720.

THE *French* have a Biſhop at *Siam*, with a Church and a Seminary for the Education of Converts. They ſtand a little above the City, on the oppoſite Side of the River. They make but few Converts, except when Corn is dear, and then ſome of the poorer Sort receive Baptiſm, which intitles them to a Maintenance from the Church, but, when Plenty returns, they throw away their Beads and brazen Saint, and bid farewel to *Chriſtianity*. *In Anno* 1720. there were not above ſeventy *Chriſtians* in and about *Siam*, and they the moſt diſſolute, lazy, thieviſh Raſcals that were to be found in the Country.

THE Biſhop was one Mr. *Ciſſee*, a Man of about 80 Years of Age, who, in a Famine that happened there *in Anno* 1708. took up about 3000 Pounds *Sterl.* from the King, to buy Corn for the Support of his Church, and ſuch poor *Siamers* as were converted by the Neceſſity of the Times, who relapſed again aſſoon as the Famine ceaſed, and the poor old Biſhop cannot leave the Country till that Debt be diſcharged. He is ſuperſtitiouſly zealous for his Religion, and would fain go to *Couchin-china* or *Tunquin* to die a Martyr, becauſe it is Death by their Law to preach any foreign Doctrine without Leave firſt obtained from their Kings.

WHAT-

WHATEVER Principles he may have had in Religion I know not, but I am ſure that he was a diminutive Moraliſt, which I knew by Experience, in ſeducing ſome of my Seamen, who were black *Chriſtians*, to leave my Ship at *Siam*, contrary to his Promiſe, which obliged me to buy Slaves to ſupply their Places; but I left him ſome Cauſe to repent of his Folly and Breach of Promiſe.

THERE were four or five Prieſts there beſides the Biſhop, one whereof always attends the College, and the others officiate daily in the Church. They live abſtemiouſly, but, I believe, rather thro' Force than Choice, for their Incomes are very ſmall, as Charity and Piety are very cold among their Flock. The *Portugueze* have alſo a Church there, built on the Side of the River oppoſite to the lower End of the Town; but their Prieſts are generally ſo ſcandalous in their Lives, that few frequent their Church, or care for their Converſation. The *Chineſe* being very numerous in *Siam*, have ſeveral ſmall Temples, but none remarkable for their Structure or Beauty.

The *Dutch* have a Factory there, about a Mile below the Town, on the ſame Side of the River. Their greateſt Inveſtments are in Tin, Sapan-wood and Deers Skins, which they buy up for the *Japon* Market. The *Siam* Market takes off but little *European* Goods; however the *Dutch* Chief makes a pretty good Figure there.

THE *English*, for many Years, had also a Factory there, till about the Year 1686. the *East-india* Company seeking Occasions to pick a Quarrel with the *Siamers*, in order to withdraw, they took hold of such as they could first find, tho' never so frivolous. The first was about *Anno* 1684. The *Carolina*, bound from *England* to *China*, had the Misfortune to lose her Passage, and coming to *Siam* to pass away the North-east Monsoons, and the King of *Siam* having Occasion for some Stores for Shipping out of the *Carolina*'s Cargo, to equip some Ships that he had built in order to humble the *Cambodians* and the *Couchin-chinese*, who disturbed the Navigation of his Country, he civilly requested the *English* Chief to supply him at the Prices the same Commodities used to be sold at to Merchants, but he could not find that Favour, which he resented, and threatned to disturb their Commerce. At length they supplied him with some Part of what he demanded, to avert the ill Consequences that might happen by a total Refusal. This was represented to the Company in the darkest Colours, and they thought that sufficient to ground a War on; but they had, at that Time, a Fleet of large Ships, which they had equipt to regain their Trade of *Bantam* and other Places, which the *Dutch* had insolently robbed them of; but they were disappointed by the deep Politicks of King *Charles* II. as is before observed.

HOW-

However, the King of *Siam* continued his Indulgence to the Company and their Servants, in much Affluence and Luxury, continually carousing in Debaucheries with Wine and Women, till their common Salaries and Gains by Trade, were in no Proportion to their extravagant Expences, however that being a free Country, they had Liberty to spend their own and their Masters Estates, as they pleased.

The King of *Siam* having formed the Design of a War, as above mentioned, with *Cambodia* and *Couchin-china*, employed a good Number of *English* who had resorted to *Siam*, to partake of the King's Indulgence and Bounty, and to help the Company's Servants to spend their Money. All the *English* who had a Mind to list themselves on board of his Fleet, had great Encouragement of honourable Posts and good Salaries well paid, and they did perform Actions in the War worthy of the Bravery and Courage of the *English* Nation, by which the King's Favour to the *English*, increased more than before the War.

One Mr. *Pots* happened to be Chief of the *English* Factory at that Time, who by his extravagant Luxury had rioted away a great Part of his Masters Goods and Money, and had run his own Credit out of Doors. He then began to form Projects how to clear Accounts with his Masters and Creditors, without putting any Thing in their Pockets. The first was on 500 Chests of *Japon* Copper, which

which his Maſters had in Specie at *Siam*, and they were brought into Account of Profit and Loſs, for ſo much eaten up by the white Ants, which are really Inſects, that by a cold corroding liquid Quality, can do much Miſchief to Cloth, Timber, or on any other ſoft Body that their Fluids can penetrate, but Copper is thought too hard a Morſel for them; however, I ſaw that Article in the Company's Accounts, as they were remitted from *Siam* to *Bombay*, and were in Mr. *Vaux*'s Cuſtody at *Surat* afterwards.

BUT that ſmall Article of 2500 Pounds, went but a ſmall Way towards clearing of his Accounts. So after Supper one Night as they were merrily carouſing, the Factory was ſet on Fire, and that balanced all other Accounts. Mr. *Pots* alledged to the King, that his Subjects the *Siamers*, had done that Miſchief, and expected the King to be accountable for Loſſes and Damages, ſuſtained by the Company and their Servants.

THE King, on the other hand, proferred to prove, that Mr. *Pots* and his drunken Companions had done it, and that he expected the Company ſhould be accountable to his Subjects for the Loſs they had ſuſtained by the Fire, which had burnt ſeveral Houſes that lay near the Factory. However, the Company adhered to the juſt Complaints of their honeſt Servants, and thought that the King's Refuſal to make good their Demands, was a ſufficient Piece of Ground to build their War on. However, the Company conſideſidering that a War could bring them no Advantage, thought it enough to bully the *Siamers*, but never declared a War.

In the Year 1685. the Company ſent two Ships to the Bar of *Siam*. One was the *Herbert* of 800 Tuns, the other the prudent *Mary* of 400. to frighten the *Siamers*, but they did no Damage to them, and the *Siamers* treated them civilly.

About the 1680. there was one *Conſtantine Falcon*, a *Greek* by Birth, that ſome Years before had ſhipt himſelf Steward of an *Engliſh* Ship at *London*, bound to *India*, and being ordered for *Siam*, and finding ſome ill Treatment on board, he deſerted from the Ship, and fled to a ſmall Village ſome Diſtance from the City, where he amuſed him; ſelf in learning the *Siam* Language. He being a ſober, ingenious, and induſtrious Perſon, ſoon made himſelf Maſter of the Language, and ſerved as an Interpreter for the *Engliſh* at Court, where he was remarkably taken Notice of, and got a Poſt there. His Behaviour recommended him to greater Preferments, ſo that in a very few Years he became prime Miniſter of State, and behaved himſelf ſo well in that high Station, that every Thing belonging to the State of the Country proſpered, ſo that *Siam* became the richeſt and powerfulleſt Kingdom in that Part of the World.

The *Jeſuits* hearing that one of the *Romiſh* Communion ſat at the Helm of the *Siam* Affairs, and it being a rich Country, brought

whole

whole Troops of them into *Siam*, who got the whole Management of Affairs into their Hands, through the Intereſt of the *Barkalong*, that being the Appellation of firſt Miniſter. They tickled themſelves with the Fancy of bringing the whole Kingdom of *Siam* under the Pope's Juriſdiction, and *in Anno* 1683. the firſt Year of his Miniſtry, they got the King to ſend an Embaſſy to the King of *France*, which Ambaſſador came alſo to *London*, and ſettled a Treaty of Commerce for the *Engliſh* that ſhould trade in *Siam*.

THE Jeſuits impoſed on the King of *France*, and made him believe, that if he would ſend an Embaſſy to *Siam*, that King would leave his own Superſtition, and embrace theirs. Accordingly an Ambaſſador was ſent, with many valuable *French* Curioſities, and among them a very fine Maſs-book, with beautiful Cuts of all the firſt Rate Saints in the *Romiſh* Kalendar.

ON the Ambaſſador's Arrival, he was received with the Reſpect due to his Character, and when the Preſents were laid before the King, according to Cuſtom, he ſeem'd much pleaſed with their Curioſity, but when he viewed the Pictures in the Maſs-book, he askt a *Jeſuit* who was Interpreter, what they were, who anſwered, that they were the Pictures of holy Men now in Heaven, and ſuch as his Brother the King of *France* adored, and as he deſigned an eternal Friendſhip with his Majeſty, he hoped that he would alſo adore thoſe Pictures, and worſhip the Images of thoſe Saints,

Saints, rather than those Idols that were worshipped all over his Dominions. The King returned Answer, that the Gods of his Country had been auspicious to them who lived in it for Time out of Mind, and as it would be unjust and ungrateful to banish those Gods that had been so long very kind to his Predecessors and himself, so he could not turn his old Gods off and take new ones in their Places that he did not so well know, and that he would oblige his Brother of *France* in any Thing but that.

THE King of *France* complimented Mr. *Falcon* with the Order of Knighthood, and in his Letter to him, wherein he recommended the *French* Affairs to his Care, particularly that of Religion, he stil'd him Loving Cousin and Counseller.

AFTER the Embassy was gone from *Siam* to *France*, the *Jesuits* thought of nothing but bringing the Trade of *Siam* under the Power of the *French*, and in order to that, got the King to order the building of a Fort on the River's Side, opposite to the Fort of *Bencock*, a Town about 20 Leagues below the City of *Siam*, and to have it mann'd with a Garison of *French*, to be paid by the Exchequer of *Siam*, and all this was granted according to their Mind.

THE Fort is a regular Tetragon, and can mount about 80 great Guns. When the *French* got Possession they grew intolerably arrogant, which made the *Siamers* uneasie, and murmured at the King's Weakness, but that was

was in private, for certain Deſtruction is the ſure Reward of talking publickly of any Miſmanagement of the State, for a King of *Siam* can no more err in Politicks, than a Pope can in Matters of Faith.

YET about the Year 1688. by ſome malevolent Planet that over-ruled his Actions, he made a War with his Neighbours the Kings of *Cambodia*, and *Couchin-china*. He ſent an Army by Land, and a Fleet by Sea, to carry on the War, but was not ſucceſsful by Land. However in the Land-army there was a mean Perſon, a Citizen of *Siam*, who kept a Fruit-ſhop, he had a bold daring Spirit, and behaved himſelf ſo well on all Occaſions, in the Land War, that he came to Preferment, and at laſt was made Generaliſſimo, and then ended the War to the Satisfaction of the whole Army abroad, and his Prince at home; but when he brought back the Army to *Siam*, ſeeing the King wrapt up in the Opinion he had of the *Jeſuits* Counſels, and the Management they had in the Affairs of State, by the Countenance of the King and his firſt Miniſter my Lord *Falcon*, he pickt a Quarrel with the King, and having moſt of the Army at his Devotion, ſeized his Maſter and put him to Death, after the Manner of royal Criminals, or as Princes of the Blood are treated when convicted of capital Crimes, which is, by putting them into a large Iron Caldron, and pounding them to Pieces with wooden Peſtles, becauſe none of their royal Blood muſt be ſpilt on the Ground, it being, by their Religion, thought

thought great Impiety to contaminate the divine Blood, by mixing it with Earth. And after he had murdered his Master, he summoned all the *Mandereens* in the City, to hold a Council in the Palace.

My Lord *Falcon*, for that was generally his Designation, had, by his civil Deportment towards People of all Ranks and Degrees, so ingratiated himself, that he had a stronger Party by far, both in the City and Country, than the General; and besides, had all the Fleet at his Devotion. Many of my Lord's Friends disswaded him from obeying the Summons, but to raise the Forces of the City, and revenge the Death of the King, and many Officers of the Army that detested the Regicide would have come over to his Party, which at least was above 50000 strong, but being infatuate, he was deaf to all good Advice, and went to the Palace, where assoon as he had set his Foot, he was seized by the General's Guards, and beheaded, so the Usurper took the Sovereignty into his own Hands, and at that Instant was by *jure divino* made an infallible Favourite of Heaven, and the Sun, Moon, and Stars, had the Honour to be his near Relations.

Had my Lord *Falcon* followed his Friends Advice, or had Courage answerable to his other good Qualities, he had certainly been honoured with the Diadem in *Siam*, and if he had introduced *Popery* in the Place of *Paganism*, he had been honoured with a Place in the Pope's Almanack, but his Pusillanimity made him unworthy of both.

I

I had this Account from my Lord Secretary Mr. *Bashpool*, who, on his Master's Death, was clapt up in Prison, and lay three Years with his Neck in the *Congoes*, which are a Pair of Stocks made of *Bamboes*, and was never taken out, but in order to be severely whipped, to make him accuse rich Men whom the Usurper had a Mind to destroy, that he might seize their Estates under the Umbrage of Justice and Law.

I saw my Lady *Falcon in Anno* 1719. and she was then honoured with the Superintendency of his Majesty's Confectionary. She was born in *Siam* of honourable Parents, and at that Time much respected both in the Court and City, for her Prudence and Humanity to Natives and Strangers, when they came into Difficulties, or under the Weight of Oppressions from the Officers of the Court or City.

WHEN the *Siam* Ambassador returned from *France* and *England*, in the murdered King's Time, his Master, among many other Questions, askt him if the King of *France* had any Palaces like his at *Siam*, for Beauty and Magnitude, and the poor Man unadvisedly told him Truth, that in *France* were many finer, nay, that the King of *France*'s Horse Stables in *Paris*, exceeded any Buildings in *India*, which his Majesty took so ill, that he disgrac'd him, and was very near losing his Head for his telling Truth.

THE King of *Siam* is as fond of lofty Titles as the King of *Pegu*. Besides his Proximity with

A prospect of the King of Siams pleasure Barge that he appears in on the River

Chap. 47. p. 177

with the heavenly Luminaries, he is a God on Earth, in whose Court are to be found Justice, Mercy, and Benevolence to Mankind, with such a Train of senseless Hyperboles, and at last, to illustrate all the rest, he is King of the white Elephant, a Title that none disputes with him but the King of *Pegu*.

THE King bestows his anniversary Blessing on his People in the Month of *September*, when he passes through the City attended with a numerous Train of Elephants, among whom is the white Elephant, but he is only of a Cream Colour, and I have seen severals at *Bangarie*, a Village near *Jonkceyloan*, as white as him. All the Elephants that Day are drest in their finest Trappings, with Drums, Trumpets, Hautboys, and other musical Instruments making a Noise as they go along, but whether it is to divert his Majesty or his Elephants, I know not, but I am sure the Noise was harsh in my Ears.

WHILE he is making his Elephantine Cavalcade through the City, the Populace dares not look him in the Face, but prostrate on their Knees and their Elbows on the Ground, with their Hands open and joyned above their Heads, and their Eyes fixt on the Ground, or shut till he has past by them, then they are permitted to rise and look on his back Parts or Side.

IN the Month of *November* he also shews himself on the River, in a *Ballong* or Barge of 30 or 40 Yards long, about two Yards broad, and two Foot deep, with a Throne

 placed,

placed near the Middle of her Length, about ſeven Foot high, and a rich Canopy over his Head, and being ſeated on the Throne, his greateſt Lords or Minions ſit under the Throne, and about 50 or 60 Rowers are ſeated a-fore and be-aft the Throne, (clothed in Carnation coloured Waiſtcoats, with fine Caps or Turbands on their Heads) to row or paddle his Majeſty wherever he orders them, and there are ordinarily above 1000 other Barges to wait on his Majeſty, beſides ſeveral Thouſands of other common *Ballongs*, inſomuch, that for 5 or 6 Miles, the River is covered with Boats, except near his Majeſty's Barge, and there is half a Mile of the River clear for his Barge to move in.

About four or five in the Evening, he goes in his Barge to a Temple about three Miles above the City, on the oppoſite Side of the River, where the Prieſts pray for him, and preſent him with two Yards and an Half of Cotton Cloth, that muſt be ſpun and woven the ſame Day that the King comes to receive it. After Sun ſets, he embarks again (leaving ſome royal Gratuity to the Prieſts for their miraculous Preſent) and is attended in State to his Palace.

His Reaſon for honouring the River and his People that Time of the Year, is to forbid the River formally to flow higher or longger than ſuch a Number of Inches in Height, or of Days in Time, as he ſets it; yet ſometimes it diſobeys his royal Commands.

All

All the *Mandarines* belonging to the Government, whose Affairs require their Residence in the City, whose Numbers generally amount to 3000. must daily attend in the Palace, except they have Leave to be absent, and if any one transgresses, he is severely whipt with split *Rottans*, which cut pretty deep into the Flesh, and leave conspicuous Marks behind them. The greater the Marks appear, the greater the Honour they take them to be. And the pretty Ladies are not exeem'd from the Flagellation, for very small Faults. And I have seen some pretty agreeable young Gentlewomen with *Rottan* Marks on their Backs, which they are so far from covering, that as they pass the Streets, they expose their Backs, tho' their Breasts, Bellies, and Necks are covered with a Scarf, seeming to glory in being so much taken Notice of by the greatest King on Earth.

The Women in *Siam* are the only Merchants in buying Goods, and some of them trade very considerably. The Husbands in general are maintained by the Industry of their Wives. And the *Europeans* that trade to *Siam*, accommodate themselves as they do in *Pegu*, with temporary Wives, almost on the same Conditions too, and it is thought no Disgrace to have had many temporary Husbands, but rather an Honour that they have been beloved by so many different Men. The *Christian* Priests cry down that Way of Marrying, and want every Heretick, as well as *Christian Catholick*, to be tied to some young Laſſes of their bringing up, but the Hereticks, according to their innate Principles, generally continue deaf and obſtinate to the grave Advice and ſound Doctrine of the holy Fathers, and marry according to the *Siam* Way. The *Catholicks* dare not do ſo for fear of Excommunication, but the *Siam* Wives generally prove the moſt obedient, loving, and chaſte, for which Reaſon, when the *Catholicks* once go from *Siam* to follow their Buſineſs in other Countries, they ſeldom return to *Siam*, but leave their beloved Wives a Legacy to the Church, who is a very indulgent Mother to her termagant Daughters.

THE Natives of both Sexes go bare-headed, and their Hair cut within two Inches of the Skin, and gumm'd, and comb'd upwards, which makes their Head ſeem very big, and all in Briſtles like a Boar's Back. They are well ſhap'd in Body and Limbs, with a large Fore-head and a little Noſe, and handſom Mouth with plump Lips, and black ſparkling Eyes. Their Ears of a moderate Size, but large thick Lappets. The Men have but little Hair on their Chins, and they are of an Olive-colour, but the Women of a Straw Complexion, and ſome of the Ladies have a little Tincture of red in their Cheeks and Lips, but whether it is natural or artificial I know not. They are very prolifick and long-lived, which may be partly imputed to their Temperance in eating and drinking.

AFTER

After the Usurper had settled himself on the Throne of *Siam*, he ordered the *French* to deliver their Fort at *Bencock*, to an Officer that he sent to take Possession of it, but they refused, without first making Terms for themselves, on which he sent a Part of his Army to attack it, and threatned every Man's Life that returned before it was taken. His Orders were punctually put in Execution, and all the *French* got, was the Honour of dying bravely in the Defence of their Liberty. The Fort stands still undemolished, but no Artillery is in it.

In *Siam* they have several Ways in punishing Criminals with Death, for Theft and other such like Peccadilloes. Beheading is the common Way. For Rebellion or Mutiny they are ript up alive, and their Guts and Intrails taken out, and their Carcases woven up in a Twig-case, and tied up to a Stake for Vultures and other voracious Fowls, or Dogs to feed on. I saw Eighteen one Morning going to be executed so for Mutiny. They were each put on a triangular Seat, with their Necks and Hands in wooden Fetters, and carried by three Slaves in Chains through the Streets to the Place of Execution, but they lookt as if they had been almost starv'd in Prison, for they were very meagre. Some were weeping, others joyful that they were near the End of a miserable Life.

For Treason and Murder, the Elephant is the Executioner. The condemned Person is made fast to a Stake driven into the Ground for the Purpose, and the Elephant is brought to view him, and goes twice or thrice round him, and when the Elephant's Keeper speaks to the monstrous Executioner, he twines his Trunk round the Person and Stake, and pulling the Stake from the Ground with great Violence, tosses the Man and the Stake into the Air, and in coming down, receives him on his Teeth, and shaking him off again, puts one of his fore Feet on the Carcase, and squeezes it flat.

In Anno 1717. the King of *Siam* made War on his Neighbour of *Cambodia*, and invaded his Country with an Army of 50000 by Land, and 20000 by Sea, and committed the Care of his Armies to his *Barkalong*, a *Chinese*, altogether unacquainted with War. The *China* Man accepted of the Charge with much Reluctancy, but the King would not be denied. The War prov'd unsuccessful, but I'll leave the Particulars till I treat of *Cambodia*, and return to *Siam*, where I had some Difficulties to meet with.

In Anno 1719. I went thither with a Cargo to dispose on, expecting to trade on the Footing of the old Treaty concluded at *London* with the King of *England*, and the King of *Siam's* Ambassador, *in Anno* 1684. but on my Arrival, I found that Mr. *Collet*, Governor of Fort St. *George*. had cancelled that Agreement by his Ambassador *Powny*, as I have already observed, and the new Conditions being too hard for me to stand to, I solicited for Liberty to depart again with my Ship

Ship and Cargo, which I could not obtain in leſs than four Months.

Collet's Attorney at the Court of *Siam*, was a *Perſian* by Birth, but had come to *Siam* with his Father when very young, and had remained about 40 Years at *Siam*. He was as complete a Raſcal as *Collet* could have found for his villanous Purpoſes, for by falſe Informations to the King, he had brought many honeſt Men into Trouble, and ſome Treaſure into the King's Coffers.

When I underſtood that he was the *Remora* that had put a Stop to my Commerce, I tried if I could remove him by large Preſents, but all to no Purpoſe, for if I traded, it muſt be on the Scheme laid down by *Collet*, by the Negotiation of *Powny*, who kept one *Colliſon* as his Reſident at *Siam*, to conſult and inform the *Perſian* of the beſt Methods to ruine the *Engliſh* Traders that had not *Collet*'s Letters of Protection.

This *Perſian*, (whoſe Name was *Oia Sennerat*) and I, were diſcourſing one Day of my Affairs in the *Induſtan* Language, which is the eſtabliſhed Language ſpoken in the *Mogul*'s large Dominions, and, among other Things, I was laying down to him the Difficulties that might attend the King of *Siam*'s Trade, carried on from *Merjee* to Fort St. *George*, becauſe if the reſt of the *Engliſh* Colonies were forbid trading with *Siam*, they had juſt Cauſe to forbid his Subjects to trade to Fort St. *George*, or any where elſe, and that other Troubles might ariſe to the King's

Affairs, by thus imposing on the King, who was ignorant of the Consequences that might follow in breaking the Agreement made in *England*, without so much as once giving Warning to the *English* Colonies of other Parts of *India*.

He answered me, that the King of Fort St. *George* could best give me an Answer, who was able to protect the King of *Siam*'s Trade thither, and that his Majesty had no other foreign Trade but *Japon*, that he valued, and the *English* had no Trade that Way to disturb his Master's Commerce, and that if I did not comply with the Agreement made by *Powny* in *Collet*'s Name, I might go away when I could.

I told him that I had a Mind to see the King, and would make him a Present of a thousand Dollars, if he could find Means to introduce me to his Presence. He answered me, that the *English* had not good Manners enough to be admitted into the Presence of so great a King, and therefore I ought not to expect to appear before him, and for fear I should have made Application to some other Court Favourite to introduce me, about two or three Days after our Confabulation, I heard that there was a Proclamation published, all over the City, that no Foreigner should dare to approach within such a Distance of the King's Palace, under very severe Penalties.

About a Week after I had a Summons to appear before a Tribunal, to answer to an In-

Indictment of ſpeaking Treaſon of the King. I knew my ſelf innocent, and appeared at the Time appointed, which was about Eight in the Morning. The Court was held in a large, ſquare, oblong Hall, open on all Sides. About Nine the Judge came with ſome Thouſands of Attendants, and, as he paſſed by me to take his Place, he viewed me very narrowly, as I did him with much Attention. He was a Man of a middle Stature, about 50 Years of Age, of a pleaſant, but grave Countenance, and had a quick ſparkling Eye. He ſpoke to my Interpreter, to bid me have a Care of my Tongue, leſt I ſhould prejudice myſelf in anſwering to intricate Queſtions. I thanked him for his Admonition, and told him, *A Word to the Wiſe was ſufficient.*

HAVING placed himſelf, he ordered my Indictment to be read, which was accordingly done, and in about half an Hour's Time it was ended. He askt me by my Interpreter, if I underſtood what was libelled againſt me. I anſwered, No. He then bade the Interpreter inform me of the Meaning of each particular Paragraph, as they were read a ſecond Time with Deliberation, and, having heard my Impeachment, which was grounded only on my ſaying, *That the King had been impoſed upon*, I thought fit to deny all, and put my Adverſary *Oia Sennerat* to prove that I had ſaid ſo; but, by the by, I found, that ſaying the King of *Siam* was capable of being impoſed on, is rank Treaſon.

THE

THE Judge chose out of the Assembly two Procurators for each of us, and there were no small Debates for three or four Hours, *Whether or not a Stranger, who was ignorant of the Laws of* Siam, *could come under the Penalty annext to the Transgression of their Laws, when they were broken through Ignorance, and not with Design*; but my Antagonist at last carried it in the Affirmative, tho' the Judge seemed to incline towards the Opinions of my Advocates.

THEN the Judge put *Oia Sennerat* to prove what I was accused of, and he produced two of his own Servants, who stood at some Distance when we were discoursing of my Affairs; but my Advocates challenged the Laws of *Siam* for their Insufficiency, for that Law admits not of a Servant's Testimony, either for or against his Master. Then he proferred to bring an undeniable Witness against me, who was the only Person with us when we discoursed, and that was *Collison*, who was presently sent for, and being fet by my Adversary, the Judge askt him by the Interpreter, if he was present at such a Time, when *Oia Sennerat* and I were in warm Discourse. He answered, He was. He then interrogated him, if he had heard me say in my Discourse, that the King had been imposed on. He affirmed he had, on which I perceived a Cloud overspread the Judge's Countenance, and many others, who had come to hear the Trial, seemed sorrowful.

AFTER a little Pause, the Judge, by the Interpreter, askt me what I had to say to *Collison*'s Evidence. I answered, that I had little Knowledge of him, but that he might be an honest Man, or otherwise, as his Interest led him. All continued mute for a little Space, and I broke the Silence by desiring the Judge to ask *Collison* in what Language I held that Discourse in with *Oia Sennerat*, which the Judge did, and was answered, that he did not well know, but that he believed it was in the *Industan* Language. I begged the Judge to ask him if he understood that Language, and he did so. *Collison*, after some Pause, answered, No. Then the Judge askt him angrily, and with an Air of Disdain, how he could come in as an Evidence of Words spoken in a Language that he did not understand, and he simply said, That he thought I had said so, at which the whole Crowd gave an Huzza, and clapt their Hands, and seemed joyful. The Judge reprimanded *Oia Sennerat* for putting him and the Court to so much Trouble, and complimented me on my safe Delivery, and so departed seemingly well satisfied.

I had two *British* Gentlemen that accompanied me all the Time of my Trial. One was Commander of a small Ship from *Bengal*, called Mr. *Alexander Dalglish*, and one Mr. *John Saunders*, who was second Supercargo under me; and when the Judge came, some Executioners followed him with their Instruments of Death, to put the Sentence in Execu-

Execution aſſoon as the Judge pronounces it. Our Debates held ſo long, that it was near Eight at Night before we got Home. Had I been caſt in my Proceſs, my Head had been a Sacrifice to my Adverſary's Reſentment, and my Ship and Cargo to the much injured King, and, to ſum up all, my Ship's Company had been the King's Slaves. On my returning Home victorious, I had the Congratulations of all my Friends, particularly the *Chineſe* Merchants, whoſe Lives and Eſtates might have been endangered by the like villanous Informations.

My Adverſaries being ſhamefully diſappointed in that Project, had one more to try their Skill in, and that was to bring me in for Piracy, for, about four Years before, Mr. *Harriſon*, then Governor of Fort St. *George*, had ſent a Ship to *Amoy* in *China*, and ſome *China* Merchants having taken Goods and Money, to the Amount of 20000 *Tayels*, or 6700 Pounds *Sterl.* when the Term of Payment came, they eloped, and the Supercargoes could have no Redreſs, which made them give Orders to the Captain of the Ship to make Repriſals, which they did on a large *Jonk* belonging to the *Barkalong* of *Siam*, which *Jonk* they carried with them to Fort St. *George*, and which Fact my Adverſaries fixed on me, tho', at that Time, I was in *Arabia* or *Perſia*, which I proferred to prove by ſome *Mahometan* Merchants that ſaw me there; but all that I could alledge would have been ineffectual, if I had not accidentally found

found ſome *Chineſe* who belonged to the *Jonk* when ſhe was ſeized, and who knew both me and Captain *Jones*, who was the Captor, and ſo it never came to a Trial.

It being high Time for me to get from *Siam* at any Rate, I applied myſelf to my Judge for his Aſſiſtance, and carried a Preſent of four Yards of ſcarlet Cloth, and ſome Pieces of *Surat* Goods, to the Value of 20 *L.* in all. He received me very courteouſly, and promiſed me his Aſſiſtance, but would accept of none of my Preſents. At laſt on my preſſing him to take it, he accepted of the ſcarlet Cloth, but would not touch any of the *Surat* Goods, tho' they were very fine in their Kind, but recommended me to two Officers more, whom I muſt addreſs to make my Requeſt be the eaſier granted, and he told me, that thoſe *Surat* Goods would ſerve to make them my Friends. I took his Advice, and in three Days had my Clearance, for paying about 200 *L.* for my Ship's Meaſurage, (an Impoſition of Mr. *Collet*'s) and ſo I fell down to *Bencock*, where, according to the *Siam* Cuſtom, I was obliged to put my Guns aſhore, before I could go up to the City. I lay there four or five Days before Orders were ſent to deliver my Guns, which, aſſoon as I had got on board, and mounted, I told the Officer that delivered them, to give my Service to *Oia Sennerat*, and tell him, that if the King's three *Jonks* arrived on this Coaſt this Seaſon, he would hear farther from me by them.

By

By that Time I was clear at *Bencock*, Captain *Dalgleiſh* arrived there alſo, in order to proceed to *Bengal*. He had fallen into the Trap laid by *Collet*, and had paid Meaſurage and Cuſtoms, beſides the uſual Preſents to the Court, according to the old Conſtitution, but he could not get ready to go ſo ſoon out of the River as I, otherwiſe I deſigned to have brought ſome Troubles on *Sennerat*, if not on *Collet* and *Powney*'s Affairs at *Siam*, but Captain *Dalgleiſh* being ſtill in their Power, tied my Hands.

Siam Bar is only a large Bank of ſoft Mud, and, at Spring-tides, not above ten or eleven Foot Water on it. It is eaſy getting into it in the South-weſt Monſoons, becauſe, in two or three Tides, with the Motion the Ship receives from the ſmall Waves and the Aſſiſtance of the Wind, ſhe ſlides thro' the Mud. My Ship drew thirteen Foot, and we had not above nine on the Bar when we went into the River, but coming out with the North-eaſt Monſoons, the Sea being ſmooth, we are obliged to warp out with Anchors and Halſers, and, if the Ship draws any conſiderable Draught of Water, we are ſometimes two Springs in warping over, but, at twelve Foot Draught, I got over in four Tides.

And now, having given ſome particular Accounts of my Obſervations on and in *Siam*, I will alſo give ſome general Remarks, and begin with the Fertility of the Country, which, on that Point, is inferior to few (if any) in the World.

There

THERE are but two Parcels of Mountains to be ſeen in the Places that I paſſed thro', and they ly between Eaſt and North-eaſt from the City of *Odia*, about ten Leagues diſtant, and they produce good Timber for building, and Agala-wood for Perfumes. They have alſo Mines of Iron, Tin, Lead, Silver and Gold, but they are all entailed on the Crown, who has the ſole Benefit of them. They breed vaſt Numbers of wild Deer, which are hunted and killed for the ſake of their Skins, which they yearly ſend to *Japon*.

THE Plains produce all Sorts of Grain neceſſary for animal and human Suſtenance. They plentifully bear as good, if not the beſt Oranges, Lemons and Limes in the World. Their Rivers ſuperabound in Fiſh of ſeveral Species, very good in their Kind. Their Villages are numerous, and well inhabited with Artificers and Peaſants; but there are but five walled Towns in all the *Siam* Dominions, and *Odia* is one of them.

THEY have Abundance of wild Animals in their Woods, ſuch as Elephants, Rhinoceroſes, Leopards and Tigers, and tame Cattle, as Bullocks, Buffaloes and Swine, in Abundance about their Farms. Temples and Prieſts are more numerous here, in Proportion to the Laity, than in any Country I ever ſaw out of the Dominions of *Portugal*. Their *Tallapoys* or Prieſts are diſtinguiſhed from the Laity by a cinnamon or orange-coloured Cloke which they wear, they again differing among themſelves by diſtinguiſhing Badges, by by which they know their Degree and Dignity. Their Heads, Beards and Eye-brows are kept close shaven. They are forbidden Marriage or meddling with Money, and if any of the Priesthood is convicted of Incontinency with Women, he is burned for it alive, and, if only suspected and brought to a Trial, he is degraded and banished.

THEY have Sermons or Lectures four Times in a Moon, the Gates of the Temples being set wide open, and the People meet in good Order. Their Sermons consist in recommending moral Duties to the People, and Charity towards one another, but particularly to the Church, by which Acts it subsists; and, after the Priests Benediction, every one goes to an Image, and kisses it, or bows to it, and marches off in good Order. They have Morning and Evening Prayers, and sing Anthems. They visit the Sick, and pray for the Dead, and accompany the Corps to the funeral Pile, and sing Obsequies. They go to Weddings, and make Sacrifices for the Prosperity of the Bridegroom and Bride, but have no Hand in joyning them together.

MARRIAGES are there made up by Parents or near Relations, without the Consent of the Parties to be married, for that Reason they are commonly married very young; but, if they are come to the Years of Discretion or Maturity, then the Spark gets some female Friend to acquaint his Mistris with his Passion for her, and if she will per-

permit a Viſit from him, the Bargain is as good as made. The civil Magiſtrate with them officiates the Prieſt's Part with us, and when once they are married, they ſeldom ſue for a Divorce, which is very hard to procure, except in Caſe of Inſufficiency in the Man, or Barrenneſs in the Woman, for Adultery, in either Party, is not reckoned infamous; and Fornication is either allowed or tolerated.

THE Children are carefully educated in Schools by Prieſts ſet apart for that Service, and it is rare to find a *Siamer* but who can write. After Schooling, they are put to ſuch Callings as ſuit beſt with their Genius and Quality: And there is generally a reciprocal Harmony between Parents and Children. The Children are obedient, and the Parent indulgent. In Childhood and Youth the Parent furniſhes the Child with what is neceſſary, and in old Age the Child ſupplies all the Wants of his Parent, as far as he is able. In Marriages they make no Account of Conſanguinity, farther than between Father and Daughter, Mother and Son, and Siſter and Brother; all other Degrees are lawful.

AND now it is Time to ſteer my Courſe to the Southward again as far as *Cambodia*. Coaſting along Shore, the firſt Place we meet with is *Bankaſoy*, a Place not frequented by Strangers, tho' it produces much Agala and Sapan-woods, and Elephants Teeth; but all are ſent to the King, who, for all his gaudy Titles, yet ſtoops to play the Merchant. I ſup-

ſuppoſe he makes Uſe of Trading in Honour of his Kinſman *Mercury*, who ſuperintends Merchandizing, but was never reckoned a fair Dealer, and in that Point the King is nearly related to him: But *Bankaſoy* is famous, chiefly for making *Ballichang*, a Sauce made of dried Shrimps, Cod-pepper, Salt and a Sea Weed or Graſs, all well mixed, and beaten up to the Conſiſtency of thick Muſtard. Its Taſte and Smell are both ungrateful to the Noſe and Palate; but many Hundred Tuns are expended in *Siam* and the adjacent Countries.

Bankaſoy River lies but 4 or 5 Leagues to the Eaſtward of *Siam* Bar, and there are two Iſlands, called the *Dutch* Iſlands, where great Ships are obliged to ſtay in the South-weſt Monſoons, when they cannot get Water over the Bar that bears off it South-caſt and by South, about nine Leagues diſtant.

I obſerved before, that the Company ſent the *Herbert* and another Ship from *England in Anno* 1685. and in 1686. as the *Herbert* lay at thoſe Iſlands, one Captain *Udal*, who commanded her, died, and the ſucceeding Captain carried his Corps aſhore, and buried it in a pretty deep Grave. Two Days after, ſome of the Ship's People going aſhore, had the Curioſity to go and ſee the Grave. When they came near, to their great Wonder, they ſaw the Corps ſtript of its winding Sheet, and ſet upright againſt a Tree. It was afterwards put again into the Coffin, and buried in the ſame Grave, with a Quantity of heavy Stones

Stones on it, and next Day they came to the Grave, and found it opened a ſecond Time, with the Corps ſtanding upright againſt another Tree, ſo they made faſt ſome Stones to it, and carried it a pretty Way into the Sea, and buried it in the Water, where it remained undiſturbed. This ſtrange Reſurrection left Room for various Conjectures, but the moſt probable ſeemed to be, that ſome Sorcerers took it up, and put it in that Poſture, whilſt they, by their Sorceries or Incantations, interrogate it about future Events, and received Anſwers thro' human Organs. The Matter of Fact I have heard often affirmed by ſeverals who were there at the Time and ſaw it, which made me enquire, if any People in *Siam* uſed to enquire about future Events after that Manner, and I was told that they did.

THE Coaſts of *Liampe* and *Chiampo* are the Territories of *Siam*, but for 50 Leagues and more along the Sea-ſhore, there are no Sea-ports, the Country being almoſt a Deſert. It produces good Store of Sapan and Agala-woods, with Gumlack and Sticklack, and many Drugs that I know but little about.

CHAP. XLVIII.

Gives an Account of Cambodia *its Trade, also of a late War brought into their Country by the* Siamer, *and the ill Success they had.*

THE first Sea-port to be met with is *Cupangsoap*, a Town in the Dominions of *Cambodia*. It affords Elephants Teeth, Sticklack and the Gum *Cambouge* or *Cambodia*; but there is no free Commerce allowed there, without a Licence from the Court of *Cambodia*.

THE next Place is *Ponteamass*, a Place of pretty good Trade for many Years, having the Conveniency of a pretty deep but narrow River, which, in the rainy Seasons of the South-west Monsoons, has Communication with *Bansack* or *Cambodia* River, which Conveniency made it draw foreign Commerce from the City of *Cambodia* hither; for the City lying near 100 Leagues up the River, and most Part of the Way a continual Stream running downward, made the Navigation to the City so long and troublesom, that few cared to trade to it, for which Reasons foreign Commerce chose to come to *Ponteamass*, and it flourished pretty well till the Year 1717. that the *Siam* Fleet destroyed it.

WHEN the *Siam* Army and Fleet threatned *Cambodia*, the King knew his Inability to withstand the *Siamers*, so the Inhabitants that lived on his Borders had Orders to remove towards the City of *Cambodia*, and what they could

could not bring with them, to destroy it, so that for fifty Leagues the Country was a mere Desert. He then addrest the King of *Couchin-china* for Assistance and Protection, which he obtained, on Condition, that *Cambodia* should become tributary to *Couchin-china*, which was agreed to, and he had an Army of 15000 to assist him by Land, and 3000 in nimble Gallies well mann'd and equipt, by Sea.

THE *Siam* Army by Land was above double the Number of the *Cambodians* and *Couchin-chinese* in Conjunction, and their Fleet above four Times their Number. The Land Army finding all the Country desolate, as they marched into the Borders of *Cambodia*, soon began to be in Distress for Want of Provisions, which obliged them to kill their Carriage Beasts, and their Elephants and Horses which they could get no Sustenance for, and the Soldiers being obliged to eat their Flesh, it being a Diet they had never been used to, an epidemick Flux and Fever seized the whole Army, so that in two Months one Half was not left, and those were obliged to retreat towards their own Country again, with the *Cambodian* Army always at their Heels.

NOR had their Navy much better Success, for they coming to *Ponteamass*, sent in their small Gallies to plunder and burn the Town, which they did effectually, and, of Elephants Teeth only, they burnt above 200 Tuns. The Ships and *Jonks* of Burden lying in the

Road, above four Miles from the Town, the *Couchin-chinese* taking hold of that Opportunity, attackt the large Vessels, and burned some, and forced others ashore, whilst their Gallies were in a narrow River, and could not come to their Assistance till High-water that they could get out. The *Couchin-chinese* having done what they came for, retired, not caring to engage such a superior Number, and the *Siamers* fearing Famine in their Fleet, steered their Course for *Siam* with Disgrace. *In Anno* 1720. I saw several of the Wracks, and the Ruins of the Town of *Ponteamass*.

THE City of *Cambodia* stands on the Side of the great River, about 50 or 60 Leagues from *Ponteamass* by Land, or by Water in the South-west Monsoons. The Country produces Gold of twenty one *Caracts* fine, raw Silk at 120 Dollars *per Pecul*, Elephants Teeth at 50 to 55 Dollars for the largest. The small are of different Prices. They have also much Sapan-wood, Sandal-wood, Agala-wood, Sticklack, and many Sorts of physical Drugs, and Lack for Japaning. They are very desirous of having a Trade with the *English*; but they will not suffer the *Dutch* to settle Factories in their Country.

PROVISIONS of Flesh and Fish are plentiful and cheap, and are the only Things that may be bought without a Permit from the King. I have bought a Bullock, that weighed between 4 and 500 Weight, for a *Spanish* Dollar; and Rice is bought at Eight Pence

per

per Pecul, which is about 140 *lb.* but Poultry are scarce, because the Country being for the most Part woody, when the Chickens grow big, they go to the Woods, and shift for themselves. Tigers and wild Elephants are numerous in the Woods, and there are also wild Cattle and Buffaloes, and Plenty of Deer, all which Animals every Body is free to catch or kill.

THERE are about two hundred *Topasses*, or *Indian Portugueze* settled and married in *Cambodia*, and some of them have pretty good Posts in the Government, and live great after the Fashion of that Country; but they have no Priests, nor will any venture to go among them, for *in Anno* 1710. a poor Capuchin went there to officiate, and finding one of the toppingest of his Congregation to have two Wives, ordered him, by virtue of his sacerdotal Power, to put one of them away, but his Parishoner would not obey in that Point, which made the Priest use the Weapon of Excommunication against him, which the other took in such Dudgeon, that he knockt his spiritual Guide's Brains out for his unseasonable Severity. Since that Time they wrote to *Siam* and *Macao* in *China* for some more ghostly Fathers, but not one will go, tho' perhaps they might have the Honour of dying Martyrs.

THEY all of them have small Pensions from the King, but too narrow to maintain them, so they go to the Woods with Fire-arms, and kill wild Elephants for their Teeth, which they ſell to Foreigners; and their Way of killing them is very ſingular, for they form a Piece of Iron like a Slug, and the foremoſt End is made ſharp. In the Woods grow certain Trees with a thick Bark of a violent poiſonous Quality. They drive the ſharp End of the Slug into the Bark, and let it ſtay a ſhort Time in it, then put the Slug into their Gun charged with Powder, and coming near the Beaſt, fire the Slug into its Body. The Elephant being thus wounded, flees from the Man, but the Man keeps Sight of it for a ſmall Space of Time, and then it drops down dead.

AND with the ſame poiſoned Slugs they kill Cattle and Buffaloes, for their Tongues. This ſubtil Poiſon has alſo another ſtrange Quality, that if Men become hungry or thirſty, (as they often do in the Woods) they ſqueeze a few Drops of it on a Leaf of a Tree, and they licking the Leaf, it gives immediate Refreſhment; but if the Skin be broken, and the Juice touch the Part, it proves mortal without Remedy.

WHEN I arrived at *Ponteamaſs*, an Officer came on board, who could ſpeak a little *Portugueze*. He brought a Preſent of Refreſhments along with him, and adviſed me to ſend to the King, to give him an Account of my Arrival, and acquaint him that I deſigned to trade with his Subjects by his Permiſſion, which I did, and in twelve Days, received an Anſwer that I might, but deſired me to ſend ſome Perſon up with Muſters of my Goods,

Goods, that he and his Merchants might see them, and sent two *Portugueze* for Interpreters, one to stay with me on board of my Ship, while I staid, and the other to accompany the Person I designed to send to him with the Musters. On their Arrival I dispatcht my second Supercargo, with an Equippage of 25 Men, well armed with Fuzees and Bayonets, with two small Bales of Musters, and Presents for the King, with Instructions to let me hear from him once a Week by an Express, if no other Opportunity offered.

After he arrived at the City, he had a large House allowed him for the Accommodation of him and his Retinue, and had store of Provisions sent him, and many Folks of Distinction visited him, but ten Days past before he could see his Majesty, who at last received him in great State, sitting on a Throne like a Pulpit, with his Face vailed below his Eyes, and after many gracious Speeches, some whereof were pertinent to my Purpose, but many not, he gave me Liberty and Encouragement to trade.

I had staid above three Weeks in Expectation to hear from my second Supercargo, but could get no Account from him. I beginning to be uneasie, got an Express to carry Letters to him, and ordered him to send it back with as much Speed as was possible, but had the Mortification to find he had been stopt at the City. I was extremely uneasie for want of Advice what was become of my People, and the approaching of the South-west

west Monsoons, which would have made that Coast a Lee-shore, and would have oblig'd me to take Sanctuary in one of their Harbours for five or six Months, and was not certain whether I was in a Friend's or an Enemy's Country. In this Labyrinth I continued a Week, and at last resolved to depart by a certain Day, and leave my People to come after me to *Malacca*, if they were alive and at Liberty. The Goods I had sent up with them, would have been sufficient to have hired a Vessel to carry them thither. I told my Resolution to my Interpreter, and that I should be obliged to carry him and some more of the King's Subjects along with me as Hostages for the civil Treatment of my People at *Cambodia*. He seemed surprised at my Resolution, and got a Person to go to the City in all Haste to give an Account of my Impatience and Design, who returned in fourteen Days, about two Days before my Term was expired, that I had set for my Departure. There accompanied him three *Portugueze*, who brought me Letters from my second Supercargo, that he had taken Leave of the King, and was coming to me with all Haste, and in three Days after the *Portugueze* came, he arrived with all his Retinue, with a Letter of Compliment to me in the *Portugueze* Language, and one directed to the Governor of *Bombay*, to invite the *English* to settle in his Country, and to build Factories or Forts in any Part of his Dominions to protect Trade.

THE

THE Reason why he kept us so long in Suspence. was, that he would enter into no Correspondence with us without the Knowledge and Consent of his Guardian the King of *Couchin-china*, who at last consented to allow us Commerce both in *Cambodia*, and in his own proper Dominions, but that the *Siamers* had destroyed the Country where they had been, and they had nothing ready for Barter with my Cargo then, but in a Year or two they would be provided.

WHEN the King bestows his Favour on any Person whom he has a Mind to honour, which he never does without a considerable Present, he presents the Person with two Swords to be carried always before him when he goes abroad in publick, one is the Sword of State, and the other of Justice. All People that meet him when those Swords are carried before him, must give him Place, and salute him by a set Form of Words, but if he meets with another Court Minion, then they compare the Dates of their Patents, and Segniority takes Place, and must be first saluted. Wherever those *Mandareens* go in the Country, they hold Courts of Justice, both civil and criminal, and they have the Power of laying on Fines, but they are paid into the King's Treasury; but in capital Crimes, his Sentence is Law, and speedy Execution follows Sentence.

THE *Cambodians* are of a light brown Complexion, and very well shap'd, their Hair long, and Beards thin. Their Women are very handsom,

ſom, but not very modeſt. The Men wear a Veſtment like our Night-gowns, but nothing on their Heads or Feet. The Women wear a Petticoat reaching below the Ancle, and on their Bodies a Frock made cloſe and meet for their Bodies and Arms, and both Sexes dreſs their Hair.

I ſaw none of their Prieſts, but underſtood from my Interpreter, that they worſhip the ſame Gods that are adored in *Siam*. They worſhip the great God under the Name of *Tipedah*, and *Praw Prumb*, and *Praw Pout*, are his Sons. The Church ſubſiſts by Free-will-offerings, and their Prieſts are not much reſpected, being generally choſen from among the lower Sort of the Laity.

THE Kingdom of *Laos* borders on *Siam*, *Cambodia*, *Couchin-china*, and *Tonquin*. It produces Gold, raw Silk, and Elephants Teeth are ſo plentiful, that they ſtake their Fields and Gardens about with them, to keep out wild Hogs and Cattle from deſtroying their Fruit and Corn. They are all *Pagans* in Religion.

THE Natives of *Laos* are whiter in Complexion than their circumjacent Neighbours. I ſaw ſome of them at *Siam*, of both Sexes. Their Women were little inferior to *Portugueze* or *Spaniſh* Ladies.

THERE are ſeveral Iſlands that ly off the Coaſt of *Cambodia*, but none are inhabited, becauſe the *Saleeters*, or Pirates that infeſt that Coaſt, rob them of what they get by Pains and Induſtry, tho' there is one about three Leagues Weſt of *Ponteamaſs*, called

Qua-

Quadrol, that has good Qualifications for a Settlement. It is about three Leagues long, and one broad. Wood and fresh Water are plentiful, the Ground of a moderate Height, the Soil black and fat, except along the East Side which faces *Ponteamass*, and that has several fine sandy Bays, and they are good safe Harbours in the rainy and windy Seasons.

About 30 Leagues East-south-east from *Ponteamass*, is the West Entrance of *Cambodia* River, generally called *Bocca de Carangera*. The shallowest Place in the Chanel in going in, is four Fathoms, and within it deepens to Twenty in some Places. The North Entrance is broader, but much shallower, and lies about ten Leagues distant from the West Chanel, but is little frequented. Between *Ponteamass* and the River, are several small uninhabited Islands. *Pullo-panjang* is the largest, and consists of a Cluster of eight Islands, which form a pretty good Harbour. *Pullo-ubi* is the Eastmost, and affords good Masts for Shipping.

Pullo-condore is the largest and highest, composed of four or five Islands. It lies about 15 Leagues South of the West Chanel of *Cambodia* River. *Pullo-condore* had once the Honour of an *English* Colony settled on it, by Mr. *Allan Ketchpole, in Anno* 1702 when the Factory of *Chusan*, on the Coast of *China*, was broke up, he being then Director for Affairs of the *English East-india* Company in those Parts.

He

HE made a bad Choice of a Place for a Colony, that Iſland producing nothing but Wood, Water, and Fiſh for catching. He got ſome *Maccaſſers* to ſerve for Soldiers, and help to build a Fortification, and made a firm Contract with them to diſcharge them at the End of three Years if they were minded to quit his Service, but did not perform what was contracted, which was the Cauſe of his own Ruin, and the Loſs of the Colony, for thoſe Eaſtern Deſperadoes are very faithful where Contracts and Covenants are duly obſerved when made with them, but in Defailiance, they are revengeful and cruel. Mr. *Ketchpole* having detained the *Maccaſſers* beyond their Time of Agreement, ſtill entruſted them with the Guard of his own Perſon and the Gariſon, and they taking the Opportunity of the Night, when all the *Engliſh* were in their Beds, who lodged in the Fort, they inhumanely murdered them all. There was ſome Noiſe made by thoſe who were awake, which a few who lodged without the Fort, hearing, took the Alarm, and ran to the Sea Side, where kind Providence directed them to a Boat ready fitted with Oars and Sails, which they imbarked in, and put off from the Shore, and were not a Stone's-throw off, till the bloody Villains on the Shore were in Queſt of them. So thoſe in the Boat, with much Fatigue, Hunger, and Thirſt in ſailing, and rowing above 100 Leagues, got to ſome Place of the King of *Johore*'s Dominions, where they were treated with Humanity.

The

The reverend and ingenious Doctor *Pound*, was one of those that escaped, and Mr. *Solomon Lloyd* (an old Acquaintance of mine) was another.

THERE were two Harbours, or anchoring Places, at *Pullo-condore*, but neither of them good. One at the North-east End, they were forced to use in the South-west Monsoons, the other on the West-side for the North-east Winds, the Bottom of which is rocky, and therefore dangerous for losing Anchors and Cables, yet that was the Place chosen to build their Fort on, but since a Factory was thought necessary to be settled on that Coast, I wonder why they chose these Islands, rather than *Quadrole* which I mentioned before.

THE City of *Cambodia* is reckoned to ly 100 Leagues up from the Bar, and the River fill'd with low Islands and Sand Banks. The Country of *Laos* is about 40 Leagues farther up, but what Navigation is used above the City of *Cambodia*, is done by small rowing Vessels, and the River being one of the longest in the World, employs great Numbers of those rowing Boats.

CHAP.

CHAP. XLIX.

Treats of Couchin-china, *and* Tonquin, *their Religion, Laws, and Cuſtoms.*

COUCHIN-CHINA is only divided from *Cambodia*, by the River, which in ſome Places is three Leagues broad. It is a Country far larger than *Cambodia*, and much richer, and the Inhabitants more couragious and hardier for enduring Fatigues in Labour or War, than the *Cambodians*, but are not ſo converſable and civil to Strangers. The *Couchin-chineſe* draw one Half of the Cuſtoms and Taxes raiſed in *Cambodia* by Commerce and Merchandizing, but they give little Encouragement for Strangers to trade with them. Their Country abounding in Gold, raw Silk, and Drugs, they bring them to *Cambodia*, to diſpoſe of there, except what they ſend yearly to *Canton* in *China*; and I have ſeen ſome of their *Jonks* trading at *Johore* and *Batavia*.

THEIR Religion is *Pagan* after the *China* Way, worſhipping the ſame Gods, after the ſame Manner as the *Chineſe* do. Their Laws are ſevere and bloody for Crimes of Treaſon, for not only the guilty Perſon ſuffers a painful Death, but the Relations within the Bounds of Conſanguinity ſuffer Death alſo. Their Cities and Towns are divided into Wardſhips, and at the Ends of each Street are railed Gates, placed to confine each Ward within its own Limits. Theſe Gates are ſhut and

lockt

lockt every Night, so that they have no Communication by Night, but if a Fire breaks out in one of the Wards, its whole Inhabitants are cut off except the Women and Children.

There are but few *Christians* tolerated in *Couchin-china*, yet there was (and perhaps is) a *French* Priest in great Esteem among them, but it is capital for any other Priest to be found in their Country. This *French* Man kept a Correspondence by writing, with Mr. *Cissie* Bishop of *Siam*, and he having a Relation of the Danger *Christian* Priests were in there, made the old Zealot half-mad to get thither, to receive the Honour of Martyrdom, and had he been honest in his Promises to me (which was only not to protect any of my fugitive Seamen at *Siam*) I would have favoured him with a Passage to *Cambodia*, from whence he might have easily gone to get that glorious Crown.

Couchin-china has a large Sea-coast of about 700 Miles in Extent, from the River of *Cambodia*, to that of *Quambin*, and it has the Conveniency of many good Harbours on it, tho' they are not frequented by Strangers; and along the East Coast it is very deep, for in several Places I sounded the Depth, and found between 60 and 80 Fathoms within Half a League of the Shore.

There are several Islands on this Coast. Those nearest the Shore are not dangerous. *Pullo-secca de terra*, lies most Southerly, and nearest the Shore. It is uninhabited, and looks

 only

only like a Parcel of ſcorcht Rocks, without either Tree, Buſh, or Graſs to be ſeen on it. I paſt within a Mile of it, and it lies about a Mile from the Shore. *Pullo-ſecca de mare*, and all the Chain of Iſlands that ſtretch from the dangerous Shallows of *Paracel*, are rather to be accounted Rocks than Iſlands. *Pullo-cambir* lies about 15 Leagues off the Shore, near the *Paracels*. It is uninhabited tho' pretty large. *Pullo-canton* lies near the Shore, and ſo do the Iſlands of *Champello*, but there are no Dangers ly off from them. There are ſtrong Currents that run to the Southward in the North-eaſt Monſoons, which makes Pilots take Care to keep near the *Couchin-china* Coaſt, for fear of being driven among the *Paracels*, which are a dangerous Chain of Rocks, about 130 Leagues long, and about 15 broad, and have only ſome Iſlands at each End. There are ſeveral Inter-currents among thoſe Rocks, but no known Marks to keep clear of Dangers by, yet I knew an *Engliſh* Ship from *Surat*, that drove accidentally through them, and neither knew nor ſaw their Danger till it was over, when they unexpectedly ſaw the Coaſt of *Couchin-china*.

In Anno 1690. a *Portugueze* Ship was loſt on one of the Northermoſt Iſlands of the *Paracels*, and all were loſt but three or four Perſons who ſwimm'd aſhore. There were many Pieces of the Wrack followed them, and ſome Caniſters of Flour were accidentally thrown aſhore, whereby they were ſupported. They

They built an Hut of what Timbers and Boards they could use for that Purpose, and they found some fresh Water in the Caverns of the Rocks, and in one Place they built a Cistern to save the Rain Water for the dry Season. They took Sea Weeds and mixt with Mud that they found about the Coast of the Island, and placing that Mixture in a convenient Part to retain the Rain Water, they subsisted by that Means a dry Season. Their Food was Sea Fowls, and Tortoises which frequented that Island in great Numbers. In three Years they all died but one, and *in Anno* 1701. a Ship bound to *Maccao*, coming near the Island against their Will, seeing the Figure of a Man waving his Hands over his Head, they had Compassion and sent their Boat to the Island, and were astonished to find the Person to be one of their own Country Men, and much more when he told them his Misfortunes, and how long he had been alone on that Island. They clothed him and fed him, and carried him to *Maccao*, where I saw him *in Anno* 1703. and had the Account from his own Mouth.

But it is Time to return back to *Couchin-china*, which about three or four Centuries ago, was but a Province of *Tonquin*, at least they were both under the Dominion of one King, who dying without Issue, divided the Government of his Dominions between a Brother and a Sister of his, whom he very much esteem'd for their good Qualities. He ordered his Brother to reside in *Couchin-china*, *na*, and take Care of Affairs there, while the Sister took Care of the Government of *Tonquin*, but to have a Meeting once a Year to consider and consult of Matters for the Good of the State.

THE Lady being young, thought fit to marry, and the Harmony of State soon ended by the Marriage. The Husband grew ambitious, and wanted the Government wholly in his own Hands, but carried fair with his Brother in Law, and one Time talking with the Queen of the Necessity of uniting both Kingdoms into one, as formerly, and that of Right both belonged to her, as being possest of the most ancient and noble Kingdom, and that in order to get both Kingdoms into her Hands, he would find a Way to cut off her Brother, without Suspicion of their being accessory to it. The Queen seeming to approve of the Design, privately let her Brother know his Danger; being then at the Court of *Tonquin*, she advised him to pretend to go a hunting for a few Days, but to make what Haste he could unto his own Government, where he might be secure from Conspiracies on his Life, which Advice he followed, and got safe into *Couchin-china*, and calling a Council of his Nobles, related the whole Affair to them.

THE *Couchin-chinese* took the designed Injury to their Prince, so ill, that from that Time they renounced all Friendship and Commerce with the *Tonquiners*, and the River *Quambin* being made the Bounds of *Tonquin* Do-

Dominions to the Southward, and of *Couchinchina* to the Northward, they both raised Armies of 40 or 50000 Men each, and they continue still facing one another, the River lying between them, and nothing of Action has happened all this while. If any *Couchinchinese* happens to flee from the Justice of his own Country, to the *Tonquiners*, they receive him kindly, and treat him civilly, but if a *Tonquiner* fall under the same Circumstances, and go for Sanctuary to the *Couchinchinese*, he is condemned to Slavery, and so must continue till he gets a Pardon from his own Court, and pay his Ransom.

Tonquin is the next Kingdom I must steer to of Course, where the *English* and *Dutch* both had their Factories, but the *English* Company's Affairs being a little out of Order, they withdrew theirs in *January* 1698. and the *Dutch* finding but little Advantage by their Trade in *Tonquin*, withdrew theirs about six Years after. However, the *English* had a private Trade pretty good till the Year 1719. that an *English* Ship from *Bengal* ruin'd it by an Act of Violence.

THE Ship being laden and ready to sail, fell down the River from *Catcheo* the capital City of *Tonquin*, and in Defiance to the known Laws of the Country, the Supercargo got a *Tonquin* Girl on board, in order to carry her with him, but her Friends missing her, informed the civil Magistrate, who sent to demand her, but the Supercargo would not resign his Mistris, whereupon Acts of Hostility ensued, and ſome were killed on both Sides, and Captain *Wallace* who commanded the Ship, had the Fortune to be one of the ſlain, however, the *Engliſh* bravely carried off their Prize, but I never heard any more of the *Tonquin* Trade ſince.

Tonquin is bounded with *Couchin-china* on the South, *Laos* on the Weſt, *Quanſi* a Province of *China* on the North, and the Ocean on the Eaſt. The Country is prodigiouſly fruitful in all Things neceſſary for the Conveniency and Support of Life.

It produces Gold and Copper, but neither of them fine. They have Abundance of raw Silk, and manufacture Part of it in wrought Silks, but none fine. Their *Baaz* is the beſt, which they generally dye black. It wears very long, becauſe it is ſoft and well ſpun, and the oftner it is waſhed, the Colour looks brighter, if blacker may be ſo called. They make Bowls, Cups, and Tables, of *Rottans*, and cover them very neatly with Lack of divers Colours, and gild them. They have alſo ſome *Porcelline*, but very coarſe and ill painted. And thoſe are the Commodities for Exportation from *Tonquin*.

There is a great Chain of impaſſable Mountains that run from the Sea above 150 Leagues, along the Confines of *Quanſi* and *Quichew*, Provinces of *China*, which ſecure *Tonquin* from any Invaſions that may come that Way from *China*, and thoſe Mountains are covered with thick Woods well ſtockt with wild Elephants, Tigers, and Deer, but the

the Use or Ostentation of training up tame Elephants, is not much minded in *Tonquin*, nor in *China*.

The *Christian* Religion is strictly forbiden to be preacht in *Tonquin*, yet there are some *Christians* of the *Romish* Church there. Their Own Religion is *Pagan*, according to the Doctrine of *China*. And they have a Tradition, that many Ages ago, *Tonquin* and *Couchinchina* were both Provinces of *China*.

The *Tonquiners* used to be very desirous of having a Brood of *Europeans* in their Country, for which Reason the greatest Nobles thought it no Shame or Disgrace to marry their Daughters to *English* and *Dutch* Seamen, for the Time they were to stay in *Tonquin*, and often presented their Sons in Law pretty handsomly at their Departure, especially if they left their Wives with Child, but Adultery was dangerous to the Husband, for they are well versed in the Art of poisoning.

The Men and Women are both well shap'd, and tolerably beautiful, but of a low Stature. The Maids keep their Teeth very white, till they have lost the blue of their Plumb, and then they dye them as black as Jet, with the Juice of a certain Herb which they hold in their Mouths for three Days successively, and the black Tincture continues ever after; but while that Juice is in their Mouths, they dare not swallow their Spittle, it being of a poisonous Quality.

CHAP. L.

Gives some Accounts of the Religion, Laws, Customs, Commerce, Riches, Cities, Temples, Gods, and Goddesses, Priests, Military Forces, Produce, and Manufactories, &c. *of* China.

THE Island of *Aynam* lies in the Bay of *Tonquin*, and not above 12 Leagues distant from its Northern Confines. The Island is large, being about 180 Miles in Length, and 120 in Breadth. It was formerly under *Tonquin*, but at present a Part of the Dominions of *China*. Its greatest Product is Salt, and is not frequented on account of Trade. There is no Passage for Vessels of Burden, between it and the Continent, being so full of dangerous Banks and rapid Currents. The mid Lands seem very mountainous. The East and South Sides are low, but clear of Danger. About two Leagues from its Shores, is from 20 to 25 Fathoms Water.

THE next Course I steer, is into *Quansi*, the Southermost Province of *China*, and as yet has not been brought to acknowledge the *Tartar* Domination. It admits of no Commerce either with Foreigners or *Chinese*, that are under the *Tartar* Government, but on all Occasions commit Acts of Hostility on them, and are so bold and couragious, that one of their little Gallies will attack four of the Emperor's, and make them flee before them, for they give Quarter to none that bear Arms under the *Tartar* Prince, as they call

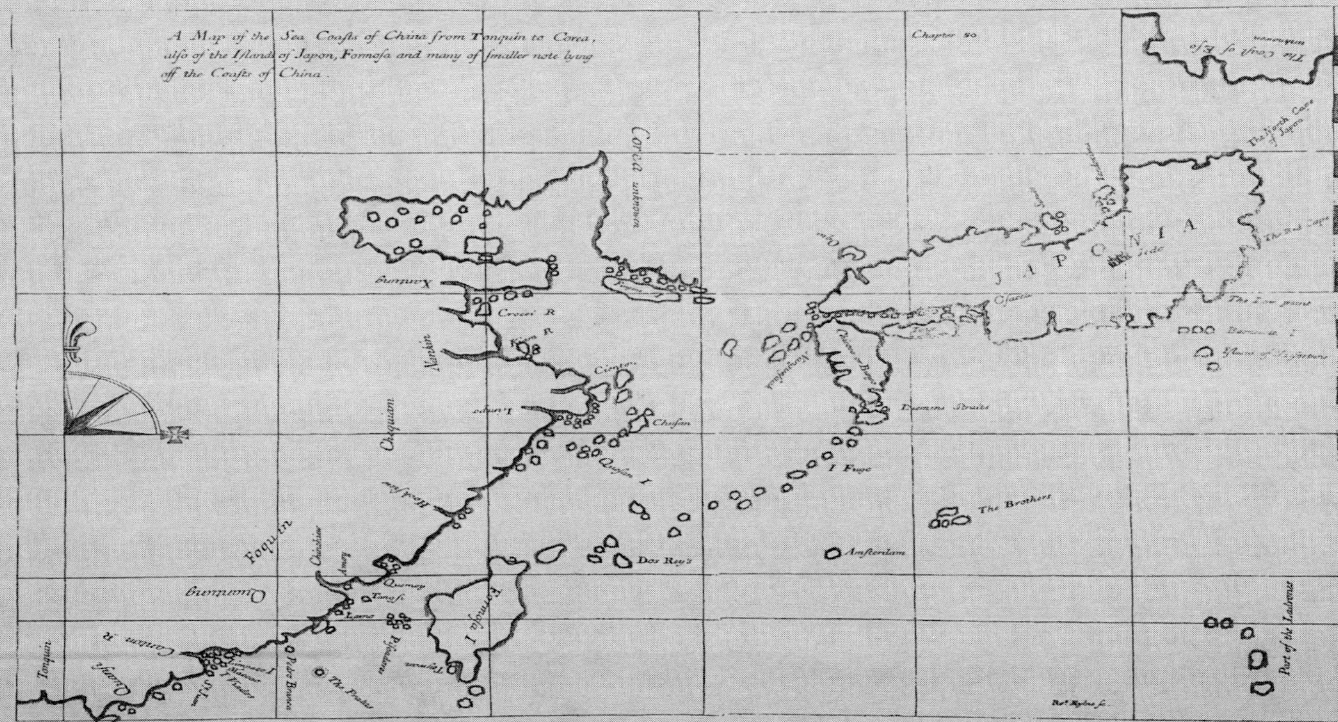
A Map of the Sea Coasts of China from Tonquin to Corea, also of the Islands of Japon, Formosa and many of smaller note lying off the Coasts of China.
Chapter 50
The Coast of Eso unknown
The North Cape of Japon
JAPONIA
Iedo
The Red Cape
The Fox point
Osacca
Corea unknown
Xantung
Crocei R
Kiam R
Nankin
Chequiam
Liampo
Cinton
Chusan
Quesan I
Dos Rey's
Amsterdam
The Brothers
I Fuge
Damons Straits
Nangasaque
Formosa I
Pescadores
Quemoy
Amoy
Chincheo
Foquin
Quantung
Pedro Branca
The Pratas
St Juan
Canton R
Tonquin
Part of the Ladrones
45
40
35
30
25
20

call the Emperor. The Country is fruitful and populous, and produces much raw Silk and Drugs, ſuch as *China* Root, *Gallingal*, &c. It has 80 Leagues of a Sea-coaſt, and is bounded by the *Limpacao* Iſlands, and *Canton* River.

Canton or *Quantung* (as the *Chineſe* expreſs it) is the next maritim Province; and *Maccaw*, a City built by the *Portugueze*, was the firſt Place of Commerce. This City ſtands on a ſmall Iſland, and is almoſt ſurrounded by the Sea. Towards the Land it is defended by three Caſtles built on the Tops of low Hills. By its Situation and Strength by Nature and Art, it was once thought impregnable. Indeed their beautiful Churches and other Buildings give us a reflecting Idea of its ancient Grandeur, for in the Forepart of the ſeventeenth Century, according to the *Chriſtian Æra*, it was the greateſt Port for Trade in *India* or *China*.

The largeſt Braſs Cannon that ever I ſaw are mounted in proper Batteries about the City. I meaſured one (amongſt many) out of Curioſity, and found it 23 Foot from the Breech to the Muzzle Ring, nine Inches and a Quarter diameter in the Bore, and it was 12250 *Rotullaes* or *lb*. Weight of ſolid Metal.

The City contains five Churches, but the *Jeſuits* is the beſt, and is dedicated to St. *Paul*. It has two Convents for married Women to retire to, when their Husbands are abſent, and orphan Maidens are educated in them till they can catch an Husband. They have alſo a Nunnery for devout Ladies, young or old,

old, that are out of Conceit with the Troubles and Cares of the World. And they have a *Sancta Casa* or the holy House of the Inquisition, that frightens every *Catholick* into the Belief of every Thing that holy Mother Church tells them is Truth, whether it be really so or no.

THE Forts are governed by a Captain-general, and the City by a Burgher, called the *Procuradore*, but, in Reality, both are governed by a *Chinese Mandereen*, who resides about a League out of the City, at a Place called *Casa Branca*. The *Portugueze* Shipping that come there, are admitted into their Harbour, and are under the Protection of the Town; but the *Chinese* keep the Custom-house, and receive Customs for all Goods imported.

THAT rich flourishing City has ruined itself by a long War they made with *Timore*, as I have observed before. They exhausted their Men and Money on that unsuccessful Project of Domination, so that out of a Thousand creditable House-keepers that inhabited the City before that War, there are hardly fifty left; and out of forty Sail of trading Vessels, they have not above five left, so that in the whole City and Forts, there are computed to be about two hundred Laity, and six hundred Priests, and about fifteen hundred Women, and many of them are very prolifick, for they bring forth Children without Husbands to father them.

In

In Anno 1703. I was bound from *Surat* to *Amoy*, and off the *Maccoa* Islands, in the Month of *August*, I met with a severe Hurricane. We had visible Signs of an approaching Storm before it came, the Air was in great Agitation by much Lightning continually flashing, but no Thunder nor Rain. We prepared for its coming from Noon to Sunset, making every Thing in the Ship fast, our Yards lowered as low as conveniently they could be, and our Sails made fast with Coils of small Ropes, besides their usual furling Lines. At Nine in the Night it laid our Ship's Gunnel under Water, and I wisht our Main-mast had been away, which about Ten was effected, and it carried our Mizzen-mast along with it. On its going over board our Ship came to Rights a little, and her lee Gunnel was clear of the Water, but much Water getting down at the Hatches, we had five Foot Water in the Ship, and no Possibility of getting it out by pumping, for our Main-mast breaking in the Parteners of the Upper-deck, disabled both our Pumps. About Midnight we had cleared the Ship of the Main and Mizzen-masts, by cutting the Rigging that kept them fast to the Ship. By this Time the Wind had shifted from North-east to South-east, and had rather increased than asswaged, and those two Winds had put the Sea in two violent Motions; however, we got our Ship before the Wind, but broaching too brought her Head almost to the Sea, which met her so violently, that it broke

broke quite over the Ship, carrying away our Fore-maſt and Boltſprit, two Anchors from the lee Bough, three great Guns of twenty two Hundred each, with our Pinnace and Yole. We ſoon cleared ourſelves of the Anchors, by cutting the Cables, and, before Day, we were quit of our Fore-maſt and Boltſprit. About Eight in the Morning the Storm abated, and at Ten I called over the Muſter-roll, and found none wanting, but between ſeventy and eighty bruiſed and wounded, who were carefully dreſt by our Surgeons, and all recovered. The Sea continued turbulent, but we having two ſpare Top-maſts, rigg'd them up, and having ſav'd our Mizzen-yard and Enſign-ſtaff, fitted them for Yards, to which we bent Sails, and ſtood towards the Land, and, before it was dark, anchored near ſome Iſlands called *Les Ilhos de Viados* by the *Portugueze*. Next Morning we had much Trouble to get our Long-boat out of the Ship. It was about 10 Tuns of Burden, and ſtrongly built; but, after 4 Hours Labour we put it into the Sea, and ſent it aſhore to try if we could get a Pilot, but found no Body on that Iſland; however, they met with two Pieces of Maſts of ſmall Veſſels that had been caſt on the Iſlands, and thoſe they brought with them, which did us very great Service in bringing us to the *Maccao* Iſlands, which were about 15 Leagues from us.

WE kept the Boat ſounding the Depths before the Ship, till we got about 8 Leagues on on our Way, and anchored in good oazy Ground, under an Island that kept the rolling Seas from disturbing us, and in the Morning, by Break of Day, we dispatched the Boat in Quest of *Maccao*, and to bring us Pilots. Before Night they landed at the City, and next Day returned with a Pilot and a *Jonk* to attend us, and, in two Days more, the Pilot brought us safe to an Anchor in *Teipe Queberado*, a very secure Place for Shipping to ride in. It is about four Miles from the City of *Maccao*, where I found a Company Ship called the *Canterbury*, commanded by Captain *Kingsford*, who had come from *Amoy* in *March*, and could not reach the Streights of *Malacca*, so was forced to pass the South-west Monsoons in this Harbour.

I went to the City, and applied myself to the Captain General and the *Procuradore* for Assistance, and they made large Promises. I addressed each of them with a Present of scarlet Cloth, and *Surat* Atlasses, which they thankfully received, but soon after I found they were in no Condition to assist me. They indeed designed to compliment me with some fresh Provisions, but had not Interest enough with the *China Mandereen* to get Liberty to send them on board of my Ship.

Nor would he suffer any Body to supply me with Necessaries, till he received Orders from the *Chontock* or Vice-roy of *Canton*. That Incivility presaged but ill Success to my Affairs there; however, I went and paid him a Visit,

Visit, and presented him with a Silver Salver and a Piece of Atlas on it, both in Value about 45 *Tayels*, or 15 *L. Sterl.* which he received, and made an Apology for his prohibiting Commerce with my Ship till he had received Advices from the Vice-roy.

He treated me with *Tartarian* Tea, which I took to be Beans boyled in Milk, with some Salt in it, and it was served in wooden Dishes, as big as Chocolate Cups. When our *Regalia* was over, I took Leave, and he loaded me with fair Promises, and sent after me a Present of an Hog, two Geese, a Goat and some Wheat Flour, and a small Jar of *Samshew*, or Rice Arrack.

Having nothing to do till the Vice-roy's Orders came, I went among some Islands to find a Watering-place, and, on a pretty high Island about a Mile long, and half as broad, I saw a fine clear Stream trickling down the Face of a Rock, about half a League from our Ship. I ordered my Men to fill about 20 Tuns of it, and being clearer than we had before, we made Use of it for drinking and boyling Rice. About ten Days after we had made Use of it, all my Men were affected with a violent Head-ach, and, among the rest, myself, which was a Distemper I never had been troubled with before.

I began to suspect that the Water might be the Cause, and ordered a large Copper-pot to be filled with it, and to boyl one Half of it away, and set the rest to cool a Day and a Night, which was accordingly done, and, on on pouring off the Water, I found about a large Handful of a dark gray Salt at the Bottom, of a ſharp unſavoury Taſte, which made me empty what remained of it into the Sea; but there was an high large Iſland about two Leagues from our Ship, that had many Springs of Water, which I tried, and found to be good.

One Day I was diſcourſing with a *Portugueze* Phyſician of the Quality of the Water we firſt uſed, and he told me, that moſt of the Springs in *China* had pernicious Qualities, becauſe the ſubterraneous Grounds were ſtored with Minerals, as Copper, Quick-ſilver, Allom, Toothenague, *&c.* and the Springs running thro' or near thoſe Mines, the Water becomes affected with their natural Qualities, which was one Reaſon why the *Chineſe* boyl'd all their Water before they drank it, and as the Boyling cauſes the Spirits of Water to evaporate, they uſed Tea to infuſe new Spirits in the Place of the old, ſo that it was more out of Neceſſity than Choice that the *Chineſe* drank ſo much Tea, tho' they do not drink it half ſo ſtrong as generally we do in *Europe*.

It was near a Month after my Arrival before the Vice-roy's Order came to ſettle my Affairs. They had repreſented to him, that our Ship was a Wrack, and, by the Laws of the Country, ſhe fell to the King; but the Vice-roy diſtruſting the Report of the *Chineſe*, ſent a *French* Gentleman to bring him true Accounts of our Condition, and what Mer-

Merchandize we had to diſpoſe of. When the *French* Man came on board, I entertained him civilly, and gave him a Sight of the Muſters of our Goods and their Quality, and we had fiſhed up ſome ſmall Fir-trees, which we had converted into Maſts and Yards.

On the *French* Man's Return, and giving the Vice-roy an Account of what he had ſeen, he ſeemed amazed at the falſe Information he had from *Maccao*, and ordered the *Hapoa* or Cuſtom-maſter to go and take an Account of our Goods, and take the Emperor's cuſtomary Dues, and give me a free Toleration to trade. Accordingly the *Hapoa* came, and brought three Merchants along with him to buy our Goods. When they came on board, they were ſurpriſed to ſee ſo large a Ship, with ſo many Guns, having forty mounted, and ſuch a Number of Men, I having above an Hundred and fifty. I ſaluted the *Hapoa* with ſome Guns, and treated him with a Dinner after the *European* Faſhion, and gave him good Store of Wine to waſh it down; but he lik'd Canray beſt, and drank of it till he was well fluſtred. Then he ordered the Length of the Ship to be meaſured on the upper Deck, and the Breadth at the Main-maſt, and departed.

Next Day I went to viſit him, and carried him a Preſent as cuſtomary. In our Diſcourſe he told me, that he had brought a very honeſt Man along with him, who ſpake the *Portugueze* Language, and that he muſt be my Interpreter at *Maccao*, and buy all my Pro-

Provisions spent in the Ship, and on my Table ashore, and that he had also brought three Merchants to agree for my Cargo, all Men of Substance. I answered, as to the Buying Provisions, I had no Occasion for any, and for making a Contract with those Merchants, I had no Mind to it, because I designed to carry my Cargo to *Canton* in small *Jonks*, and when I arrived at *Canton* with my Goods, and had enquired into the Market, it would be Time then to make Bargains. He seemed to be angry that I was not directed by him, and told me, that he had taken much Pains to serve me, but that I slighted his Service. I answered, that being a Stranger, I might be allowed to walk cautiously till I had informed myself of the current Prices of Goods, and the King's Duties to be paid on them, but I should always have a great Regard to his Friendship. He alledged that there was great Danger in carrying Goods between *Maccao* and *Canton*, because there were many Pirate Vessels in the Way, belonging to *Quansi*, and that neither the Emperor nor the Vice-roy could be accountable for what Robberies might be committed by these Pirates. I replied, that I desired none to answer for such Losses, but would be very glad to meet with those Scar-crows, that I might have an Opportunity to make a Present of some of them to the Vice-roy.

When he found that none of his Arguments prevailed, he gave Orders to have my

Goods put on board of ſmall *Jonks*, and that I might put five Men of my own in each Boat for a Guard, and ordered one of his Merchants to accompany me in that which I went in, ſo that we were twenty five *Europeans* well armed, in our little Fleet. We took the inland Paſſage, which was the neareſt, and ſailed by ſeveral Iſlands on both Sides of us. I kept in the headmoſt *Jonk*, and a good Officer in the ſternmoſt; and every Veſſel we ſaw, they told us they were Pirates. I anſwered them, I wanted to be near them, but I could not perſwade them to ſteer towards them.

After we had ſailed about 18 Leagues from *Maccao*, we came to a ſmall City called *Janſan*. The *Teytock* or Governor ſent me a Compliment, and invited me aſhore; but I excuſed myſelf, becauſe the Wind was fair, and I was in Haſte to be at *Canton*. About 5 Leagues above *Janſan*, we entred into a Canal cut thro' a large Plain of Cornfields, where we ſaw many large flat-bottom'd Boats built to breed Ducks, which they bring up for Sale, and to weed the Rice Grounds for Hire. They have three or four Stories over one another, where are the Ducks Neſts. On the uppermoſt they ſit and hatch Eggs. In the others they lodge all Night; and it is wonderful to ſee what Order and Oeconomy thoſe Ducks keep; for ſome old Drakes (on the Winding of a Whiſtle) drive all the younger Novices into the Water, ſome going foremoſt to ſhew the Way, while others

thers take Care that none loiter behind. There is a ſmall Port made about a Foot high from the Water, and a Piece of Deal Board laid in it, whoſe other End lies in the Water on a gentle Deſcent, that ſerves them for a Bridge to go out, and come in at when they are out about Service. The Maſter goes in a ſmall Boat among the Rice Grounds, (for that Grain always grows among Water) and winding his Whiſtle, they all follow his Boat, and fall to their Work, to deſtroy Frogs and ſmall Fiſh, with the Weeds that would hinder the Growth of the Corn. About Noon he winds his Whiſtle again, on which they all repair on Board of their own Veſſel in good Order, ſome of the old Drakes bringing up the Rere, whilſt others guard the Bridge, to take Care that no Stranger Ducks enter with their own Tribe; and when all are in, the old Guardians enter alſo and take their proper Poſts.

SOMETIMES when two or three of thoſe Boats are employed in one Field, and their Ducks mingle, and ſome young Novices, which do not underſtand their proper Maſter's Whiſtle, chance to come in Company to another Boat, and would enter with the reſt, the old Guardian Drakes ſoon ſpy them out, and beat them away from the Bridge, and on no Account will they ſuffer them to enter, more than an eſtabliſhed Company will admit Interlopers to enter into their Trade.

BETWEEN *Janſan* and *Canton*, which is about twenty Leagues, there are many pretty ty Villages ſeated in the Plains, and the Peaſants bring Fiſh, Fowl, Eggs, &c. Eatables to ſell at very moderate Prices; and there are alſo ſome ſmall high Towers built on high Grounds. The Reaſons why they were built I could not be informed of my by Companions, but the Foot of their Covering is hung round with Pieces of Glaſs of ſeveral Sizes, ſo near, that, with a ſmall Gale of Wind, they beat againſt one another, and make a pretty agreeable Noiſe.

WHEN I arrived at *Canton* the *Hapoa* ordered me Lodgings for myſelf, my Men and my Cargo in an *Haung* or Inn belonging to one of his Merchants, where none but the *French*, who had then a Factory there, had Liberty to viſit me, and when I went abroad, I had always ſome Servants belonging to the *Haung* to follow me at a Diſtance. I had ſtaid about a Week, and found no Merchants came near me, which made me ſuſpect, that there were ſome under-hand Dealings between the *Hapoa* and his Chaps, to my Prejudice, but I could not be informed what they deſigned. At length, one Night I had ſupp'd in the *French* Factory, and began to make my Complaint to Mr. *Petchbertie* the Chief, of the ſtrange Method I was treated in, that all Merchants ſhunned my Company, but for what Reaſon I knew not. He winkt on me to follow him into his Bed-chamber, and, ſhutting the Door, told me, that thoſe three Merchants, or rather Villains, *Linqua*, *Anqua* and *Hemſhaw* had paid to the *Hapoa*

4000 *Tayels* for the Monopilization of my Cargo, and that no Merchant durst have any Commerce with me but they, but withal advised me to carry fair with them, and bargain with them on whatsoever Terms they would allow me.

ACCORDINGLY I had a Meeting with my Chaps, and, in my Discourse, I told them what the current Price was in Town for every Species of my Goods, and desired to know what they would give. They seemed surprised that I knew the Market, and would fain have known who had informed me of the Prices, but I desired to be excused on that Point, and to proceed to bid for themselves. My Cargo consisted in Cotton, *Putchock* or *Radix dulcis*, *Rosamalla* or liquid *Storax* and *Surat* coarse *Chints*, which, according to the current Market, would have come to 14000 *Tayels*, but they would not come within 80 *per Cent*. of the Market Price.

I finding myself insulted, had a Mind to wait on the Vice-king, who resided at a Town called *Sachow*, about 20 Miles up the River, and, in order to go thither, I applied myself, by the Assistance of the *French* Linguist, to a *Mandereen* called the *Chumpin*, for Licence to go to *Sachow*, and for his Letter of Recommendation to the Vice-roy. The News of my being with the *Chumpin* alarmed the *Hapoa* and my Merchants, who found no Way to impede my going but by seizing any Linguist that should serve me either in *Canton* or in my Journey, and accordingly, as I was going next Day to receive my Letters, and the *French* Linguist along with me, he had a small Iron Chain thrown over his Head, (a Custom that is among the *Chinese* when they arrest a Man) and he was dragged before the *Hapoa*, and was accused of assisting the *French* in running Goods on board of their Ships, for they had two lying at *Whampoa*, a Village about 4 Leagues below the City. The poor Man was kept in Prison as long as I staid at *Canton*, and his Imprisonment so terrified others, that I could get none to serve me but whom those Villains of Merchants recommended to me, and none durst serve me as Linguist.

I finding no Remedy, but Patience, to my disturbed Mind, was forced to comply with the unjust Impositions of the *Hapoa*, and so struck up a Bargain at the villanous Merchants Rates, but to receive Silver for my Goods; and after I had delivered them, I desired to settle Accounts, and to have my Money according to Contract. They made up a large Account of Charges, as 3000 *Tayels* for the Measurage of my Ship, 1000 for Liberty to buy Masts, Cordage and Provisions, and 1000 *Tayels* for Presents to some *Mandereens*, and then they told me, for what remained I should have Goods at the current Price of the Market, tho' I was obliged to take them between 40 and 50 *per Cent*. higher. They made me pay 13 *Tayels per* Chest for *Japon* Copper, which I could have bought for 9 *Tayels*, and for *China* Copper I was charged

charged ten and an half, which I bought at *Maccao* for ſeven, ſome Fir Maſts that I cheapned for 60 *Tayels* they made me pay 250. It was the Middle of *January* 1704. before I had ended my Accounts with them, and I wanted Permiſſion to go to *Maccao*, but that I could not have. They put me off, from Day to Day, about a Week. At length I viſited the *French* Chief, and he frankly told me, that they would not let me go till I laid out ten thouſand *Tayels* of Silver with them, which they were informed I had on Board of my Ship, and that my Merchants had told him ſo. I anſwered, that being bound to *Amoy*, I had Bills on Merchants there for near that Sum, which, with my Goods, had been ſufficient to have loaded my Ship there, for which Reaſon I had brought no Silver with me; but I found there was no End to their Villany, and therefore I would go without Leave, if I had it not in three Days. He told me of many ill Conſequences that would attend violent Courſes; but I anſwered him, That I could no longer bear their Inſults, and, if I had not my Permiſſion in three Days, I would run a *Muck*, (which is a mad Cuſtom among the *Mallayas* when they become deſperate) and that I thought twenty five Men well armed, were ſufficient to go off by Violence, when by fair Means they could not obtain it, that being the laſt Remedy, what Blood might be ſpilt in the Action, the *Hapoa* and his Chaps would anſwer to the

Emperor for, who, no Doubt, would enquire into the Cause.

I then bade farewel to all the Gentlemen of the *French* Factory, and left a Present of 50 *Tayels* for the Linguist that lay in Prison, and came Home to my Inn, and acquainted my Men with my Resolution, who unanimously approved of it, promising to live and die with me, and immediately we new cleaned our Arms, and new loaded them with Powder and Ball, which the Servants of the *Haung* taking Notice of, went and informed my Merchants what we had been doing, and that we lookt brisker than usual. The Merchants went to the *French* Chief, to see if he knew what Design we had, and he frankly told them all that I had told him. They immediately acquainted the *Hapoa*, who forthwith sent us a Permit for ourselves and Goods, and next Day I departed with twelve of my Crew, and some Goods, leaving the rest to follow with the rest of my Goods and Masts.

In three Days we got to *Maccao*, and got all Things in Readiness to sail. There were two *Portugueze* lay in *Tiepe-queberado* waiting for me to accompany them for fear of a *French* Cruiser of 32 Guns, that had been at *Manila*. One Mr. *Burno* commanded her, who had made his Brags to the *Spaniards*, that he would bring all the *English* and *Portugueze* that were bound from *China* to the Streights of *Malacca*, into *Manila*, and make a Present of our Ships to the *Spaniards*, which frightned the *Portugueze*. One was a Ship of two

two and twenty Guns, and the other of sixteen.

However, some *China* Merchants contracted with me to carry them, and about 150 Tuns of Bricks and *China* Ware, to *Pullo-condore*, and were to pay me 1000 *Tayels*. Three Days after my Arrival came my Masts, and as they were passing through the Harbour of *Maccao*, towards my Ship, they were stopt by the Procuradore of the City. When Word was brought me, I sent my Purser, who spake good *Portugueze*, that if my Masts were not delivered the same Day, I would take the Masts out of their Ships that lay close by me, let the Consequence be what it would. So to avoid Trouble, my Masts were cleared.

Two of my Merchants came to *Maccao*, under Pretence of clearing Accounts fairly. I invited them on board to dine with me, but they would not do me that Honour. They had heard of the Contract I had made with the *China* Merchants, to carry them and their Goods to *Pullo-condore*, which Contract they broke, for that strong Reason, that they had bought me of the *Hapoa*, and that Freight I had no Power to contract for, but they would furnish them with a Passage for them and their Goods, on the same Terms that I had agreed on, so I was obliged to lose my Freight.

I received what Goods they were pleased to bring me, but I found wanting 80 Chests of *Japon* Copper, and some Toothenague that I had weighed off at *Canton*, and put the

Stocks

Stocks Mark on them. I askt the Reaſon why they did not deliver thoſe Goods, ſince, according to their own Account, there was a Balance due to me of 1800 *Tayels*. They told me that they would give no more, and the Balance they would keep, for fear they ſhould loſe on my imported Cargo. I bid them farewel, and promiſed to let them hear from me by the firſt *Jonk* of theirs that I met with. Next Day I ſent them my Account, wherein I ſhewed that they and the *Hapoa* had cheated me of 12000 *Tayels*, and that I ſhould not fail to make Repriſals when I met with any Effects of theirs. Accordingly I did at *Johore*, by the King's Permiſſion, ſeize a Jonk of theirs, and ſecured their Books of Accounts, having two *Portugueze* Natives of *Maccao*, who could ſpeak and write *Chineſe*, and they found out what Merchandize belonged to thoſe Villains, which I took on board of my Ship, among which was my 80 Cheſts of Copper, and 200 *Peculs* of Toothenague, with my own Mark on them. I drew out a fair Account, and ſent them with a Letter of Advice, that I had received but one third Part of the Balance due to me, but upon their fair dealing with the *Engliſh* for the future, I would forgive the reſt, but if they continued to act like Villains, I would proſecute my Reſentment till I had recovered the laſt Peny of my Balance.

WHEN I gave the King of *Johore* an Acount how they had uſed me in *China*, he wondred that I did not ſeize all the other Merchant

Miglect the God of Voluptuousness or Pleasure

near Chap. 51

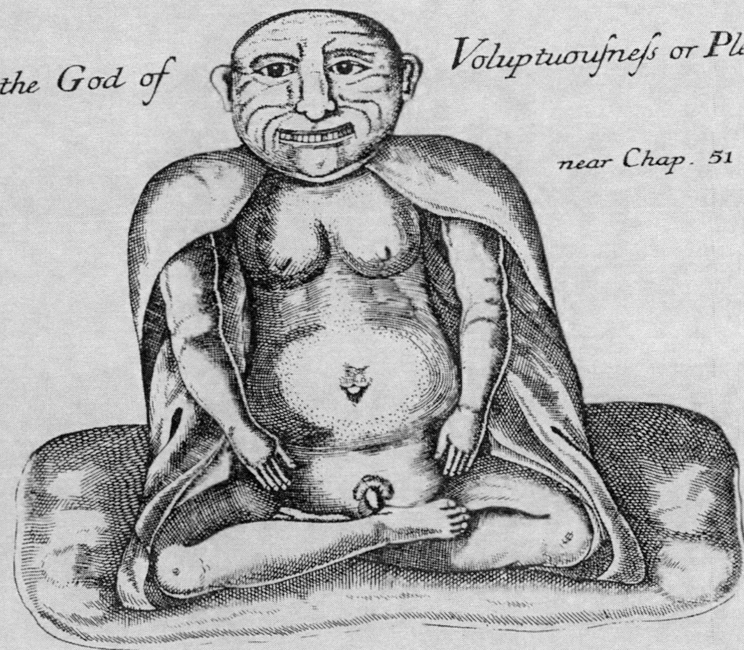

Rot. Mylne sc.

Chap. 51

A China Triumphal Arch

chant Goods that were in the *Jonk*, and sell the Men for Slaves. So having ended this short Digression to *Johore*,

I return back to *Canton*, to give an Account of my Observations on that fine City and Country.

CHAP. LI.

Some Observations and Remarks on the Province and City of Canton *or* Quantung, *and of the Province of* Fokien, *with some Occurrences that happened there.*

CANTON was once a Kingdom of it self, and was called *Nangvee*. It had been several Times conquered by the Emperors of *China*, and shak'd off the Yoke when they found Opportunity. At last, about three Centuries ago, it was subdued and made a Province of *China*. It borders on *Quansi* to the Westward, *Kiangsi* to the Northward, *Fokien* to the Eastward, and the Ocean washes about 100 Leagues of its Coast to the Southward. The Country is as pleasant and profitable as any in the World. The Ground yields two Crops a Year of Rice, Wheat, and Legumen. The People are ingenious, industrious, and civil, but are too numerous, which makes them tolerate a base and cruel Custom, that when a Man thinks he has too many Daughters, he may destroy as many as he pleases of them, but they do not kill them

out

outright, but serve them as *Moses* was in *Egypt*, by laying them on an Ark of Reeds, and letting them flote on the Stream of a River, while they are Infants, and if any charitable Persons see them, and commiserate their Condition, they may take them out, and bring them up as their own, either for Marriage, Concubinage, or Slavery.

THE abominable Sin of *Sodomy* is tolerated here, and all over *China*, and so is *Buggery*, which they use both with Beasts and Fowls, in so much that *Europeans* do not care to eat Duck, except what they bring up themselves, either from the Egg, or from small Ducklings. Whoredom is not punished in this Province, tho' very severely in some others.

THE City of *Canton* stands upon the East-side of a pretty large River called *Taa*. Its Walls are high towards the River, but towards the East the Ground is a little hilly, and the Walls are much lower. The Walls are about ten Miles in Circumference, but some reckon them Twelve, tho' there are large Spaces towards the East and South, kept for Gardens, and no Buildings but Summer-houses are there.

THERE is a large Building of Timber on the highest of the little Hills to the East, that stands close to the Wall, and it bears the Name of the King's Banqueting-house. It is four Story high, supported with great Fir Masts, very finely painted with Vermilion, and japann'd and gilded, as are all the Walls and Ciel-

Cielings within it. From it a very fair Prospect of the City and Suburbs may be had. The Suburbs are so large, that some of them look like Cities. Half of the Number of Houses built in the Garden Plots, would fill them up, and all the other vacant Places in the Town.

There are many stately Buildings in the City of *Canton*, and above a Dozen of triumphal Arches in several Places of the City, and a great Number of Temples, well stockt with Images. The *Italian* Church makes an handsom Figure, but the *French* Chapel is but mean on the out-side.

There was a new Temple built by the King of *Couchin-china*, and dedicated to one of his Gods called *Migleck*, whose Image is placed in it, in a lazy Posture, sitting on a Carpet, with his Heels drawn almost to his Buttocks, clothed in a loose Robe, with his Breast and Belly bare, and leaning on a large Cushion or Bolster. He is very corpulent, and always laughing, which merry Aspect made me think that he might pass for *Democritus* of *Abdera* in *Greece*. There is another Image of a young God that died before he reacht Twenty. He is plac'd sitting on a Chair, and as we approach near him, he nods his Head, by Means of some Springs that reach from the Pavement that we tread on: However, this young dead Fellow shews as great a Wonder in nodding to his Visitants, as St. *Charles* of *Millan* does to his Devotees on the anniversary Day of his Canonization.

Can-

Canton was the laſt great City of *China* that the *Tartars* conquered, when they over-ran that Country about the Year 1650. and had it not been for the Cowardice and Treachery of the Governor, it might ſtill have been an independent Province as well as *Quanſi*. The *Tartars* loſt above 100000 Men in reducing it, for they lay nine Months before it, and the City nowiſe diſtreſt for Want of Proviſions, having the River free for Communication with foreign Places; but upon the Governor's Surmiſe that it might be taken at laſt, and he and his Family ſacrificed to the Reſentment of a barbarous Enemy, he ſecretly articled with the General of the *Tartars*, and perfidiouſly opened two Gates in one Night, and the *Tartars* entring Horſe and Foot, ſoon made the City a Theatre of Horror and Miſery.

I made a Calculation of the Number of Inhabitants within the Walls of *Canton*, by the Quantity of Rice daily expended in it; for they reckon 10000 *Peculs* is the daily Import of that Grain. It is alſo reckoned, that every Perſon conſumes one *Pecul* in 3 Months, ſo that by that Calculation, there muſt be above 900000 People in it, and the Suburbs one Third of that Number, and there is no Day in the Year but ſhews 5000 Sail of trading *Jonks*, beſides ſmall Boats for other Services, lying before the City.

A little Way below the City, are two ſmall Iſlands in the River; they have each a Caſtle built on them, and their Gariſons examine all Veſſels and Boats that paſs by them. THE

THE Product of the Country, besides Corn and Fruits, is Gold, Quick-silver, Copper, Steel, Iron, raw and wrought Silks, and besides the Silk Manufactories, there are lack'd or japann'd Ware; and at *Sachow* there are much *Porcelline* or *China* Ware made. We have the same Sort of Clay in several Parts of *Great Britain*, that *Porcelline* is made of, but we want the warm Sun to prepare it.

THEY reckon that the Province of *Canton* or *Quantung*, pays yearly to the Emperor 1200000 *Peculs* of Rice, and 20000 *Peculs* of Salt, out of which is served out to the Military (who are reckoned 80000 continually kept in the Emperor's Pay) 320000 *Peculs* of Rice, and 8000 *Peculs* of Salt. The rest is sold in Markets, at the common Price of 5 *Macies* a *Pecul*, which may amount to 446000 *Tayels*, which is appropriated towards the Payment of the military Expence, which may amount to 1000000 of *Tayels* yearly. The Customs on Merchandize and Poll-money amounts to prodigious great Sums, all which are gathered according to the Book of Rates, and sent to the Treasury of the Province, for the Use of the Empire, which makes the Emperor's Treasury always full.

Fokien is the next maritim Province to the Eastward of *Canton*, a very mountainous Country, and has about 90 Leagues of a Sea-coast. It reaches from the Island *Lamoa*, which lies directly under the Tropick of *Cancer*, and makes a very spacious secure Harbour for

for Shipping, between it and the Continent, but no Stranger frequents it, but to ſhelter them from Storms, becauſe they admit of no Trade with Foreigners. About 3 Leagues without the great *Lamoa*, are ſome ſmall Iſlands uninhabited. They are called the ſmall *Lamoas*. There is a good clear Chanel between thoſe ſmall Iſlands and the great one, of 15 Fathoms, on a good oazy Bottom.

THE next Place of Safety for Shipping, is the Iſland of *Amoy*, where the *Engliſh* once had a Factory, and a good Trade, but now it is ſhut up from foreign Trade, by the Emperor's Order. There are ſeveral ſmall Iſlands ly off it, particularly the Iſland *Tang ſi*, by the *Engliſh* called *Chapel* Iſland, and by ſome the *Hole in the Wall*, becauſe there is a large Hole that paſſes quite through it, being undermined by the Sea below, but above all is faſt without Fracture. It appears like the Arch of a large Bridge. About ſeven Leagues within it, is the inner Harbour of *Amoy*, where Ships ly very ſecure in 12 Fathoms oazy Ground, within 200 Yards of the Shore. The Town is built cloſe to the Sea, and ſome Houſes in it at high Water, are waſhed by the Sea.

ABOUT the Year 1645. the *Dutch* had a great Mind of poſſeſſing *Amoy*, for the Conveniency of its Situation and Trade. They came to an Anchor with five large Ships in the outward Harbour, and landed about 300 Men. There were none to oppoſe them but a few Merchants and Mechanicks, who were ſoon

ſoon frightned, but were ſo cunning, that before they left their Town, they left their Houſes well ſtor'd with *Samſhew*, a Kind of ſtrong Arrack made of Rice, and with *Hockſhew*, a Kind of ſtrong Ale made of Wheat-malt, by Fermentation.

THE *Dutch* fearing no Enemy, or Deſign againſt them, entred the Town, and ſome inconſiderable People being left in it, were civilly treated by the *Dutch*, and thoſe poor *Chineſe* ſhewed their new Maſters the beſt Houſes in the Town, where the *Dutch* took up their Lodgings, and, according to Cuſtom, carouzed heartily, that before Midnight there were but few of them ſober, and ſo went to ſleep. The *Chineſe* who were left in the Town, went and informed their Country-men what Poſture the *Dutch* Affairs were in. They armed all they could get, with Swords, Lances, Bows, and Arrows, to the Number of 2000. and came on the *Dutch*, before they could put themſelves in a Poſture of Defence, and cut them all off, which Diſaſter made the *Dutch* depart without making any farther Attempt.

THIS Hiſtory is written in large *China* Characters, on the Face of a ſmooth Rock that faces the Entrance of the Harbour, and may be fairly ſeen as we paſs out and in to the Harbour.

Amoy was famous in the *Tartar* War, betweeen the Years 1648. and 1675. by the Diverſion it gave to the *Tartar* Forces at Sea, by the Courage and Conduct of one *Cockſing* a Native of *Amoy*, who gave them many Defeats, and could never be brought to comply with the *Tartar* Uſurpation, tho' he had many advantagious Offers to ſubmit, but his Death gave the *Tartars* a quiet Poſſeſſion of the whole Province.

About the Year 1648. the *Tartars* took *Chinchew*, a very large City, reputed to be as large and rich as *Canton*. They did not ſtand out above nine Weeks, becauſe they foreſaw that Want of Proviſions would compel them to a Surrender at laſt, upon worſe Terms than they might have had, if the Siege had been but ſhort, however, they capitulated to have their Lives and Fortunes ſecured, and ſubmitted in all other Things to the *Tartar* Government and Cuſtoms.

This Province of *Fokien*, borders on *Chequiam* to the North-eaſt, on *Kiamſi* on the North-weſt, on *Quantung* on the South-weſt, and the Sea waſhes the South-eaſt Part of it. There are ſeveral Iſlands ly on its Coaſt, and *Quamoy* is but two Leagues from *Amoy*, and is much larger, but not ſo well inhabited, becauſe of the near Neighbourhood of *Chinchew*.

In Anno 1693. I was at *Amoy*, and then the Iſland was governed by a *Chungcoun*, or a General of 10000 Men. He was a Man of about 80 Years of Age, of a very agreeable Aſpect. He had done many ſingular Services to his Country, particularly in ſuppreſſing Pirates that mightily diſturbed the Province, and governed with much Juſtice and Moderaration, but next Year he died, and was succeeded by a *Teytock*, or a deputy General of 5000. *In Anno* 1697. I went thither again, and found a new Temple built in Honour to the old *Chungcoun*, and his Image placed in it, as much like his Person while alive, as ever I saw any Thing represented in my Life, with every Lineament and Feature in his Face, and I saw many Votaries worship his Image. It seems the *Chinese* are speedier in their canonizing than the *Romans* are.

The *Teytock* has a Deputy called the *Chungnae* by Title, and another Officer called the *Chumpin*, who superintends the Affairs of the Sea and Rivers. In those three Persons Hands is the Management of the Affairs of the Island, except the Customs on Goods imported and exported, and these are in the Hands of the *Hapoa*, who farms those Customs of the Court at *Peking*, but the other three are put in by the *Chungtock*, who keeps his Court at *Hocksew*, a large City about 200 Miles North-east of *Amoy*.

There are no beautiful Buildings in or about *Amoy*, but some Temples, in one of which I saw Hell painted *in Fresco*, on a Wall according to *Des Cartes*'s System of *Demonology*, the Demons being painted in the same Shapes and Figures as are in the Cuts of *Des Cartes*'s Book, their Methods of tormenting the damned, very near the Notions delivered by *Christian* Doctors, and *Purgatory* better represented according to the Doctrine of the Church of *Rome*, than I saw it in a Church in the City of *Antwerp*.

THERE are some Curiosities in *Amoy*. One is a large Stone that weighs above forty Tuns, that is set so dextrously on a Rock, in such an Equilibrium, that a Youth of twelve Years old can easily make it move, but an hundred Men can make it move in no greater Motion, than that single Youth can. I saw it tried with a Pair of Hand Screws, but to no Purpose.

ANOTHER Rarity is of five large Stones, as big, or bigger than the last mentioned, placed in an Hollow at the Foot of a Mountain (whether by Nature or Art I cannot tell) they are each about thirty Foot long, and Twelve or Fourteen Diameter. They lean their Heads against one another, and form an Alcove at their Feet, wherein is placed a Table, and Benches around it, of Stone, and there is a pretty clear Rivulet runs close by the Table. We *Europeans* frequented that Table on *Sundays*, for we often dined there.

THERE is a fine large Citadel at the Backside of the Town, with good high thick Stone-walls, and two Gates that face one another, and in the Middle stands the *Teytock*'s Palace. The Front of it is built of Wood, and the Back and Sides of Stone, as most *Mandareens* Houses are in this Province, as well as the Temples. There are Sentinels and Guards always in the Gate-ways, but I saw none any where else, except when he gave pub-

publick Audience to Strangers, then he had about 50 Men attending at the Palace.

THERE are about fifty *Christians* in *Amoy*, and they have a Chapel served by *French* Missionaries, but the Parishoners are of the Scum of the People, as they are of *Christianity*.

I heard a pleasant and true Story about the famous *Chunghee*, who died *in Anno* 1723. and the *Chungtock* of *Fokien*, who was alive *in Anno* 1700. which I had from Mr. *le Blanc*, a *French* Missionary, as well as from some eminent *China* Merchants, and it happened about the Year 1690. the *Chungtock* being then *Chungnae*, or Deputy-governor of the Island of *Quamoy*, that Island having about 30000 Inhabitants, not reckoning Women and Children, they were all poor, and had their Sustenance by their hard Labour, in manuring the Ground, and Fishing.

A great Part of the Island being low and marishy, by the Overflowings of Spring-tides, made Travelling very incommodious. The *Chungcoun* being a Man of Pleasure, could not bear living at Home in rainy Weather or Spring-tides, and in going to hunt, he was obliged to go a great Way about, before he could reach the Places where the Game was.

ONE Day in Council he proposed to take one Half of the miserable Inhabitants from their daily Labour, to bring Stones from some neighbouring Mountains, to build a Bridge or Causey over the Morass, which was above three Leagues long, and being the Emperor's Work, it must be done *gratis*.

THE *Chungnae* oppoſed it, laying down the the Difficulty, if not the Impoſſibility for thoſe poor People to carry on ſuch a Work, which could not be finiſhed in leſs than three Years. He laid before the Council, that the Inhabitants could hardly live by their Labour, when every one of them were imployed, and how could they ſubſiſt on the Labour of one Half, that he could foreſee the Ruin of the Whole by taking off the Half from their manuring the Land, and Fiſhing. However, it was put to the Vote, and the *Chungcoun* carried it, on which the *Chungnae* laid down his Commiſſion, and proteſted that he would not be acceſſory to the Deſtruction of ſo many Innocents, whom he foreſaw would be wrought and ſtarv'd to Death, and ſo bade the *Chungcoun*, and the reſt of the Council, adieu.

THE *Chungnae* having ſpent moſt of his Time in the Study of Letters and Philoſophy, had made a good Progreſs in both, and having a ſmall Fortune of ten or twelve thouſand *Tayels* in Money, took a Journey to *Pecking*, to try if he could get into ſome convenient Poſt in the Government there, but found that none was to be got, without Friends and Money, ſo that he took a Reſolution to lead a private Life on the Intereſt of his Money, and to follow his Studies.

AND hiring a Chamber in a By-lane of the City, he fell to writing a Tract of moral Philoſophy, being well qualified in writing a good Hand, and a good Stile. He began to write on the Imbecillity of human Nature, when our

our Paſſions were more followed than Reaſon; of the diſmal Conſequences of Tyranny when ſupported by Power, and ſeveral other ſuch uſeful and commendable Topicks, and having carried his Work pretty well forward, one Morning he went to a Neighbour's Houſe to drink Tea, and forgot to ſhut his Chamber Door or Windows, which being on the lower Story of the Houſe, and facing the Lane, any Body that paſt by could ſee what was in the Room.

THE Emperor had gone abroad that Morning *incognito*, to hear what News paſt current in the City, and accidentally came into that Lane while the Gentleman was at his Tea, and looking in at the Window ſaw a Book lying open on the Table, and the Writing ſeem'd to be extraordinary fine, which made him have the Curioſity to enter at the Door, and to ſit reading till the Owner ſhould come in, that he might know both the Subject written on, and the Author.

IT is the Cuſtom in *China* for a Stranger, to read on any Book that he ſees lying on a Table. If it be a Merchant's Book of Accounts, they take that Liberty; and the Emperor having read above half an Hour, was mightily pleaſed with the fine Writing, and ingenious Reflections made on each Subject by the Author. At laſt the Gentleman came in, and was ſurpriſed to find another in his Chamber, but the Emperor addreſt him in ſo obliging Terms for his intruding into his Chamber without Leave, led by the ſtrong

Chains of Curiosity, and the Opportunity that offered to give him Satisfaction, by the Door being accidentally left open, that the *Chungnae* could take nothing ill that was done.

The Emperor asked him of what Country he was, and what had brought him to *Peking*, and the *Chungnae* satisfied him that he was a Native of *Fokien*, and re-counted the History of his Affairs in *Quamoy*. The Emperor was much taken with his Story, and the modest Way he exprest himself in it, and told him that he found his Actions to quadrate with his Doctrine. Then he askt the *Chungnae* if he had an Employment, or if he had a Mind to accept of one. He answered, that he had been in *Peking* above a Year, and could observe, that Merit was but a weak Recommendation to Preferment, and he did not design to buy it.

The Emperor told him, that he was nearly related to a great *Mandereen* at Court, and that if he would accept of a Post, he would use his Endeavours to procure him one, for he found him recommended by two good Qualifications, Ingenuity and Honesty. The *Chungnae* thank'd him in very obliging Terms, and told the Emperor, that he was willing to accept of a Post, providing it was not too high, because his Fortune was too low to support the necessary Expence, nor too low, lest it should make him contemptible. The Emperor assured him, that his Kinsman had several Posts to dispose of, and that he might depend on one suitable to his

his Mind, and giving the *Chungnae* his Fan, ordered him to call at a Gate of the Palace, called the *Elephant* Gate, and deliver that Fan to the Captain of the Guard, and tell him, that you want to ſpeak to a *Mandereen* of ſuch a Name (as the Emperor borrowed for that Time) and the Captain would conduct him to his Apartment; but withal he begg'd the Uſe of his Book for a few Days, and, as he was a Man of Honour, he would return it.

THE *Chungnae* complimented him with the Uſe of the Book, making a modeſt Apology for its Incorrectneſs, and ſo they parted for a ſhort Time.

THE Emperor ſent for ſome *Coleas*, *Mandereens* of the firſt Order, and gave them a pleaſant Account of his Morning's Adventure, and ſhewed them the Book, which they were highly pleaſed with, and the Emperor told them, that he had promiſed the Author an handſom Poſt, and deſired to know if any were vacant. One *Mandereen* told his Majeſty, that he had received private Advices that Morning, that the *Chungtock* of *Fokien* was dead, and that there would be certain Information next Day at Court, if it was ſo or not, and that if it was true, his Majeſty might beſtow that Poſt on him, he being a Native of that Country, and conſequently knew the Manners and Cuſtoms of his own Country better than a Stranger could. His Majeſty approved of his Advice.

AND

And next Morning, according to Appointment, the *Chungnae* went to the *Elephant* Gate, and enquired for the Emperor by the borrowed Name, and, on Sight of the Fan, was conducted by the Captain of the Guard to an Apartment in the grand Palace, and was ordered to ſtay till the Captain came back to him. When the Emperor knew of his being in the Palace, he ordered a Council of *Mandereens* to be ſummoned forthwith, and when they were convened, and himſelf ſeated on the Throne, the *Chungnae* was ſent for, and he paying the uſual Compliment of falling on his Knees, and bowing his Head three Times to the Ground, the third Time to continue in that Poſture till he was ordered to riſe, the Emperor ordered him immediately to ſtand up. The *Chungnae* ſoon knew who had been his Gueſt the Day before, and would have begg'd Pardon for the Freedom of Speech he had uſed to the Emperor in Diſguiſe; but the Emperor prevented him by beginning an allegorical Diſcourſe, recounting the *Chungnae*'s Adventure at *Quamoy*, as if it had happened in a foreign Country, and when he had made an End, he askt the Opinion of the Aſſembly, what both the *Chungcoun* and *Chungnae* deſerved. They unanimouſly condemned the *Chungcoun*, and commended the *Chungnae*, and were of Opinion, that the *Chungnae* deſerved a better Poſt than he had before.

The Emperor told them, that this was the Caſe of the Perſon before them, and that the Govern-

Government of *Fokien* was vacant by the Death of the *Chuntouck*, which Advices he had received that Morning, and that he had Thoughts of beſtowing that Place on him before them, which they all approved of, on which he ordered Robes of the ſecond Order to be brought, and inveſted him in the Office and Dignity, and ordered 100000 *Tayels* to be paid to him, in order to equip him for his Journey, and withal told him, that he expected he would govern his Province according to the Doctrine that he preached to others.

ACCORDINGLY the new *Chuntouck* took his Journey to *Hockſhew*, where, on his Arrival, all the *Mandereens* of Note in the Province came to compliment him, and none muſt come to wait on him till firſt introduced by a Preſent, which is punctually ſet down in a Book kept for that Purpoſe.

AND among the Crowd of Viſiters came his old Friend the *Chungcoun* of *Quamoy*. After the common Compliment of Genuflexion and Proſtration was done, he ordered him to ſtand up, and asking him if he did not remember him, he received a negative Anſwer. He askt him how his Government of *Quamoy* thriv'd, and how far the Bridge was brought forward. The *Chungcoun* gave him a ſad Account of the State of his Iſland, which, he alledged, was occaſioned by a raging Plague, that had ſwept off above the half of the People, and the Bridge was not carried one Quarter of the Way forward.

THEN

THEN the *Chungtock* made himſelf known to him, and upbraided him with his Cruelty, and the *Chungcoun* having little to ſay in his own Defence, fell at his Feet, and implored Mercy. The *Chungtock* bade him riſe, and told him, that for the ſake of his Family, he would ſave his Life, which he had juſtly forfeited, but withal baniſhed him to a Palace on the Side of an Hill on the Iſland of *Quamoy*, where he ſhould be allowed 2000 *Tayels* yearly, for the Subſiſtence of his Wives and Children, but he was never to meddle in Government again, and ſo diſmiſt him, and ſent one along with him to take Poſſeſſion of his Government, with Orders to rectify all Things that had been amiſs in his Government, and to invite People to the Manuring of the Ground and catching of Fiſh, on better Terms than had been before. Thoſe juſt and generous Actions of the Emperor and *Chungtock* were worthily admired by all who loved Juſtice and Generoſity; and I have born no ſmall Veneration for both their Perſons ever ſince.

I muſt now give an Account of the *Chungtock*'s Juſtice and Generoſity in an Affair relating to ſome ſhip-wrackt *Engliſh* Men at *Amoy*.

CHAP.

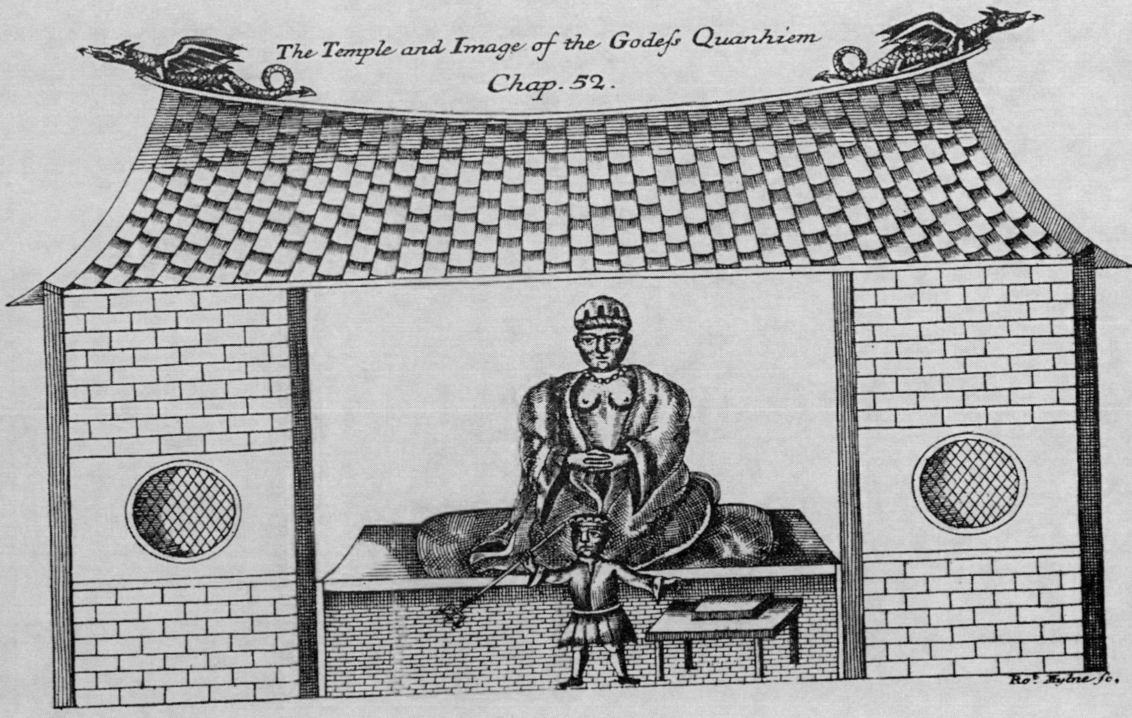

The Temple and Image of the Godefs Quanhiem

Chap. 52.

CHAP. LII.

Is a Continuation of the History of the Chung-tock *of* Fokien, *in relation to some Occurrences that happened among the* English *at* Amoy *in Anno* 1700.

I Being then bound to *Amoy* in a Ship from *Surat*, employed by Sir *Nicholas Waite* the new *East-india* Company's President there, and Commodore *Littleton* being then at *Surat* with a Squadron of four Men of War, by some considerable Reasons was perswaded by Sir *Nicholas* to let one of his Squadron go as far as *Amoy* to look after the *English* Pirates that then infested the Streights of *Malacca*.

The *Harwich* was the Ship pitcht on, a 50 Gun Ship, commanded by Captain *Cock*, and we sailed in Company as far as *Atcheen*, and there we were parted by a Storm. He called at *Atcheen*, but I made what Haste I could for the Port of *Malacca*. I staid there above a Fortnight for him, and when he had taken in such Provisions as he wanted, and that I had paid for them, we sailed from *Malacca*, in order to proceed for *Amoy*.

When we arrived there, we found three *European* Ships, and a Country Ship from *Surat*, employed by Sir *John Gayer* President for the old *East-india* Company. The Supercargoes of those Ships, on Sight of a Man of War, sent a Compliment of 500 *Tayels* to the *Teytock*, to disswade him from giving

ving the *Harwich* Permiſſion to come into the Harbour, for fear of loſing a Feather that they had put in their own Capes, of wearing a Pendent at their Top-maſt Heads, ſo that when I went to pay my Compliment to the *Teytock*, and give him an Account of our Cargo, and to deſire Liberty for the Man of War and my own Ship to come into the Harbour; he told me, that my own Ship was welcom, but he could not, with Safety, admit of the King's Ship into the Harbour, but that ſhe might be ſupplied with what ſhe wanted, in the Road.

I told him, that the King's Ship's Bottom wanted Repair, and that if he would not permit her to come into the Harbour, both ſhe and I muſt go to *Canton*, and if the Captain of the Man of War reſented the ill Uſage he was like to meet with at *Amoy*, thoſe ought to anſwer who had given the *Teytock* that ill Advice, and ſo I took Leave very ill ſatisfied.

The Linguiſt and I had been acquainted ſome Years, and, on our Way from the Citadel, I told him, that if the *Teytock* continued his Reſolution of denying our King's Ship the ſame Civilities that he granted to Merchant Ships of our Nation, I could not anſwer for the ill Conſequences that might attend that Affront, and, if ſhe had not Permiſſion in three Days to come in, on the fourth we would proceed for *Canton*.

He then very frankly told me, that it was none of the *Teytock*'s Fault, but the *Engliſh* Captains and Supercargoes, who had ſent him

him with a Meſſage to the *Teytock*, to acquaint him, that if the Man of War was permitted to come into the Harbour, their Men would be rude to the Merchants, and would be tied up to no Rules or Laws which the Merchant Ships obſerved, that the Women would be debauch'd, and many other aggravating Crimes, they alledged, the Man of War's Men would commit, and withal had ſent the *Teytock* a Preſent of 500 *Tayels* to keep her out of the Harbour.

I carried the Linguiſt into a Merchant's Houſe that was my Acquaintance, to conſult with that Merchant about removing that *Remora* that ſtopt the Man of War from entring into the Harbour, which could be done no other Way than by my being bound for the good Behaviour of the People belonging to the Man of War, and to give a Preſent ſuperior to theirs, which I conſented to.

THEN we conſulted how the Captain of the King's Ship ſhould be received by the *Teytock*, when he ſhould make his Viſit, and we agreed, that all the Captains and Supercargoes ſhould be called to the *Teytock*'s, in Company with Captain *Cock*, and that he ſhould enter before us, and have an high Chair placed a little before the *Teytock*'s Chair, on the left Hand, which, among them, is the Place of Honour, and we Captains and Supercargoes to be ſet on felt Cuſhions on the Floor, and on the right Side of the *Teytock*'s Chair, which was raiſed on a plat Form of Deals, with three Steps of Aſcent.

WE

We had no ſooner done with our Conſultation than I diſpatcht my Friend *Shawban*, for that was the Merchant's Name, with the Linguiſt, to acquaint the *Teytock* with what we had reſolved on, and he approved of all, and two Days after ſent a Summons for the Captains and Supercargoes to accompany Captain *Cock*, and all obeyed but one, who pretended Indiſpoſition; however he ſent his ſecond Supercargo to ſupply his Place.

Assoon as we were in the Citadel, we were conducted to the *Teytock*'s Palace, and entred the Chamber of Audience, and were ſeated according to the Method before agreed on. The *Teytock* being ſeated before, he made a Speech pretty long, wherein he told how he had been informed of the looſe Behaviour of Men of War's Men, which had armed him with Caution, but that he knew of a more convenient Place on an Iſland within three Leagues of the Town, for the Man of War to hale aſhore, if we would be ruled by his Advice. The Captain made a Bow, and acceded to that Motion.

He then wanted to know who would be Surety for the Captain and Men belonging to the Man of War, that they ſhould obſerve the Laws and Cuſtoms of the Place, without being Moleſtation to the Natives. I found none cared to enter on ſo hazardous an Affair, ſo I ſtood up, and proferred myſelf, Ship and Cargo for Security. The reſt not expecting that the Captain could have found ſuch Security, one, who made a good Figure among us, told

told me, I was too forward in my Profer. I anſwered him, that I only engaged what I had the Command of, but meddled with no Body's Affairs elſe.

THE *Teytock* ſeemed well ſatisfied, and gave us a very handſom Entertainment, and then diſmiſt us. The Man of War went to the Iſland, and landed ſome of her greateſt Guns, but found ſo much Difficulty in carrying Things aſhore, that we got an Order from the *Teytock* to bring her into the Harbour, and accordingly ſhe came in.

THERE is an Iſland oppoſite to the Town of *Amoy*, called *Cullemſhoe*, about half a Mile diſtant, and it has two convenient Places to lay Ships on, in order to clean their Bottoms, or repair them, and there are ſome Rocks that ly between thoſe Places, that appear dry at low Water. In one of thoſe Bays the *Harwich* was haled aſhore, and cleaned, and her Sheathing being much worm-eaten, it was repaired with a great Deal of new Sheathing, all which Charges I had Orders from my Employers to disburſe on their Account, in Expectation, that carrying back 200 Tuns of *China* Goods would ſufficiently reimburſe them; but Captain *Cock* being a young Man, not very well verſed in the Affairs of Shipping, took Advice of ſome other Captains of better Knowledge, and daily carouſing with them on board of his Ship, chanced, that Day that his Ship haled off, to be a little inebriated, as well as his Tutors. I was none of the Cabal, and ſo ſtaid in my Factory. The Tide of Ebb was made before they began to remove the Ship from the Bay that ſhe had been fitted in, and in haling off, the Tide ſet her upon the Rocks above mentioned, and on them ſhe was loſt.

As soon as the Ship ſat faſt on the Rocks, his Counſellers left him to think on his Miſfortune. Next Morning all the Captains and Supercargoes went over to the Iſland (where he and all his Men were lamenting their Condition) to condole his Misfortune, but not one had the Charity to invite him to a Dinner. About Ten I went over to viſit him, and found him weeping. I diſſwaded him from grieving at what could not be remedied, and invited him to dine with me, if he was not pre-engaged. He then wept very bitterly, and told me, that not one of all his Companions that had been viſiting him, had the good Manners to give him an Invitation, and that I, who had juſt Cauſe to be angry with him for his Folly and Contempt of my Counſel, had ſhewed him more Humanity than thoſe who had ſworn eternal Friendſhip to him.

I carried him and his two Lieutenants along with me to Dinner, and allowed them a Chamber in my Factory to lodge in, and, to ſhew a good Example to the reſt of the Captains, I took forty of the poor Seamen on board of my Ship, and gave them Proviſions. They were in all One hundred and eighty two Men and Boys in the Crew, and there

there being five Ships, I thought, I had taken a large Quota for my Share, but not one of the rest would follow my Example, so the Remainder of the Crew were in Distress for Want of Food and Raiment. I went over one Morning to see what Condition the poor Men were in, who had made Tents of the Ship's Sails, and I saw one newly dead for Hunger and Cold.

I used all my Rhetorick amongst my Brethren the Captains and Supercargoes, to take Pity on the poor ship-wrackt Men, but they were all deaf to my Petitions, which obliged me to allow them a Pound Weight of Rice *per* Day each Man: And to clothe them, I bought three thousand Yards of blue Cotton Cloth about a Groat *per* Yard Value, and bought them Needles and Thread, and gave them about 1000 *lb.* Weight of Cotton for quilting, and so every Man was his own Taylor.

But finding my Charges would be very great in maintaining such a Number of Men, and in carrying them Passengers would take up too much Room in my Ship, which I could much better employ in carrying *China* Goods to *Surat*, I went to my old Friend *Shawban*, with my Confident the Linguist, and held a Consultation how we might compel my Brethren to be humane, and force them to take their Quotas of the poor distrest Men, and we fell on the Project to write to the noble and just *Chungtock* at *Hocksew* before mentioned, to get an Order from

 him,

him, that no Ship ſhould have Liberty to lade their Goods aboard, that did not firſt take their Quota of the ſhip-wrackt Men. We went to the *Teytock*, and acquainted him with our Deſign, who much approved of the Project, and he ſeemed ſurprized, that any of thoſe Ships durſt go into our King's Dominions, who had denied to aſſiſt, not only his Subjects, but immediate Servants. He was very human, and ſent the poor Seamen Preſents of Pork and *Hockſew*, (a ſtrong fermented Liquor like our ſtrong Ale) for me to diſtribute among them, and thoſe Preſents he frequently ſent.

I provided a Preſent to accompany my Letter to the *Chungtock*, to the Value of 40 Pounds *Sterl.* and got the beſt Scribe in the Place to write my Letter, laying down the Miſery the poor Men were in, and how eaſily and juſtly they might be reliev'd by ſuch an Order.

I ſent my Letter and Preſent by an Expreſs, who returned in ſixteen Days with a ſatisfactory Anſwer, and an Order to the *Hapoa*, to ſuffer no Goods to be ſhipt off without conſulting me. The *Hapoa* came to my Factory, and congratulated me on the Honour that the *Chungtock* had done me, and promiſed to obey his Orders in relation to ſhipping Goods off.

A Gentleman who was Supercargo of the Ship *Dorrel*, bound directly from *Amoy* to *England*, was the firſt that was denied a Permit to ſhip Goods off. He had ſent for the

in Chap. 52

The Godess Pusa a China Diety

Rot. Mylne sc.

the Ship's Boat to carry off ſome Cheſts of Silk, but the Waiters ſtopt them from putting them into the Boat, on which the Linguiſt was ſent for to know the Reaſon; and he told the Supercargo, that the *Hapoa* had received Orders to let no Goods be ſhipt off without conſulting me firſt about taking a Quota of the Man of War's Men; on which my Antagoniſts held a Council, and reſolved to continue obſtinate, and that Supercargo before mentioned came early next Morning to my Houſe. When my Servants informed me that he was in the Court, I went and invited him in. I gueſs'd his Errand by his Countenance, and askt him to ſit down, but he refuſed. I askt him if he would drink any Coffee or Tea, but he would not. He then, in a Fret, askt me if I was Governor of his Affairs. I anſwered, no, nor did I know how he could ask me ſuch a ſimple Queſtion. He ſware that he found I was, and that if I were in another Place than *Amoy*, I durſt not act as I had done, and ſware again, that not one Man of them ſhould be entertained on board the *Dorrel*. I told him, that I durſt do any Thing that was honeſt and juſt, and was always ready to defend what I had ſo done; but as to his taking his Quota of the ſhip-wrackt Men, he muſt comply with it, if he had a Mind to ſave his Paſſage to *England* that Seaſon. He ſtill continued curſing himſelf if he took any of them, and went away in a very great Huff, which I little regarded.

It was, and, I believe, is ſtill the Cuſtom on board the *Engliſh* Company's Ships, for the Captain to give a Remonſtrance and a Proteſt thirty Days before the Expiration of the Term for their Departure, to the Supercargo or Factor for the Company, according as it is ſtipulated by Charter Party. Accordingly the Captain of the *Dorrel* gave in his Proteſt about that Time to the aforeſaid Supercargo, which aggravated his Chagrin, and he told the Captain, who was my Friend, what Troubles I had brought him and the reſt into. The Captain adviſed him to conſider what Time might be ſpent in Contention, and that I, having the Government on my Side, would certainly carry my Point in ſpite of all the Oppoſition they could make, and that it would be much better to comply in Time than to ſtand out, and be forced to comply at laſt.

He told the Captain, that he might do as he pleaſed, but he was reſolved to give him no Orders on that Head. The Captain bade him look what was agreed on in Charter-party, where they found, that the Commander of a Company's Ship was to take no Paſſengers on board of his Ship, on Penalty of 100 *L.* for each Paſſenger, without a written Order from the Company's Agent where he ſhould happen to be; but where no Agent was, he was then at his Liberty.

After a little Deliberation, he bade the Captain ſpeak to me of the Hardſhips they would be under in carrying ſuch a Number of Paſſengers ſo long a Voyage, and to try me, whether I would favour them in the Number of the Quota that they muſt be obliged to carry: And the Captain came to diſcourſe me about it, and I agreed, that Captain *Cock*, his Lieutenants, and ſeventeen more ſhould have their Paſſage on board his Ship to *England*, and that thoſe ſeventeen ſhould be ſuch as Captain *Cock* ſhould chooſe, that the Captain and his two Lieutenants ſhould have Captain *Hide*'s Table, they paying him 20 *L*. each for that Favour, all which the Captain conſented to, and the Supercargo and I became Friends again.

THE other Sticklers ſoon complied, and took thirty ſix each for their Quota, and the reſt I provided for, and they were as forward to work and obey my Orders as my own Seamen, tho' they were not ſo on board of the other *Surat* Ship, where they were like to mutiny for Want of Victuals, even before they went to Sea, for the Captain of that Ship pretended, that he would allow them no Victuals before they went to Sea, and the poor indigent Fellows faſted twenty four Hours on that Pretext. At laſt Hunger compelled them to make their Complaint to me, and I furniſhed them with a Supper, and bade them be eaſy till next Noon, and if there was no Proviſion made for them, when the Ship's Company's Dinner was ready, to ſeize on it for their own Uſe, and let the others ſtay till more was dreſt, which Advice they took to be very wholſom, and punctually followed it.

THE Captain complained to me of the Paſſengers Rudeneſs. I told him, that they only followed my Advice, for I could not ſee what Pleaſure he could take in ſtarving poor Men, ſince what they did eat was nothing out of his Pockets, for I knew the Charges would be allowed in his Accounts with his Employers, and adviſed him to treat them civilly at Sea, ſince they being ſuperior in Numbers to his Ship's Company, might make them uſe Force to obtain what they ought to have by fair Means: Nor was I out in my Conjecture, for at Sea he put them to ſo ſmall an Allowance, that they mutinyed, and threatned to carry him and the Ship to *Madagaſcar*, and deliver him to the Pirates.

ABOUT *Chriſtmas* I brake up Houſe-keeping, and paid Houſe Rent for Captain *Cock* and his Officers to remain in it a Month after me, and knowing the Scarcity of Money among him and his Family, I gave him a Bag with 1000 *Spaniſh* Dollars for his Subſiſtence on his Voyage to *Europe*, on condition, that when he was in a Capacity to pay me, he would not forget to repay me. I gave his firſt Lieutenant 100. and the ſecond Lieutenant 50 of the ſame Pieces, but without Proviſion of Repayment.

THE Captain made his Acknowledgments in the moſt emphatical Words he could expreſs, imprecating Vengeance to purſue him if he did not thankfully repay with good Intereſt,

tereſt, when he was able. I alſo wrote to the Lords Commiſſioners of the royal Navy, about the Charges I had been at on acount of the Loſs of his Majeſty's Ship in *China*, and petitioned that I might be reimburſed, and made Mr. *Matthew Cock*, a Brother of the Captain's, my Attorney, to ſolicite for, and receive what their Lordſhips would pleaſe to allow me.

I received a Letter from the Captain, then at Cape *Bona Eſperance*, in his Way home, wherein he gave me an Acount of their hard Uſage aboard of the Ship, and of the Death of his ſecond Lieutenant, and that was all I had from him in 23 Years. When I arrived in *England*, I did my ſelf the Honour to write him from *London* to *Leather-head*, to try if I could furbi h up his ſhort Memory with the Remembrance of what had paſt between us in *China*, but he proteſted that he had quite forgot it. I anſwered him, that his firſt Lieutenant, Captain *Falconar*, ſtill remembred it very well, and had made a grateful Acknowledgment of the ſmall Favour he received above twenty Years before. My Affairs calling me to *Holland*, *in Anno* 1724. he called for me at *London*, when he knew I was in *Holland*, and before I returned to *England*, he had paid his great Debt to Nature, without taking Notice of the ſmall one due to me.

CHAP.

CHAP. LIII.

A Continuation of Obſervations on the Gods, Clergy, and Devotion of the Chineſe.

AND now I have followed him to his Grave. I'll return back to *Amoy*, and obſerve ſome of their Cuſtoms, religious, civil and criminal. Their Temples are built all after one Form, but, as in other Countries, very different in Beauty and Magnitude. Their *Joſſes* or Demi-gods are, ſome of human Shape, ſome of monſtrous Figures, but in the Province of *Fokien*, they are more devoted to the Worſhip of Goddeſſes than Gods. *Quanhiem* has the moſt Votaries. She is placed in State, ſitting on a Cuſhion with rich Robes, and her little Son ſtanding before her, with a charged Trident in his right Hand, ready to throw at Offenders of the Laws of Humanity and Nature, and alſo at thoſe who make no Free-will-offerings to his Mother. The *Chineſe* who have ſeen the *Roman Catholick* Churches and Worſhip, ſay that ſhe is the *Chineſe* Virgin *Mary*.

THERE is another Goddeſs called *Matſoa*, who ſwimm'd from a far Country, through many Seas, and came in one Night to *China*, and took up her Reſidence there. She ſits on a plat Form, with a Cuſhion laid on it, and her Head is covered with blue Wooll inſtead of Hair. She is the Protectreſs of Navigation, for which Reaſon none go a Voyage but

but they first make a Sacrifice of boiled Hogs Heads, and Bread baked in the Steam of boiling Water. It is set before the Image when reeking-hot, and kept before her till it is cold, she feeding on the Smoke, and the Devotees on the Substance, when it is cold. On their Return from a Voyage, they compliment her with a Play, either acted on board of the Ship, or before one of her Temples.

THEY have another Goddess in Form of a Virgin, called *Quonin*, who has many Votaries, but is mostly worshipt in the Provinces of *Peking* and *Nanking*, but being a Virgin, she has many Lovers all over *China*.

THE God *Fe* has an human Shape, except his Head, which has the Figure of an Eagle's. *Gan* has a broad Face, and a prodigious great Belly. *Fo* is a very majestick God, and is always placed with a great Number of little Gods to attend him. *Minifo* in *Fokien*, I take to be the God *Miglect* at *Canton*, being alike in Shape and Countenance. He is called the God of Pleasure. *Pussa* is set cross-legged on a Cushion, bespangled with Flowers and Stars, and she has eight or nine Arms and Hands on each Side, and two before that she holds in a praying Posture. In every one of her Hands (except the two that are dedicated to Prayer) she bears some Thing emblematical, as an Ax, a Sword, a Flower, *&c.* The great God that made the Heavens and Earth, they bestow an human Shape on him, like a young Man in Strength and Vigour, quite opposite to the Church of *Rome*, who

make

make his Picture like *Salvadore* Winter, old, cold, and hoary. I have seen many more whose Names I have forgot, some with human Bodies, and Dragons, Lions, Tigers, and Dogs Heads, and one I saw like *Stour Tonker* in *Finland*, with a Man's Body and Clothes, and with Eagle's Feet, and Talons in the stead of Hands.

THE Priesthood are in no great Esteem among the People, being generally of low Extract. They have many different Orders among them, which are distinguished by Badges, Colour of Habit, or Fashions of their Capes. They are all obliged to Celibacy while they continue in Orders, and that is no longer than they please. But while they continue in Orders, and should, or chance to be convicted of Fornication, they must expiate the Crime with their Lives, except their high Priest, who is called *Chiam*, and he always keeps near the Emperor's Person, and is in very great Repute, and he has Liberty to marry, because the high Priesthood must always continue in one Family, as *Aaron*'s did for a long While, but not half so long as it has been in this Family, who has kept up the Custom above 1000 Years successively, without the Intrusion of Interlopers.

THERE are no Persons of Figure or Fortune that care to have their Children consecrated to serve at the Altar, so that the Priests who can have no Issue of their own, are obliged to buy Novices of such mean Persons as Necessity forces to sell their Children, and their

their Study being in the large Legends of their Divinity, and not having the Benefit of Conversation with Men of Letters or Polity, they are generally ignorant of the Affairs of the World, which makes them contemptible among so polite a People as the ingenious and conversible *Chinese* Laity are.

Confucius, or, as the *Chinese* call him, *Confuce*, was the Prince of their Philosophers. He was near contemporary with *Artaxerxes*, *Nehemiah*, and *Malachi*, about 450 Years before our Saviour *Jesus Christ*. He both taught and practised moral Philosophy to Perfection, and acquired so great a Veneration among his Countrymen, that his Sentences are taken for *Postulata* to this Day, not one since having offered to contradict any Thing that he has left behind in Writing. They have another Doctor of Philosophy called *Tansiw*, who was almost as ancient as *Confucius*, and wrote many excellent Tracts of a virtuous Life, and the Methods to attain to it, but his Character is inferior to *Confucius*'s.

THEIR Preachers take some Apophthegm out of those great Mens Writings, for Texts to comment and exspatiate on. They live very abstemiously, and rise early before Day to pray. Every Temple has a Cloister or Convent annext to it, and has a certain Stipend allowed by the Emperor to support the Priests and Novices, but they get much more by letting of Lodgings to Travellers, who generally lodge in their Cells, than the Emperor's Allowance. Besides, they have a genteel Way of begging from

Stran-

Strangers, by bringing Tea and Sweet-meats to regale them.

The *Chinese* don't bury in or near their Temples, but in the Fields, and when *Bouzi* or Priest tells a rich dying Person, that such a Piece of Ground is holy, and that the infernal Spirits have no Power to haunt such Ground, they'll perswade the poor Man that is distemper'd both in Body and Mind, to buy it at any Rate to be buried in, and sometimes they will pay a thousand *Tayels* for ten Yards square of such holy Ground.

The Fishers and Carriers by Water, who are born and bred in their Boats, and on the Water, must also be buried in it, unless they have Money enough to purchase a Burying-place ashore.

They have many Sects among them, but all agree in the Transanimation of Souls, yet not one Sect persecutes another, but allow free Liberty to believe what they think best, and it is very natural for Men to embrace what they think is best, whether it is the best or not.

The *Christian* Missionaries have converted many by the Indulgence of several Emperors, particularly of *Chunghee*, and those Apostles indulge their Proselytes in many Things opposite to the System and Canons of the Western *Christianity*, as Poylagmy, Concubinage, and the Invocation and Adoration of *Pagan* Saints, as well as *Christian*, in their Apotheosis, which has caused no small Disturbance at *Rome*.

When

When a *Mandereen* of any Consideration, passes through a Street or High-way, he goes in great State, either on Horse-back, or in close or open Chairs, carried by Men, and he has Flags carried before him, and large Peels lacquered, and painted black or red, with large golden Charactets writ on them, that gives the Designation of his Titles and Dignity The foremost of his Retinue in their particular Habit, with an high crown'd Hat in Form of a close Stool-pan, and two long Feathers of a Pheasant's Tail, standing upright in it, and they make an hideous Noise as they go along, crying incessantly Ho----ot, to warn every one to go off the Streets or High-way, till he pass by. Next to them are Fellows with small Chains in their Hands, ready to throw over any Body's Head, and catch them by the Neck, that do not obey the Call of the foremost Men. And next them are Executioners with their Ensigns of Cruelty, as a great Sword, an Ax, and some large Pieces of Wood, painted black, and trailing on the Ground as they pass along, to *bambow* the Delinquent, which is by throwing them on their Faces, and giving their Buttocks as many Blows with those Batons as his Worship the *Madereen* shall order, and they have Caps like Sugar-loaves. I knew an *English* Gentleman now alive in *England*, that underwent the Chastisement of the *Bambow*.

Yet I heard of a comical Passage that happened at *Amoy*, between a *Mandereen* and an *English* Sailor. The *Mandereen* going

ing in his Chair, with his usual Retinue, met a Sailor coming with a *Keg* of Arrack under his Arm. Every Body went off the Street but the jolly Sailor, who had been tasting his Arrack, he was so mannerly as to walk aside, and give the *Mandereen* the Middle of the Street, but one of the Retinue gave the Sailor a Box on the Ear, and had almost shov'd him down *Keg* and all. The Sailor d----n'd him for a Son of a Whore, and askt what he meant by it, and at the same Time gave the Aggressor a Box on the Ear in Return. The poor Seaman was soon overpowered by the Retinue, but the *Mandereen* ordered to do him no Harm, till he had sent for the *English* Linguist, who forthwith came. The *Mandereen* told the Linguist what had happened, and bid him ask the Sailor why he gave him that Affront. The Sailor sware that the *Mandereen* had affronted him, in allowing his Servants to beat him, while he was walking down the Streets civilly, with his *Keg* of *Samshew* under his Arm, and sware by G---d that he would box the *Mandereen*, or every one of his Gang, for a *Spanish* Dollar, and with that put his Hand in his Pocket and pull'd a Dollar out.

THE *Mandereen* ordered the Linguist to tell him *verbatim* what the Sailor said, and why he pull'd his Money out. When the Linguist had told him all, the *Mandereen* was ready to fall off his Chair with laughing. And after he had composed himself, he asked if the Sailor would stand to his Challenge, who sware

ſware he would. The *Mandereen* had one *Tartar* in his Retinue, famous for boxing, who had won many Prizes at it, and called for him to try his Skill on the *Engliſhman* The *Tartar* was a luſty Man, and the Sailor ſhort, but well ſet. The *Tartar* promiſed an eaſie Conqueſt, and to the Combat they went. The *Tartars* uſe to kick high at the Guts, and the firſt Time he kickt, the Sailor had him on his Back. The *Tartar* was much aſham'd of the Foil he had received, and at the Sailor again, but *Jack* ſoon tripp'd up his Heels again. He deſired then to have a fair Bout of Boxing without Tripping, which *Jack* agreed to, and batter'd the *Tartar*'s Face and Breaſt ſo with his Head, that he was forc'd to yield to old *England*. The *Mandereen* was ſo pleaſed with the Bravery and Dexterity of the Seaman, that he made him a Preſent of ten *Tayels* of Silver.

In the Puniſhment of Crimes there are Laws made to proportion the Puniſhment according to the Notoriety or Quality of the Crime. For Faults not capital, they uſe the *Bambow* and Whip, or a Pair of wooden Stocks, or a wooden Collar, being ſome Boards fixt together, with a Hole in the Middle for the Head to go through. It is generally about five Foot ſquare, and betwen 60 and 80 Pound Weight, that they are obliged to carry a conſiderable Way in the Day, and ſleep in it at Night, ſitting with that continual Weight on their Shoulders, becauſe there is no lying down, which Puniſhment laſts as long as the Judge

 de-

determines in his Sentence. Some they lay in the Stocks by the Neck, laid flat on their Back in the open Sun, with their Face continually towards it while it ſhines, and this laſts for one, two, or three Days, as the Judge thinks fit to order.

TRAITORS, Murderers, and Pirates, are carried to *Nankin* to be tried and puniſht, except a ſpecial Order from the Emperor carry Cuſtom out of her Road. Thoſe Goals in *Nankin* are only cleared of Malefactors once in three Years. In thoſe Priſons they live in great Miſery, and often wiſh for Death before it comes.

EVERY one of thoſe Sort of Criminals has particular Priſons belonging to ſuch Crimes, and when the Judge receives the Emperor's Orders to reprieve ſuch a Number, the Judge has it in his Power to ſave whom he pleaſes of that Number ſpecified, and the reſt are immediately put to Death, as faſt as they can diſpatch them with the Sword and Ax. I have been credibly informed, that 30000 have been executed in one Month, and half that Number reprieved.

WHEN the Emperor gives ſpecial Order for the Puniſhment of Piracy or Murder, the Delinquent is tied to a Stake, and an Executioner cuts the Skin of his Forehead round from Ear to Ear, and pulls it over his Eyes, and then delivers him to the Friends and Relations of thoſe that had ſuffered Injuries by him, and they have the Pleaſure of torturing him as they pleaſe. I have heard of ſome

who

who have been tortured three Days and Nights before they expired. Others have had a Brick or Stone Cloke built round them close to their Bodies, by the Side of an Highway, and a Guard set over them, who commanded all Passengers to spit on their Heads as they past by, and they are generally much longer a dying than the others.

PARENTS have the Power of the Life and Death of their Children till they marry, and then that Power ceases. Husbands have the same Power of their Wives, if they are convicted of Adultery. I knew an Instance of the latter in *Amoy*, by a *Chinese* that went a Voyage to Fort St. *George*, and from thence to *England*. He had a good agreeable young Woman to his Wife, and he pretended when he returned, to make his Wife use the Freedom of *England*, in bringing his Wife into *English* Mens Company when they came to his House, and made her eat at Table, or drink Tea with them, but not when any *Chinese* Strangers were in his House. However, she did not know how to behave her self prudently in that State of Freedom, but was debaucht by severals, and he going a Voyage to *Canton*, had staid ten Months after the *English* Shipping was gone, and found her big with Child at his Return. He sent for her Relations and feasted them, and then before them upbraided her for her Disloyalty, and took a Piece of heavy Wood that they use in pounding Rice, and gave her a Blow on the Head that killed her outright.

I heard of an Inſtance of the other at *Canton*. A rich Merchant had a profligate Son, whom he ſent abroad with a conſiderable Stock to employ in Trade. In a few Months he had conſumed all the Stock, and run in Debt. He gave his Creditors Bills on his Father, who anſwered them for his own Credit. The Son came back, begged his Father's Pardon, and proteſted, that for the future he would lead a virtuous Life. The kind indulgent Father intruſted him with a ſecond Stock, and he, in a ſhort Time, deſtroyed that alſo, and when his Credit was gone, returned to his Father, who ſeemed to paſs by his Folly. But one Day he made an Entertainment for all his Relations, and when the Entertainment was over, he began an Apologue that came pretty near his own Caſe with his Son, and asked their Opinion what in Juſtice the Son ought to ſuffer for abuſing his Father's Kindneſs, and ruining his Eſtate. They did not know that he and his Son were the Perſons mentioned in the Fable, under borrowed Names, unanimouſly agreed that the Son ought to be puniſhed with Death. On which the Father took a Knife and cut his Son's Throat, before either the Son or his Relations had the leaſt thought of it, and then he thanked them for paſſing ſo juſt a Sentence, for that he and his Son were the real Perſons repreſented in the Apologue.

If Children grow incorrigible, and deſpiſe the Threats or Admonitions of their Parents according to Law, the Parents are to com-

complain of them to the Magiſtrate, and upon full Conviction, the Magiſtrate will ſeverely correct them. For if a Son break the eſtabliſht Laws, the Parent ſuffers Puniſhment as well as the criminal Son, if he had not before made the Magiſtrate acquainted with his Son's Vices.

AND if a Parent is brought to Poverty and Want, and has not brought his Son up to ſome Calling, whereby he might get his Living, the Son is not obliged to aſſiſt his Father, but otherwiſe he is.

IN their Marriages the Bridegroom never ſees his Spouſe till they are married, for the Match is made by Matrons of both Sides, and he is obliged to pay a Sum of Money to the Bride's Relations, before he can have her, and when all Obſtacles are removed, her Relations make a Feaſt for the Bridegroom and his Friends, and after that is over, ſhe is brought vail'd into the dining Room, and he preſents her with ſome Jewel of ſmall Value, or ſome Pieces of Silk Stuffs, and a Prieſt ſacrifices a Cock, by cutting his Throat, and ſprinkling ſome of the Blood on them both, and then they are married by Law, and he ſeldom marries another while ſhe lives, except in caſe of Barrenneſs, and then he may take another, and ſo on in caſe of Failure in Iſſue, as far as four, but they cannot go beyond that Number; yet he may buy as many Concubines as he pleaſes, and the Wives are ranked according to Priority, and the Concubines muſt attend and ſerve the Wives.

THE Ladies Drefs is very becoming. They wear fine Linen Breeches that reach to the Ancle, but they are covered with a Petticoat handfomly platted, that reaches below the Ancle, and a Gown that reaches mid-leg down, tied with a filken Belt round their Middle, and each Sleeve fo large, that one would ferve to put their Body in, and reaches almoft to the Ground. They have a Collar of Embroidery handfomly cut, that comes round their Neck, and covers the Neck of their Gown, and reaches half-way between the Neck and Shoulder-bone. They have naturally a great Deal of Hair as black as Jet, which they fet on Wiers fitted to their Head, raifed four or five Inches, and covered with their Hair in a becoming Manner, and thofe who can afford Pearl, have fome of them bored on one Side, and fet in their Hair, and they have two or more Gold Bodkins which keep all the handfom Fabrick faft.

THEIR Feet are bound up with Rollers of Cloth when they come to three Years of Age, and are always kept hard bound, fo that all the other Parts of their Body grow in their natural Shape and Magnitude, but their Feet, which by Reftraint, are always as fmall as they were when firft bound up. Their pretty little Shoe has a Piece of Wood placed in the Middle between the Heel and the Toe, that ferves for both Heel and Sole, which makes them rather trip along when they go, for their Ambulation cannot be called Walking.

THEIR Forehead is large, pretty fmall Eye-

Eye-brows, well arched, their Eyes black, but almoſt hid with the Lids, their Noſe ſmall and flat at the Eyes, their Mouth little, and pretty plump Lips of a deep Vermilion Colour, their Cheeks and Chin in a good agreeable Symmetry, and their Neck ſmall, their Arms long and ſlender, a fine little Hand, and to grace the whole Structure of their Perſons and Ornaments, the Nails of their Fingers are never pair'd, but are let grow to two or three Inches in Length, to ſhew that they are not employed in ſervil Works.

AND this Faſhion of long Nails is followed by the Men of Diſtinction, and are carefully kept clean, and formerly, before the *Tartars* were their Lords, they wore their Hair long, rolled up behind (as our Women in *Britain* formerly wore theirs) and a Net of Hair or black Silk to cover their neat Rolls and Gold Bodkins, with double or treble Prongs ſtuck in their Hair, to keep it in Order, but now they have only a Lock at their Crown, platted and hanging down their Back, and none are without that Lock, for if they have not Hair enough growing naturally on their Heads, they take ſmall Locks of borrowed Hair, and twiſt in with their own to be in the Faſhion.

THE Men of Figure have a Coat of Silk that comes down to their Knees, and a ſhort Doublet over that, that reaches no farther than their Loyns. Their Breeches are large and full, which come under the Tops of their Silk Boots, neatly made and quilted, for great

Men wear no Shoes. They generally wear on their right Thumb a thick Ivory or Agate Ring, very convenient for drawing their long Bows made of *Buffaloe*'s Horn, they being all bred to Archery, and exercise themselves much in shooting at a Mark. They wear their Swords on the left Side, with the Point forward, and when they draw them, they lift up their lacqued Scabbard, that the Handle may reach above their Shoulder behind, so that at the drawing of them with their right Hand, they can make a good and nimble Stroke on whatsoever they attack.

AND to dress our *China* or *Tartar* Gentleman completely, he wears a Cap made of fine Mat for that Purpose, in the Form of a blunt Pyramid, with a Tassel of Horse Hair dyed red, that reaches from the Crown almost to the Bottom, and often an Amber or coral Button fastned to the Crown of the Cap, and they use a Piece of Hair-tape to come under the Chin, to keep it from blowing off by the Wind, and to their Girdle they have a Purse for their little Tobacco-pipe, which is made of some Metal, and two other Purses, one small for their Tobacco, and the other pretty large, with several Divisions in it for their Money and Papers, all drawn close by silken Strings, and their Handkerchief is a Piece of coarse Cotton Rag stuck between their Girdle and Side, one End hanging to the Knee, and that serves for a Towel and a Napkin also, and so I have equipt him either as a Courtier or Cavalier.

BUT

BUT the *Mandareens* of the Pen have a long Gown to their Heels, with Badges or Blazons on their Backs and Breasts, to distinguish their Degree or Dignity, and before they are admitted to the Degree of Doctor, they must pass thro' several Trials and Examinations. They also wear a distinguishing Cap on their Head, and look as grave as an old Advocate.

A Merchant and Mechanick wear the same Cap as the Courtier, but their Habit is a long Robe with narrow Sleeves, and Stockings made of coarse Cotton Cloth, with square-toed Shoes, without Heels or Latchets to tie them on. The Peasant and Fishers are not tied up to sumpture Laws, but wear what they please.

EVERY House, Ship and Fishing-boat keep a domestick God that they pay Adoration to Evening and Morning, and he has always a small flat Table with Ledges before him, filled with Wood-ashes smoothed over, and small Furrows drawn thro' the Ashes in Order, and those Furrows filled with Powder of *Putchock* or *Radix dulcis* mixt with Powder of Sandal, Myrrh or *Olibanum*, and the Composition is fired at one End, and it gives a little, but pleasant Smoke the whole four and twenty Hours, without the least Need of mending or renewing it.

WHEN two *China* Men quarrel, (for they are naturally a little cholerick) if the Breach is so wide that it will be difficult to be made up again, then they'll threaten not

to

to pay anv Reverence or Reſpect to one anothers God, and that Word cuts off all Means of Communion and Society ever after. And ſo I leave them, and proceed to my Obſervations on other Things.

CHAP. LIII.

Gives an Account of the natural Rarities of China, *and of the Emperor's Revenue and common Expence.*

THERE are many artificial as well as natural Rarities in *China*. Their artificial ones are in ſtupendous Bridges, that give ſafe and convenient Paſſages over great and rapid Rivers, and over Vallies between the Tops of Mountains, to make Roads eaſy and pleaſant that would otherwiſe be very ſteep, crooked and dangerous; but I never ſaw any of them, tho' I have heard much Talk of them.

THEY have alſo great and convenient Sluces to check the Violence of Floods from Lakes and Rivers, and to ſerve out their Waters to lower Grounds, to moiſten them and make them fit to yield good Crops of Corn, but I being confined to the Iſland of *Amoy*, could not have an Opportunity to ſee them, ſo that what I add more to my Obſervations, is only by Informations and Reports from others, (who had travelled where I had no Per-

Permiſſion to go) whoſe Acquaintance I caſually ſought after to be informed.

I now begin again to continue my Courſe along the Sea-coaſt to the Northward: And in the ſame Province of *Fokien* is the River and City of *Hockſew*; but whether the City of *Hockſew* be the ſame with *Fochew*, I know not; it is very large however, and is famous for being the Reſidence of the *Chungtock*, and in brewing a Sort of good ſtrong Ale in ſmall Pots of coarſe *China* Ware luted over with a Clay Head as big as the Pot.

ABOUT twenty Leagues to the Northward of *Hockſew* begins the Province of *Chequiam*, whoſe chief City is *Limpoa*, by ſome called *Nimpoa*, and by others *Ningpoo*; however, it is a large City, and drives a great Trade. Here the *Portugueze* were once well ſettled, and had a numerous Colony. When the *Chineſe* were Maſters of their own Country, and the *Portugueze* of the Seas, it is reported, that they had above one thouſand *Portugueze* Families ſettled in *Limpoa*, and were governed by their own Laws. Their Trade thro' *China* and *Japon*, which they carried in Shipping to *India* and *China*, made them prodigiouſly rich, which brought them into Luxury and Debauchery, and, at laſt, was the Cauſe of their Expulſion from *Limpoa*.

THEY began to be notorious Raviſhers of Women. They would go into the Country Villages, and carry off young Virgins by Violence, from their Parents, and when they had

had abuſed them as long as they pleaſed, ſent them back to their Friends. Many Complaints had been made, but no Redreſs could be obtained. At length, when a Parcel of Virgin Hunters had gone into the Country upon an Expedition of that Nature, the Peaſants fell on them, and killed them every Man.

THIS Slaughter made the *Portugueze* very loud in their Complaints, and demanded Juſtice to be done on the Peaſants. The Peaſants made ſolid Replications to the Complaints of the *Portugueze*, and deſired their Caſe might be laid before the Emperor, which was accordingly done, and the *Portugueze* were ordered to clear themſelves of the Crimes laid to their Charge, and they not being able to do it, were baniſhed *Limpoa*, but had Liberty to carry off their Effects: And thus ended the moſt opulent Colony, at that Time, in the World.

Nanking is the next Province to *Chequiam*, and the City of *Nanking* is ſtill reckoned one of the largeſt Cities in *China*, or perhaps in the World. I have heard many ſay, that ſaw both *Peking* and *Nanking*, that it occupies a larger Spot of Ground than *Peking*, and that the triumphal Arches, Palaces, and other publick Edifices, are nobler than thoſe at *Peking*.

THE Province begins at *Souchew*, a large City, and one of the greateſt trading Cities in *China*, in Gold, wrought Silks, *Porcellein* or *China* Ware. It ſtands near the Lake of *Ham-*

Hamchew, which is about 20 Leagues long, and 16 broad, of fine clear freſh Water, and it produces many excellent Sorts of Fiſhes, ſome whereof are daily ſent in Boats to *Peking* for the Emperor's Table.

Nanking City ſtands on the Banks of the River *Kiam*, the greateſt, but not the longeſt River in *China*. It is ſituated about 100 Miles from its Mouth, in a fine, pleaſant, fertil Plain. It was formerly the Metropolis of all *China*, till the *Tartars* grew troubleſom and formidable, which drew the Court to *Peking*, to be nearer the Frontiers, in order to check their Inſolence.

THE Diſtance between *Nanking* and *Peking* is about 500 *Engliſh* Miles. They have a Communication by Water in two royal Canals, one from *Nanking* to the yellow River, ſo called from the Colour of its Water, and the other from that River to the City of *Peking*, or very near it. They are the Work of Art, done by the hard Labour of many Thouſands of poor Workmen, in Obedience to their Emperor's Order, to facilitate the Carriage of Merchandize between thoſe great Cities.

THE yellow River, or *Corcei* River, is much longer than any River in *Aſia*, or perhaps in *Europe*, for there are 30 Degrees Diſtance between its Source and its Mouth: And I heard one Mr. *Fountanay* a Miſſionary, who went to *France* on the Emperor of *China*'s account, about the Year 1694. ſay, that, he believed, there were as many People that lived

lived in Boats and Veſſels on the Rivers of *Kiam* and *Corcei* as in the three greateſt Provinces of *France*, for in their Veſſels they keep Fairs on theſe Rivers, one Seaſon at one Place, and in other Seaſons at other Places; and tho' there may be 10000 Veſſels aſſembled at a Fair, yet there is as good Order and Decorum kept, as in a well governed City. All Ships and Boats who have the ſame Species of Goods are moor'd together along a certain Place on the River's Side allotted for them, by proper Magiſtrates, and, at Night, Watches are ſet to prevent Thieving and Diſorder, and Offenders are ſeverely puniſhed, without Reſpect of Perſons.

There are alſo Fairs kept on the Royal Canal, between the *Yellow River* and *Peking*, in which all the Sorts of Commodities that *China* produceth are to be ſold.

The Magnitude, Beauty, and Opulency of *Peking*, are ſo fully deſcribed by ſome who have been there, that my Hear-ſay Account can be of no Uſe, and for that Cauſe I omit it, but the aforeſaid Mr. *Fountanay* told me, that the Winter Seaſon is much colder than in *France*, and, that in the Month of *November*, the Fraternity bought three Deers, and hung them up in a Pantry without Salt, and, when they had a Mind for ſome Veniſon, they cut what they wanted for their Uſe till the Beginning of *March*, and what was left then began to grow ſtale, but not before, which ſhews the ſubtil Coldneſs and Dryneſs of the Air there.

And

And now being at the End of my Journey on the Continent of *Asia*, I'll make some more general Observations on the Product of *China*, and return to the Southward, to take a View of the Islands that face the Sea-coasts of *China*, and steer back to the Northward as far as *Japon*.

As there are many Mountains in *China*, so they have many different Qualities. Some by their Situation and prodigious Height, shew their lofty Tops above the Clouds, always clear and serene, but none dare presume to go to their Tops, because the Air being too much rarified, insensibly takes away Perspiration, and causes Death. Others, tho' as high, by nitrous and sulphurous Mines in their Bowels, send up thick Vapours that always hide their Tops: And at the Foot of those Mountains are Springs and Wells of Fire, that continually burn in their own Cells, but never break forth in any other Places.

Other Mountains are cover'd with Trees of various Sorts. The Pine is the largest, some being six Foot through, and four or five Score *Covets* high, or according to *English* Measure, an hundred and fifty Foot in Length, and they produce *Bambows*, as long, and so big, that one Joynt between the Inter-nodes or Knots can contain above ten *Catties* of Water, which are of great Use to Sea-faring Men, to hold their fresh Water in. They also produce the Rose Tree, which preserves an agreeable Smell and Colour as long

long as the Wood lasts, which is not less than a Century or two.

In the southern Provinces, I have been told, that a Tree called *Quanlang*, has a soft Pulp growing within it, which the Inhabitants dry and pulverize, and apply it to all the Uses that Wheat-flour serves for, having the same Taste and Quality. I heard a Missionary assert, that not far from *Limpoa* in the Province of *Chequiam*, he saw some Trees that bare a Fruit pretty hard on the Outside, but within a fat Pulp, which being put a While in the Air, becomes good white Tallow; and it serves for all Intents and Purposes, for the same Uses that Tallow is put to, only with this Advantage, that it does not defile the Hand, nor grease and stain Clothes.

All the Provinces of *China* are well stor'd with Fruit-bearing Trees, and being of so large an Extent, and the Seasons so different, that in one Place it is Summer, while in another Place Winter predominates, as in the Provinces of *Quansi* and *Quantung* it is pleasant Summer, while in *Zansi* and *Peking* the chilling Colds of Winter, and Storms disturb the Air, and shut up the Pores of the Earth.

All the Provinces produce Tea in abundance, but *Nanking* and *Chequiam* afford the best. I saw four or five Tea Shrubs growing on the East Side of *Amoy*, but it was in the End of *September*, when all the Leaves were off. It is pretty like a young Willow; and I was informed, that they plant once in three

three Years, and pull all up, or cut down all that are above that Growth. I was alſo informed, that, about the Middle of *June*, they pulled off the firſt and beſt Leaves, and about the Beginning of *Auguſt* they had a Crop of *Sungloa* Tea, which is ſomewhat groſſer than the *Bing* or firſt Crop. Both thoſe Sorts are put under a Shade to dry with the Wind, and in *September* they ſtrip the Buſh of all its Leaves, and, for Want of warm dry Winds to cure it, are forced to lay it on warm Plates of Iron or Copper, and keep it ſtirring gently, till it is dry, and that Sort is called *Bohea:* And I have heard others ſay, that ſome Grounds will produce none but fine Tea, and others again none but coarſe; but they all agreed in drying the the *Bohea* on hot Plates.

On the Skirts of the Mountains they plant their Mulberry-trees for their Silk-worms, and cut them down at two Years Growth, becauſe the Inſect delights moſt in a tender Leaf.

There are many uſeful Trees in *China* that bear no Fruit. Some bear Beans, but of thoſe I have ſeen in *India* at *Surat* and *Bengal.* One Sort they have that provokes Sleep; by laying ſome of the Leaves in the Bed near the Patient. The Iron-wood Tree is commodious for making Anchors for Shipping. It is prodigiouſly ſtrong and hard, and has natural Gravity enough to ſink it to the Bottom of the Sea.

On the Mountains of *Zensi*, near the famous Wall that divides *China* from *Tartary*, grows Abundance of that uſeful and valuable Root Rhubarb, whoſe Uſe is ſo well known in *Europe*. The Root *Genſing* grows alſo in Woods there, and when the Natives go in Queſt of it, to find it, they are forced to go in the Night Seaſon, with Torches in their Hands, for fear of being aſſaulted by the wild Inhabitants of the Woods, ſuch as Lions, Tigers, Leopards, Rhinoceroſes, *&c.* of the brutal Kind, beſides dangerous Reptiles, as Serpents and Snakes, which all flee from Fire. I have heard of Serpents thirty Foot long, and five in Circumference, which lurk all Day in their Dens, and come out in the Nights, to prey on Animals that ly ſecurely in theirs.

This Root *Genſing*, when dried, is like a little Carrot, of a light yellow Colour, and, about Mid-way down, it branches in two, which makes the *Chineſe* call it the *Man-herb*. It has a ſweetiſh Taſte, but, being much chew'd, it ſeems bitteriſh. It is cut in Shreds, and drunk with Tea, and then it is eſteemed a very great Reſtorative of the animal Spirits. It is exceeding hot in Quality, and therefore to be avoided by thoſe of ſtrong Conſtitutions. It is excellent in Conſumptions, and, for its ſeveral good Qualities, is ſold at a great Price, ſome at three Times its Weight in Silver; but, after it is a Year old, it goes off at a Shilling *per* Ounce, becauſe it is difficult to keep the Worm out of it.

it. *Radix China* or *China* Root grows in many Parts of *China*, but the Island of *Aynam* yields the best.

THE Emperor's Revenues, by Report, amount to 180000000 of *Tayels*, out of which he maintains fifty *Caloes* or Privy-counsellers, at 100000 *Tayels* yearly. The Princes of the Blood are honoured with the Government of Provinces, and are allowed, out of the royal Treasury, from 500000 to 1000000 *Tayels* yearly. He has fourteen Provinces, wherein he maintains 80000 Soldiers in each, and each Soldier is allowed 10 *Tayels per Annum* in Silver, and a *Catty* of Rice, and an Ounce of Salt *per* Day, which are delivered monthly out of the Emperor's Granaries. In a Word, I look on *China* to be the richest and best governed Empire in the World. And so having given the best Account I can of it, I steer my Course to the Southward among the *Philippine* Islands, whose Descriptions I take by Report.

CHAP. LIV.

Gives some Account of the Islands of Mindanoa, Luconia, Formosa *and* Japon, *with some remarkable Occurrences that have happened on them.*

MINDANOA is both the southermost and eastermost of all the *Philippines*. It has little or no Commerce with

Strangers, and I never heard of any *European* Ship that went to it ſince Captain *Swan* called there in his Way from *Panama* to *India*, when Captain *Dampier* was with him, who, no Doubt, has given a good Account of it in his Travels: And I know no more of it, but that it is divided into many ſmall Principalities, and that the Sea-worm eats ſo greedily Ships Bottoms, that in three or four Months they eat quite thro', and that there is Abundance of Rice and other Proviſions to be had very cheap there, and that it produces very good *Caſſia-lignum*, or baſtard Cinnamon. It is about 140 Leagues in Length, but of a very unequal Breadth, having many large deep Bays running into it, which afford many Harbours for Shipping.

Papa-goa, or little *Borneo*, is a very long narrow Iſland, being 90 Leagues long, and but 14 or 15 broad. It breeds the beſt Soldiers and Seamen that the *Spaniards* have in the *Philippines*, but produces nothing for Exportation. The *Spaniards* have a Fort on the North-eaſt End of it, and ſo they have on the Iſlands of *Panay*, *Negroſs*, *Cobu*, *Leyte* and *Samar*. They are all large Iſlands, but have no Commodities for Export. And *Mindora*, that lies cloſe to the Iſland *Luconia*, affords nothing for Trade.

Luconia is the largeſt of all the *Philippine* Iſlands, and is richeſt in its Productions, for it affords Corn, Fruits and Roots in great Plenty, as well as wild Game and Fowl. It produces Gold, but of a low Touch. It is not fore either the Prince or the *Dutch* Captain knew any Thing of the Matter; and an Officer bringing the News, the Prince ordered a Search to be made for the Ringleader, and being found, he sentenced him to be smeared over with Hony, and made fast to a Cocoa-nut Tree in the Sun till he died. Next Morning the Sentence was put in Execution. These Cocoa-nut Trees producing a sweet Liquor called *Toddy*, bring vast Numbers of Wasps and large red Ants to drink the Liquor. Those Ants bite as painfully as the Stinging of Wasps. When the Sun begins to be hot, they leave the Top of the Tree, and burrow in Holes about the Root. In their Passage downward they fixt on the Carcase besmeared with the Hony, and soon burrowed in the Flesh. The poor Miscreant was three Days in that sensible Torment before he expired. The *Dutch* Captain begged every Day for a Pardon, or at least for a milder or quicker Death; but the Prince was inexorable.

In Anno 1702. I hired a Ship called the *Albemarle*, in Service of the new established *East-india* Company, to serve me three Months and an half on a Voyage from *Surat* to the *Malabar* Coast, and back; and having Occasion to call at *Cannanore*, I accompanied the Captain of the Fort and an *English* Factor from *Tellicherry* to the Court of *Omnitree*, Successor to the eldest Son of the *Samorin* before mentioned, who died in his Voyage towards *Mecca*.

CAPTAIN *Beawes*, who commanded the *Albemarle*, accompanied us alſo, carrying a Drum and two Trumpets with us, to make our Compliment the more ſolemn. This was a Viſit paid him by all his Tributaries and Friends, to wiſh him many happy Years, it being his Birth-day. We travelled eight or ten Miles before we came to his Palace, which was built with Twigs, and covered with *Cadjans* or Cocoa-nut Tree Leaves woven together. We were admitted to his Preſence aſſoon as we arrived, in an open Green juſt by his Palace Window, which lookt into it, where ſat his Majeſty, with his Queen, and three or four of his Children, pretty well grown up. We paid our Compliment each with a *Zequeen* in Gold, and a few Grains of Rice laid on it, and ſo, by an Interpreter we had ſome frivolous Diſcourſe. He treated us with *Toddy*, ſome *Plantains*, and young Cocoa-nuts; and then, after an Hour's Stay, we had Audience of Leave, and ſo departed.

Omnitree himſelf was a Man of a good Aſpect, about 40 Years of Age, of an Olive Colour. His Dreſs was only a Silk *Lungie* or Scarf made faſt by a Girdle of Gold Plate, about his Middle, that reacht to his Knees, with great Jewels of maſſy Gold, ſet with Rubies, Emeralds and Pearl, hanging at his Ears, but no Ornament on his Head, but a very beautiful Head of Hair hanging over his Shoulders. His Queen and Daughters were in the ſame Habit, only their Hair was tied

tied up behind. They were all naked above the Navel, and were bare-footed. The Queen had a cheerful Countenance, and very affable to us and others, who had the Honour to ſtand near her, diſtributing *Bettle* and *Arecka* with her own royal Hands, to Strangers, who came, as we did, to compliment the Prince her Husband.

About the Year 1680. there were three Princes of the Blood royal, who conſpired to cut him and his Family off, to poſſeſs themſelves of the Government of *Calliſtree*; but being detected, they were beheaded on Altars built of Stone. About two Miles from *Cannanore* the Altars were ſtanding when I was there. They were only ſquare Piles of hewn Stone, about three Yards high, and four Yards each Side.

Adda Rajah's Dominions reach but ten Miles to the Southward of *Cannanore*, to *Tellicherry* River, near which he has an Harbour called *Dormepatam*. Its Paſſage inward is deep enough, but embaraſſed with Rocks in its Entrance. It has an Iſland againſt its Mouth, called *Cacca Diva*, about half a League from the Shore, invironed with Rocks.

Adda Rajah has alſo the Dominion over the *Lacca Diva* Iſlands, which ly about 40 Leagues off the *Malabar* Coaſt, between the Latitudes of eight Degrees and an half and twelve and an half. I have ſeen eighteen of them. They are all very low, and have many dangerous Sholes among them, and to the

Northward of them. The Chanel between them and the *Maldiva* Islands, is called the eight Degree Chanel. There are no Dangers in it, and sometimes we pass through without seeing either the *Maldivas*, or them. There is another Chanel through them in 11 Degrees Latitude.

THEIR Product is only Cocoa-nuts and Fish. Of the Cocoa-nut Kernels they express Oyl, which is fine and clear, fitting for Lamps; and, when it is new, serves their Kitchins. Of the Rind of the Nut they make *Cayar*, which are the Fibres of the Cask that environs the Nut spun fit to make Cordage and Cables for Shipping, and for several other Uses. Their Fish they dry, and export to the Continent. Sometimes in the Southwest Monsoons they find Amber-grease floting on the Sea. I saw a Piece in *Adda Rajah*'s Possession, as big as a Bushel, and he valued it at 10000 Rupees, or 1250 *L. Sterl.* What Religion they have is *Mahometan*, for no other Reason but because their Prince is so, which Complaisance may teach others a Lesson of Conformity.

THE next Province to *Adda Rajah*'s Dominions is *Tellicherry*, where the *English East-india* Company has a Factory, pretty well fortified with Stone Walls and Cannon. The Place where the Factory now stands belonged to the *French*, who left the Mudwalls of a Fort built by them, to serve the *English* when they first settled there, and for many Years they continued so, but of late

no

no ſmall Pains and Charge have been beſtowed on its Buildings; but for what Reaſons I know not, for it has no River near it that can want its Protection, nor can it defend the Road from the Inſults of Enemies, unleſs it be for ſmall Veſſels that can come within ſome Rocks that ly half a Mile off, or to protect the Company's Ware-houſe, and a Punch-houſe that ſtands on the Sea-ſhore a ſhort Piſtol-ſhot from the Gariſon.

THE Town ſtands at the Back of the Fort, within Land, with a Stone Wall round it, to keep out Enemies of the Chief's making, for in 1703. he began a War that ſtill continues, at leaſt there were Folks killed in 1723. when I was there; and I was informed by a Gentleman of Judgment there, that the War and Fortifications had taken Double the Money to maintain them that the Company's Inveſtments came to.

THE Occaſion of the War, as I was informed, began about a Trifle. The *Nayer*, that was Lord of the Mannor, had a Royalty, for every Veſſel that unladed at *Tellicherry*, paid two Bales of Rice Duty to him. There was another Royalty of every tenth Fiſh that came to the Market there, and both together did not amount to 20 *L. Ster. per Annum.* The Chief either appropriated theſe Royalties to his own, or the Company's Uſe, and the *Nayer* complained of the Injuſtice, but had no Redreſs. Theſe little Duties were the beſt Part of the poor *Nayer*'s Subſiſtence, which made it the harder

to

to bear, so his Friends advised him to repel Force by Force, and disturb the Factory what he could, which he accordingly did (by the secret Assistance of his Friends) for above 20 Years. The Company are the best Judges whether the War is like to bring any Profit to their Affairs there, or no.

THE established Religion of this Country is *Paganism*; but there are a few black *Christians* that live under the Protection of the Factory, and some of them serve for Soldiers in the Garison. They have a little Church standing within the outward Wall of the Factory, served by a *Portugueze* Priest or two, who get their Subsistence by the Alms of the Parish. And the *English* have Punch-houses, where the *European* Soldiers make Oblations to *Bacchus*, and if they want Devotion, which their Accounts can certify at Pay-day, they are forced to commute with their Officer, or undergo some wholsom Discipline or Chastisement.

ABOUT four Miles to the Southward of *Tellicherry*, is a small *French* Factory lately settled at the Mouth of a small River, but for what End I know not; but I believe more to employ a little Stock for the Gentlemen of *Calecut* Factory's Account, than for the *French* Company's.

AND eight or ten Miles farther to the Southward, is *Burgara*, a Sea-port in the Dominions of *Ballanore Burgarie*, a formidable Prince. His Country produces Pepper, and the best *Cardamums* in the World. I once called

called at his Port, and bought about 40 Tuns of *Cardamums* for the *Surat* Market. My Ship was large, and of good Force, so he sent me a Present of Poultry and Fruits, and sent me Word, that he had a Mind to see me on board my Ship. I returned Answer, that his Visit would do me great Honour, and I sent my Barge to wait on him. He came on board in her, and brought about 100 Attendants in other Boats, along with him. I carried him to the great Cabbin, and would have treated him with Coffee, Tea and Wine, or Spirits, but he would taste none, telling me, that my Water was polluted by our Touch, but he thanked me. He desired to see the Ship every where; and I ordered he should have free Liberty, and he went for an Hour to and again, making his Observations; and, when he had seen what he thought fit, he told me, that he would build a Ship of the same Dimensions, but there wanted Water enough in his Rivers to flote her.

THIS Prince, and his Predecessors, have been Lords of the Seas, Time out of Mind, and all trading Vessels between Cape *Comerin* and *Damaan*, were obliged to carry his Passes. Those of one Mast paid for their Passes about eight Shillings yearly, and those with three paid about sixteen; but when the *Portugueze* settled in *India*, then they pretended to the Sovereignty of the Seas, which occasioned a War between him and them, that has lasted ever since. He keeps some light

light Gallies, that row and sail very well, which cruize along the Coast, from *October* to *May*, to make Prize of all who have not his Pass. In our Discourse, I asked him if he was not afraid to venture his Person on board of a Merchant Ship, since he himself was an Enemy to all Merchants that traded on these Coasts. He answered, that he had heard of my Character, and that made him fearless, and that he was no Enemy to Trade, but only vindicated his Sovereignty of those Seas before mentioned, and that our own King was invested with the like Sovereignty, not only on his own Coasts, but on those of *France*, *Holland* and *Denmark*, and could have no greater Right than he had, only he was in a better Condition to oblige the Transgressors of his Laws to Obedience than he was: However he would maintain his Claim and Right the best Way he could, and whoever lost their Ships or Vessels for Contempt of his Authority, might blame their own Obstinacy or Folly, and not him.

He stayed about three Hours on board, and, at his going away, I presented him with five Yards of scarlet Cloth, a small Carpet, a Fowling-piece and a Pair of Pistols finely gilt, which Present he seemed highly pleased with; and he took a *Manila*, or Wrist-jewel off from his left Arm, on which was engraven something of their Language, in their own Characters, and putting it on my left Arm, declared me a free Denizon in all his Territories; and all his Attendants paid their

their Compliments to me with profound Reſpect. At his going over the Side, he gave the Boatſwain ten *Zequeens* for waiting on him while he viewed the Ship, and ten more for the Seamen to make a Feaſt, and when my Barge landed him, he gave the Cockſwain five *Zequeens*, and loaded her back with Poultry and Fruit. He was a very well ſhaped Man, about 40 Years of Age, of a very dark Colour, but not quite black, his Eyes very lively and ſparkling, and ſomething of a majeſtick Air in his Deportment.

NEXT Day I waited on him aſhore, and he carried me to his Palace, which was very meanly built of Reeds, and covered with Cocoa-nut Leaves, but very neat and clean. He had two Rows of *Bettle* Trees, which are very tall and ſtraight, ſet in Order about fifty Yards from the Door of his Palace, for it was not large enough to be called a Gate, and there he treated me with Rice, Fowl and freſh Fiſh dreſt after their Way; and, after Dinner, he ſhewed me ſeveral Warehouſes like Barns, full of black Pepper and *Cardamums*; and he told me, he wondred why the *Engliſh* did not ſettle a Factory in his Dominions rather than at *Calecut* or *Tellicherry*, for he ſupplied both theſe Countries with his Commodities; and, conſidering the Cuſtoms paid to him were but 5 *per Cent.* and what was carried into their Countries muſt pay other Cuſtoms to the Princes, the Company would find Pepper and *Cardamums* much cheaper in his Dominions than they

they could poſſibly have them at their Factories where they were ſettled. I told him, that ſending his Veſſels to cruize on Merchant Ships had blaſted the Reputation of his Country. He anſwered, that if the Company would make a Trial of a few Years in trading with him, they would be convinced of his fair Dealings; or, if I would come and ſtay in his Country, he would build a good Stone Houſe at his own Charge, and make a Fortification round it, in any Place that I ſhould chooſe in his Dominions, and that I ſhould be Superintendent of all the Commerce and Trade in his Country. I told him, that I could not accept of his Favours without the Approbation of our Company, and that would require Time to be got. This happened in *January* 1703.

In 1707. he built a new Ship, which I had a Mind to buy. I was then at *Couchin*, and ſent him Word, that I deſigned him a Viſit. He returned an Anſwer, that I was a Freeman in his Country, and might be aſſured of an hearty Welcom. About ten Days after I came in a ſmall Boat, to a Place belonging to him, called *Mealie*. When News of my Arrival were carried to him, he ſent a Perſon of Diſtinction, with twenty armed Men, to receive me, and ordered me to be lodged in a Stone Houſe, the common Place for Ambaſſadors to lodge in, when any had Buſineſs to come to him. The Bedding was only ſome Mats ſpread on a Couch; but it is the common Bedding of the Country, and his

his Highneſs has no better. Before I was conducted to my Lodgings, there was a Preſent of Rice, Butter, Hens, Fruits and Roots put into a Pantry for me, and my Retinue and Guard, for Supper. Next Morning he ſent a Compliment, that he deſired to ſee me at his Palace. I went accordingly, and he received me very graciouſly, with many Proteſtations of his Friendſhip, and told me, he would make good all that he had promiſed before, if I would continue in his Country. I returned his Compliment in the propereſt Terms I could, and told him, I came to kiſs his Hand, and to buy his new Ship, if he and I could agree. He told me, that I ſhould have her at a very reaſonable Price, but that his Religion forbad him to ſell any Ship that he either built or bought, till he had firſt employed her in one Voyage himſelf. I ſtayed ſeven Days in his Country, and he treated me after the ſame Manner as if I had been an Ambaſſabor, in defraying all my Charges, and allowing his own Servants to attend me.

When I went to his Palace the firſt Time, I was innocently guilty of ill Manners, for, walking with him near his Lodgings, I chanced to touch the Thatch with my Hat, which polluted it ſo much, that, aſſoon as I went away, he ſtript it of its Covering, becauſe Religion forbad him to ſleep under it when it was thus polluted; but it was ſoon re-ſanctified by a new Thatching. If any of his own Subjects had been guilty of the ſame Fault,

Fault, they might have run in Danger of losing their Lives for the Offence.

I daily received for my Table six Hens, two Pounds of Butter, five and twenty Pound Weight of Rice, a Quarter of a Pound of Pepper, and some Salt, some *Bettle* Leaves, and green *Arecka* with twenty young, and ten old Cocoa-nuts, but no Fish, which was a favourite Dish of mine. I sent my own Servants to the Fishing-boats, when they came from fishing, to buy some; but the poor Fellows durst not take a Peny of Money, yet supplied me with what Fish I wanted, and my Servants took their Opportunity to pay for them, when none of the Prince's Servants were present.

WHEN I took Leave to depart, he seemed to be sorry that I stayed so short a Time with him, and ordered two Days Provisions to be put into my Boat, and I presented the Officer that waited on me to the Sea Side with five *Zequeens* for a Feast of *Bettle* to him and his Companions. I do not certainly know how far southerly this Prince's Dominions reach along the Sea-coast, but I believe to *Tecorie*, about 12 Miles from *Mealie*, and in the half Way is *Cottica*, which was famous formerly for privateering on all Ships and Vessels that traded without their Lord's Pass.

THERE is a Rock lies off *Cottica* about 8 Miles in the Sea, which bears the Name of *Sacrifice Rock*. There are no Dangers near it for Ships to be afraid of. How it came by try its Name is uncertain; but common Tradition tells us, that when the *Portugueze* settled first at *Calecut*, which lies about seven Leagues South-east of this Rock, the *Cottica* Cruizers surprised a *Portugueze* Vessel, and sacrificed all their Prisoners on that Rock, which gave Name to it. It is observable, that tho' the *Portugueze* got Footing in all the Dominions of the Princes whose Lands reach to the Sea-shore of *Malabar*, yet they never could get a Foot of Ground in the *Balanores* Country, tho' many Trials have been made, and fair Means used to effect it.

CHAP. XXV.

Observations on the Samorin *and his Country, their Religion, Laws and Customs, Product of the Country and its Commerce; an Account of their War with the* Dutch, *begun* in Anno 1708. *and the Consequences of it.*

THE *Samorin*'s Country reaches along the Sea-coast from *Ticori* to *Chitwa*, about 22 Leagues. His chief City (if it may be called one) is *Calecut*, where he generally resides. His Palace is built of Stone, and there is some faint Resemblance of Grandeur to be seen about his Court. He is reckoned the powerfullest King on the Sea-coast of *Malabar*, and has the best Trade in his Country, which makes both himself and

People richer than their Neighbours. The *English* had a Factory there many Years, but now the Chief and the Factors are removed to *Tellicherry*, and what Quantities of Pepper they procure there by their black Servants, is ſent by Sea to *Tellicherry*. The *French* have alſo a ſmall Factory, ſettled *in Anno* 1698. but they are not in a Condition to carry on a Trade for want of Money and Credit: And the *Portugueze* have a Church, but poorly decorated, and pitifully endowed, for *Chriſtian* Charity is much decayed there as well as in other Places; and the Prieſts Perquiſites are but ſmall by Converts.

THE Product of the *Samorin*'s Country is Pepper in Abundance, *Bettle*-nut and Cocoa-nut, and that Tree produceth *Jaggery*, a Kind of Sugar, and *Copera*, or the Kernels of the Nut dried, and out of thoſe Kernels there is a very clear Oyl expreſt; alſo Sandel-wood, Iron, *Caſſia-lignum* and Timber for building, all which Commodities they export to the great Benefit of the Inhabitants.

MANY ſtrange Cuſtoms were obſerved in this Country in former Times, and ſome very odd ones are ſtill continued. It was an ancient Cuſtom for the *Samorin* to reign but twelve Years, and no longer. If he died before his Term was expired, it ſaved him a troubleſom Ceremony of cutting his own Throat, on a publick Scaffold erected for that Purpoſe. He firſt made a Feaſt for all his Nobility and Gentry, who are very numerous. After the Feaſt, he ſaluted his Gueſts,

Guests, and went on the Scaffold, and very decently cut his own Throat in the View of the Assembly, and his Body was, a little While after, burned with great Pomp and Ceremony, and the Grandees elected a new *Samorin*. Whether that Custom was a religious or a civil Ceremony I know not, but it is now laid aside.

And a new Custom is followed by the modern *Samorins*, that a Jubilee is proclaimed throughout his Dominions, at the End of twelve Years, and a Tent is pitched for him in a spacious Plain, and a great Feast is celebrated for ten or twelve Days with Mirth and Jollity, Guns firing Night and Day, so at the End of the Feast any four of the Guests that have a Mind to gain a Crown by a desperate Action, in fighting their Way through 30 or 40000 of his Guards, and kill the *Samorin* in his Tent, he that kills him, succeeds him in his Empire.

In Anno 1695. one of those Jubilees happened, and the Tent pitched near *Pennany*, a Sea-port of his, about fifteen Leagues to the Southward of *Calecut*. There were but three Men that would venture on that desperate Action, who fell in, with Sword and Target, among the Guards, and, after they had killed and wounded many, were themselves killed. One of the *Desperados* had a Nephew of fifteen or sixteen Years of Age, that kept close by his Uncle in the Attack on the Guards, and, when he saw him fall, the Youth got through the Guards into the

Tent, and made a Stroke at his Majeſty's Head, and had certainly diſpatched him, if a large Braſs Lamp which was burning over his Head, had not marred the Blow; but, before he could make another, he was killed by the Guards; and, I believe, the ſame *Samorin* reigns yet. I chanced to come that Time along the Coaſt, and heard the Guns for two or three Days and Nights ſucceſſively.

When the *Samorin* marries, he muſt not cohabit with his Bride till the *Nambourie* or chief Prieſt has enjoyed her, and, if he pleaſes, may have three Nights of her Company, becauſe the firſt Fruits of her Nuptials muſt be an holy Oblation to the God ſhe worſhips: And ſome of the Nobles are ſo complaiſant as to allow the Clergy the ſame Tribute; but the common People cannot have that Compliment paid to them, but are forced to ſupply the Prieſts Places themſelves. Any Women, except the firſt Quality, may marry twelve Husbands if they pleaſe, but cannot have more at one Time, and they muſt all be of her own *Caſt* or Tribe, under Pain of Excommunication and Degradation of Honour, if ſhe marries into a lower Tribe; and the Men are under the ſame Penalty if they tranſgreſs that Law, but they are not confined to a ſet Number of Wives, as the Women are to Husbands.

When a Woman is married to the firſt of her Husbands, ſhe has an Houſe built for her own Conveniency, and that Husband cohabits with her till ſhe takes a ſecond, or ſo

many

teen Years, and three were ſent in Company with a *Corean* Ambaſſador to *Peking*. Thoſe three profeſſed themſelves to be good *Catholicks*, and the Church at *Peking* got them Paſſage for *Canton*, where they met with Opportunities to get Paſſage for *Batavia*. And now having made my Obſervations on all the maritim Coaſts and Cities between Cape *Bona Eſperanza* and *Japon*, I conclude, and bid you Adieu.

F I N I S.

A

TABLE

OF

Weights, Measures and Coins used in several Parts of the *East Indies*.

Weights used in *Mocha* for gross Goods.

1	*Casilla* is	16 *Kerrats*
1	*Vakea*	10 *Casillas*
1	*Maund*	40 *Vakeas*
1	*Frasella*	10 *Maunds*
1	*Bahaar*	15 *Frasellas*

N. B. A *Frasella* is 29½ *lb. Averdupois*.

The *Banyan* Weight.

1	*Rotulla* is	15 *Vakeas*
1	*Maund*	2 *Rotullas*
1	*Frasella*	26⅔ *Rotullas*
1	*Bahaar*	400 *Rotullas*

Magiet, a Root for dying, is weighed.

1	*Vazena* is	1½ *Frasella*
1	*Bale*	13½ *Vazenas*

Am-

Ambergrease Weight.

1 *Bea* is	-	$1\frac{1}{2}$ *Vakea*
1 *Vakea*	-	9 *Zequeen* Weight

N. B. 1 *Vakea* is equal to 21 Peny Wt. *Troy.*

For *Agala*-wood, which is much used in *Arabia* for Perfumes

41 *Vakeas* is a *Maund*, equal to 3 *lb. Troy* Weight.

The Gold and Silver Weight.

1 Dollar Weight	is	22 *Dab*
1 *Zequeen* Weight		56 Grains

The Coin current is the *Cammassie*, which is heightned and lowered at the *Sheriffs* or Bankers Discretion, from 50 to 80 for a current Dollar, which is but an imaginary Species, being always reckoned $21\frac{1}{2}$ *per Cent* lower than *Spanish* Dollars.

The Grain at *Moha* is measured by the *Tomaan*, which is 40 *Kella*.

Kella	is	-	4 *Rotullas*

Weights used in *Persia*.

Maund.				*lb. Averdupois*
1	-	*Taverize* is	-	$6\frac{3}{4}$
1	-	*Capaar*	-	$8\frac{3}{8}$
1	-	*Shaah*	-	$13\frac{1}{2}$

Their

THEIR current Coins.

1 *Shahee* is	- -	10 *Gaaz* or *Cosbegs*
1 *Mamoody*	-	2 *Shahees*
1 *Abashee*	- -	2 *Mamoodies*
1 *Tomaan*	- -	50 *Abashees*

in Value 3 *L.* 2 *sh.* 6 *d. Sterling*.

THEIR Pearl Weights.

1 *Miscal* is	-	24 *Kerracks*
1 *Kerrack*	-	4 Grains,

or 3 *Abashee* Weight.

6 *Miscal*	-	1 Ounce *Troy*

THE Prices current for Pearl at *Cong* in *Persia*, Anno 1715.

Abashee Weight.	Price in *Mamoodies*.
1	1
2	6
3	12
4	from 20 to - 30
5	40 to - 50
6	70 to - 80
7	90 to - 100
8	120 to - 150
9	160 to - 200
10	220 to - 250
11	280 to - 320
12	400
13	700
14	1100
15	1600
18	2200
21	2500 to - 3000

WEIGHTS

WEIGHTS used in *Bassora*.

1 *Miscal* is	-	1½ *Derhams*
1 *Vakea*	- -	500 *ditto*
1 *Maund-bassora*	-	24 *Vakea*
3 *Maund-attarie*	-	1 *Maund-bassora*

N. B. A *Maund-attarie* is 27½ *lb. Averdupois.*

Bagdat Weights are sometimes used in *Bassora.*

1 *Vakea* is	-	400 *Derhams*
1 *Maund-attarie*	-	10 *Vakea*
1 *Maund-bagdat*	-	6 *Vakea*

SPECIES of Coins current in *Bassora* and *Bagdat*.

1 *Derham* is	-	10 *Fluce*
1 *Mamoodie* from	10 to	12 *Derhams*
1 *Abashee-bassora*	-	1½ *Mamoodies*
1 *Croush*	- -	4½ *ditto*
1 *Lyon* Dollar	-	7 *ditto*
1 *Spanish* ditto, from 9	to	9½ *ditto*
1 *Zequeen* from 16 to		16¼ *ditto*
1 *German* Duckat	-	15½ *ditto*

A *Bassora Tomaan* 75. and a *Bagdat Tomaan* 100 *ditto.*

WEIGHTS used at *Sindy*.

The common Weight is 40 *Sear* to the *Maund-pucah*, 75 *lb. Averdupois*, but, for Elephants Teeth 84 *lb. ditto.*

OF

Of the Weights in Use at *Surat*.

The groſs Weight is 20 great *Pice*, or 32 ſmall to a *Sear*.

40 *Sear* is	-	1 *Maund*
20 *Maund*	-	1 *Candy*

Amber and Coral Weight.

1 *Sear* is 18 *Pice*, or	-	35 *Tolla* Weight.
1 *Tolla*	- -	32 *Valls*

Diamond Weight.

1 *Rutty* is	- -	$3\frac{1}{2}$ Grains *Engliſh*
1 *Vall*	- -	3 *Rutties*
1 *Tank*	- -	8 *Valls*
1 *Tolla*	- -	32 *ditto*
1 *Miſcal*	- -	$1\frac{1}{8}$ *Tank*
1 *Kerrack*	- -	3 Grains

The current Money in *Surat*.

Bitter-almonds go 32 to a *Pice*.

1 *Annoe* is	-	4 *Pice*
1 *Rupee*	- -	16 *Annoes*

The Price of Gold riſes and falls, according to the Plenty or Scarcity of Silver.

The *Rupees* current in Payments are

The *Chillany* always the ſame
The *Hundea* $\frac{1}{2}$ *per Cent*. leſs.
The *Harſanna* and
The *Magarie* from 1 to 2 *per Cent*. leſs.

Weights

Weights in Use at *Bombay*.

1 *Sear* is - - $10\frac{2}{3}$ Ou. *Averdupois*
1 *Maund* - - 40 *Sear*
1 *Candy* - - - 20 *Maund*

Their Accounts are kept by *Rayes* and *Rupees*.

1 *Rupee* is - 400 *Rayes*

But there are several other Species of Money current there, as *Xerephins*, *Larees* and *Fēdees*.

Decan Weights are equal to *Bombay* Weights, but for Silver and Gold

1 *Ickery Pagoado* is - 48 *Jettals*
1 *Darwary Pagoado* - 33 *ditto*

An *Ickery Pagoada* formerly was reckoned at $3\frac{1}{2}$ *Rupees*, or 8 *sh.* 3 *d. Sterl.* but now they are reduced below 3 *Rupees*.

Goa Weights are

24 *Rotullas* to - 1 *Maund*
20 *Maund* is - 1 *Candil* of 520 *lb. Averdupois*.

Their Coin.

1 *Vintin* - - 15 *Budgeroocks*
1 *Tango* - - 5 *Vintins*
1 *Xerephin* or *Pardoa* - 5 *Tangos*

1 Gold

1 Gold St. *Thomae* - 5 *Xerephins*

But they keep their Accounts in *Rayes.*

Calecut Weights are

The *Maund* of 28 *lb. Averdupois.*
20 *Maunds* to a *Candy.*

The Coins are
10 *Tar* to a *Fanam*
$4\frac{1}{2}$ *Fanams* to a *Rupee*

But most Sorts of foreign Money pass there in Payments as the Bankers value them.

All the Coasts of *Malabar* and *Chormondel* use near the same Weights with *Calecut.*

Orixa and *Bengal* have the *Puckah* Weight, fully weighed by the Natives at 80 to 84 *lb.* to a *Maund*, but the *English* Factory Weight is but 75 *lb.*

Their current Money and Coins are

80 *Couries* to a *Poan.*

32 to 36 *Poan* to a *Rupee* current.

But 1 *Secca Rupee* is 11 *per Cent.* better than current.

A *Surat Rupee* 9 *per Cent.*

An *Harsanna Rupee* 8 *per Cent.*

A *Piet Rupee* 5 *per Cent.*

In

A Table of Weights, &c.

In *Bengal* their Accounts are kept in *Pice*,

12 to an *Annoe*
16 *Annoes* to a *Rupee*.

Pegu Weight.

1 *Viece* is	-	-	39 Ou. *Troy*
or 1 *Viece*	-	-	100 *Teculs*
140 *Viece*	-	-	a *Bahaar*.

The *Bahaar* is 3 *Pecul China*.

Atcheen Weights.

1 *Catty* is 20 *Bankaals*, or 29 Ou. *Averdupois*.
1 *Bankaal* is 3 *Tolla* 18 *Vall Surat*.

Their Coin is

From 12 to 1600 *Cash* to 1 *Mace*, 16 *Maces* is 1 *Tayel*, valued at 18 *sh. Sterl.* but in Accounts reckoned commonly at 1 *L.*

The *Atcheen* and *China* Weights are used on *Sumatra*, *Java*, &c. Islands, among the Natives, and in the Dominions of *Johore*.

Siam Weights and Coin have the same Denomination.

1 *Miam* is	-	-	2 *Foads*
1 *Tecul*	-	-	4 *Miams*
1 *Cattee*	-		80 *Teculs*

1 *Pe-*

1 *Pecul* is 100 *Cattees*
or 133 *lb. Averdupois.*

THE *Cattee* and *Pecul* are uſed in *Cambodia, Couchin-china, Tonquin, China* and *Japon*, not differing above 2 *per Cent.* in all thoſe Countries.

ON *Sumatra* Pepper is ſold by the *Bahaar* but on *Java, P rneo* and *Johore* it is ſold by the 100 *Gantams*, a *Gantam* being a certain wooden Meaſure that contains about 4 *lb.* 5 *Ou. Averdupois*; and I have bought 100 *Gantams* in *Johore* for 11 *Macies*, or 1 *L.* 18 *ſh.* 6 *d. Sterl.*

ON *Java* and *Malacca*, and in *Siam* Rice is ſold by the *Quoins* of 40 *Peculs*; but in *Johore* and *Cambodia* 32 *Peculs.*

IN *Malacca Dutch* Coins paſs, and *Spaniſh* Dollars alſo: According to their Plenty or Scarcity they are in Value, but the *Medium* is 25 *per Cent.* better than *Dutch.*

IN *Johore* their *Macie* is a Gold Coin, in Value about 3 *ſh.* 6 *d. Sterl.* and the *Coupang* is one fourth of a *Macie.*

IN *Siam* a *Tecul* is in Value about 3 *ſh. Ster.* and they are divided into *Maiams* and *Foads*, all ſuperfine Silver.

In *Cambodia* their only Coin is *Galls*, a ſmall Piece of coarſe Silver with Characters on one Side. Its Value 4 *d. Sterl.*

I never ſaw any *Couchin-china* or *Tonquin* Coins, ſo I can ſay nothing of them.

China has only *Peties* of Coin, being a ſmall Piece of coarſe Braſs caſt round, with Characters on each Side, and a four-ſquare Hole in the Middle. They riſe and fall often, but Accounts are kept in *Tayels*, *Macies* and *Condereens*, 10 *Condereens* to a *Macie*, and 10 *Macies* to a *Tayel*

FINIS.